D1248514

Jerusalem Stone

Insights into the Weekly Parsha From The Old City of Jerusalem

Jerusalem Stone
Insights into the Weekly Parsha From The Old City of Jerusalem
Sefer Bereishis

HaRav Avigdor Nebenzahl

Translated and Adapted by Nehemiah Klein

ROSSI PUBLICATIONS

First Edition MMX

Copyright © MMX by Yeshivat Netiv Aryeh

Editing and Layout by Rossi Pub.
Editor: Caroline Fletcher
Technical Editor: Ricahrd L. Sine

Cover Design: Adam Simon
Cover Photo By: Yosef Gillers

Production Manager: Adam Simon

ISBN13 978-0-9779629-5-2

ROSSI PUBLICATIONS

6265 Rose Street Suite 101
San Diego, CA 92115
619-663-3233

www.RossiPublications.com

10 9 8 7 6 5 4 3 2 1

לזכרון עולם

In loving memory of
my grandfather
Abraham Adelsbberger ז״ל
and
my father
Alfred Isay ז״ל
Who stood firm with courage
In the terrible times of The Shoah
For the sake of their family and
The future of the Jewish People

Ruth Fass–Isay
and children

Contents

Preface

It is with praise and gratitude to the Almighty that we present the English speaking public with this publication of HaRav Avigdor HaLevi Nebenzahl Shlit"a's *sichos* on *Sefer Bereishis*.

These are timeless, classical essays on *hashkafa*, *machshava*, *mussar*, and *halacha*. These are thought-provoking discussions that plumb the depths of human nature. They contain brilliant, analytical, sometimes novel, occasionally humorous, but always inspiring insights into the five books of the Torah and the people that inhabit them.

This book is the result of a project which began 13 years ago. The Rav would speak in the *Yeshiva* in Hebrew. Each *sicha* was then edited and translated and sent to a limited email list of alumni. Due to the popularity of the Rav's words, that small list soon grew into thousands of addresses.

This volume is a compilation of the *sichos* on *Sefer Bereishis* heard in the *Yeshiva's Beis Midrash* since the year 5758. In the interests of practicality we were forced to limit ourselves to two (in one case three) *sichos* for each *parsha*. It is no easy task to whittle down 13 years of Torah into just a few representative *sichos*, as each of the Rav's discourses is עולם ומלואו – they encompass an entire world of *machshava*. We have attempted to present you with as wide a variety of the Rav's insights as possible, with the emphasis on what we consider HaRav Nebenzahl classics.

מה אשיב לה' כל תגמולוהי עלי – "How can I repay Hashem for all His kindness to me." I would like to thank the Almighty for all His kindness throughout the years, especially for the privilege of being associated for the past 13 years with the dissemination of the Rav's weekly *sichos* on the *parsha*. It has been a tremendous *zechus* as well as a great learning experience.

I would like to single out a number of people who were instrumental in bringing the Rav's *sichos* to publication.

I would first of all like to express my appreciation to HaRav Nebenzahl Shlit"a himself. His brilliant insights and lucid understanding are an increasing source of inspiration. His presence in our *Beis Midrash*, his humility and overall devotion to *HaKadosh Baruch Hu* are a shining example to all who come in contact with him. May Hashem grant him and his family many long and healthy years of disseminating Torah to *Klal Yisrael*.

HaRav Aharon Bina Shlit"a, Rosh Yeshiva of Yeshivat Netiv Aryeh, sees this as a vital labor for Klal Yisrael and has been a constant source of encouragement in this and other projects. His life of Torah, *Avodah*, and *Gemillus Chassadim* are a hard act to follow. May *HaKadosh Baruch Hu* grant him and his family the strength to continue their life of service to the Jewish people.

Thank you to Richard and Anita Grossman who have been our weekly sponsors since the inception of this project. May *HaKaodsh Baruch Hu* grant them many more years of benefiting *Klal Yisrael* with their many acts of chesed.

I would like to thank Mrs. Caroline Fletcher for a superb editing job.

Thank you to Adam Simon of Rossi Publications for his efforts in bringing this book to publication.

Last but certainly not least, I would like to thank my wife Rina for her encouragement as well as her input into this endeavor. May *HaKadosh Baruh Hu* grant us many years of *nachas* from all our children and may we be *zoche* to see בנים ובני בנים עוסקים בתורה ובמצות.

Nehemiah Klein
Jerusalem
Menachem Av 5770

Parshas Bereishis

"On Three Things The World Stands"

בראשית ברא אלקים את השמים ואת הארץ
"In the beginning of God's creating the heavens and the earth..."[1]

The World Was Created For The Torah And For Yisrael

In the very first *pasuk* in the Torah we learn that there was a creation and Who the Creator is. As we read further in the Torah we learn how He created the world. The Torah does not inform us explicitly why Hashem created heaven and earth and all that they contain. Rashi states that the word בראשית in this context poses grammatical difficulties. He posits that the word is a contraction of the words בשביל ראשית – "For ראשית – for the Torah, which is called ראשית דרכו – 'the beginning of His way'[2] and for Israel who are called ראשית תבואתו – 'the first of His crop'[3] i.e. in their merit."[4] However, this does not tell us the purpose of creation. Of course we know that the whole notion of purpose – cause and effect – has no meaning in reference to Hashem's acts, for Hashem is above and beyond everything – "higher than all heights."[5] Nevertheless, the Torah was given to us to study with our human intellect, which is the tool we must use to try to understand the meaning behind the creation.

It seems clear that Hashem created the world in order to do *chessed*; כי חפץ חסד הוא – "for He desires kindness."[6] Before there was a world, there was no one in existence who could be the focus of Hashem's *chessed*. Hashem set many types of creatures in this world in order to provide for them and to bestow kindness upon them.

"The World Is Built On Kindness"

Chessed is the foundation for all the other attributes. Hashem is a God of justice and of mercy as well as other *middos*, yet all this stems from His desire to shower us with good. The Attribute of Justice, for example, was created out of His desire to do good for us, to prevent the world from sinking into anarchy, for if there were no justice, every evil person would do as he pleased. Had the Attribute of Justice been the only guiding force, however, the world would not be able to continue, thus Hashem guides us with His Attribute of Mercy as well. One of the foundations on which the world is built is *chessed* – as Dovid HaMelech said: עולם חסד יבנה.[7]

"On Three Things The World Stands"

Shimon HaTzaddik used to say, "On three things the world stands: on the Torah, on the Temple service, and on deeds of lovingkindness."[8] Why did he choose these three specifically? Does the world not stand on the merit of any of the other 613 *mitzvos*? It seems to me that these are three primary categories of achieving closeness with Hashem and all other ways may be viewed as subcategories. Let us analyze each of these categories individually.

Al Ha'Torah

Torah study is our opportunity to become close to Hashem through our intellect in order to gain some insight into His thoughts, although as we mentioned, no human being can comprehend Hashem's thoughts. The prophet says, "As high as the heavens over the earth, so are My ways higher than your ways, and My thoughts than your thoughts."[9] When a brilliant scholar, wise in the ways of Torah, or, *lehavdil*, in the sciences, speaks, we may have difficulty understanding his profound words, but in the final analysis, his thought process is no different from that of other human beings. He thinks in terms of cause and effect. The Gemara asks a question, and therefore provides an answer. *Tosafos* poses a difficulty and as a result reaches a conclusion. We live our daily lives in such a manner as well: we are hungry, so we go and buy food. Man's life is based on reasoning and logic. Our intellect and methods of analysis use causality as a frame of reference. Hashem is above all reason and He is the Reason for all reasons. No cause can require Hashem to do anything. Hashem's thoughts differ totally from our understanding of the term "thought," so not only are we unable to reach the depths of His understanding, but we cannot even attribute the notion of "thought," as we know it, to Him.

Torah Is The Blueprint Of The World

The *Midrash Rabba* opens its commentary on the Torah by quoting the *pasuk* from Mishle: ואהיה אצלו אמון – "I was then His אמון."[10] This *pasuk* appears in Mishle where the Torah has just described herself as: ה' קנני ראשית דרכו – "Hashem made me as the beginning of His way."[11] The *midrash* offers several meanings for the word אמון. One interpretation points out that the word אמון is made up of the same letters as the word אומן, – 'a craftsman.' The *midrash* explains that the Torah is saying: "I am Hashem's tool." When a craftsman wishes to construct a building, what does he do? He draws up a blueprint and he constructs the building based on that. Similarly, the Torah is the blueprint for the world; as the *Zohar* says: "Hashem looked in the Torah and [from that] He created the world."[12]

A wise man once concluded that since the world was created according to the Torah, it is not correct to say that we eat matzoh on Pesach in commemoration of the Jewish people's leaving Egypt on that day. In fact, the opposite is true – because the Torah commanded us to eat *matzos* on the fifteenth of Nisan, Hashem orchestrated history so that on that day, the Jewish people left Egypt in haste, with no time for their dough to rise.

In my humble opinion, he is both correct and incorrect. Does the craftsman really construct a particular type of house only because that is what is outlined in the plan? Is the opposite not true? Does he not draw up the plan in response to his customer's specifications? Different plans would be drawn up for a customer desiring a residential dwelling and for one wanting to build a shul. The building is not constructed because of the plan, rather the plan is based on the needs of the building. The same is true of the world and the Torah. The desire to create the world is the reason for the contents of the Torah; the Torah is not the reason for the existence of the world. In reality, this is also not totally correct – for as we said, the thought process of cause and effect does not apply to Hashem. We must therefore conclude that Hashem gave us this type of Torah because He wished to create this type of world, and the converse is also true: Hashem created the world in this manner, because He wrote the Torah in this particular way.

Another concept of ours that doesn't apply to Hashem is chronology, for Hashem is above the notion of time. Although Chazal teach us that the Torah preceded the creation of the world by two thousand years,[13] or according to one view by nine hundred and seventy-four generations[14], these are purely spiritual concepts, since time did not exist prior to creation. The concepts of time and causality do not apply to God, yet His desire to create this world and the Torah means that the world corresponds to the Torah and the Torah corresponds to the world. Man's soul corresponds to both, for he is both a microcosm of this world and a reflection of the Torah. Because Avraham Avinu was such a pure reflection of the Torah, he was able to master the Torah on his own – "I can see God from my flesh."[15]

"God Has Made Man Simple"

If Avraham Avinu was able to study the Torah and understand it on his own, why can we not do the same? Why did we need Moshe Rabenu to bring the Torah down to us? Shlomo HaMelech, wisest of all men, explains: "God has made man simple, but they sought many intrigues."[16] When man is straightforward, everything comes out the way it should, but when man searches for "intrigues," he will not find the true Torah. A merchant was once asked: "What is the sum of two plus two?" to which he answered, "That depends. If I am buying, it is three. If I am selling, it is five!" With calculations like these, we cannot hope to attain an understanding of Hashem's wisdom.[17] Avraham Avinu thought in an honest manner. In fact, all the forefathers were referred to as *yesharim* – straight. Every morning we recite about Avraham Avinu: "You found him faithful before You."[18] Someone who is one hundred percent faithful to Hashem has no personal bias. His only wish is to serve Hashem in order to arrive at the Absolute Truth. Even though he lived in a generation of idol worshippers, Avraham Avinu came to recognize Hashem because he was faithful and straight thinking. Such a person can declare, "I can see God from my flesh." He can perceive the Torah and realize how it is reflected in man.

Our true will and desire, which comes from our *neshama*, is to follow the *mitzvos* of the Torah, because the Torah is a reflection of our soul. *Mesilas Yesharim*[19] explains that the soul is constantly striving to return to its rightful place under the Throne of Glory. Our problem is that we do not have the clarity always to know what we truly want. The *yetzer hara* foists his desires upon us as if they are our will, and entices us to do what he wants. In reality, the inner desire of each Jew, and even that of a non-Jew to some extent, is to cleave to Hashem. The Torah teaches us how to achieve that closeness, therefore it is our true desire. The Torah reflects man and man reflects the Torah, as long as the man we are speaking of follows a straight path and does not corrupt himself with all types of calculations emanating from the *yetzer hara*.

The Torah is thus the way in which we become close to Hashem's thoughts.

V'al Ha'avodah

Avodah – 'service' – is the way in which we approach Hashem emotionally. When man brings an offering on the Altar, he should feel as if it is himself that he is sacrificing. If the offering is a *chatas* – a sin offering, then he should feel as if he himself deserves to be slaughtered on the Altar. If he is bringing a *nedava* – a donation, it should be as if he were giving himself as a gift to Hashem. Avraham Avinu was ready to offer his only son, and would have done so had Hashem not prevented him by saying, "Do not stretch out your hand against the lad."[20] If Avraham Avinu was not permitted to offer his son, then we certainly are prohibited to make any form of human sacrifice. Instead, Hashem gave us the possibility of bringing animal, fowl, or *mincha* offerings. Our desire, however, should be to sacrifice ourselves on the Altar.

Prayer As A Substitute For *Korbanos*

Today, when we are no longer able to offer sacrifices, we try to achieve that same closeness with the Almighty through our prayers. Three times a day we are granted the opportunity to stand before Hashem and to speak to Him, as a son stands before his father. We thank Him for all the good He has given us, and request that He continue to shower us with good – with wisdom, repentance, forgiveness, redemption, and whatever we may need. Many people travel great distances to receive the *beracha* of a Rebbe or *talmid chacham* on special occasions like the *Yomim Noraim*, or when searching for a *shidduch*. In our case, one hundred times a day Hashem lowers Himself, so to speak, to us – the dust of the earth – in order to receive our *beracha*! This is a special opportunity for closeness. We should desire to make our prayers last longer and longer, rather than trying to finish them as quickly as possible. We are obligated to study Torah as well, but if we had the opportunity, "Would that man could spend the entire day in prayer."[21] Since we are unable to pray all day, the least we should do is make sure to utilize the little time we do set aside for prayer and not waste it in daydreaming. They tell the story of a Jew who was standing in shul davening, when suddenly he felt somebody hitting him in the chest, not once but twice! Shocked, he looked around to see who it was, only to discover that it was himself! He was in the middle of *Shmone Esrei* and had reached 'selach lanu.' This is clearly not what our *tefillah* should look like!

V'al *Gemilus Chassadim*

Gemilus Chassadim is the way we cleave to Hashem through our actions. We have said that we cannot apply the idea of causality when speaking of Hashem, yet our minds can comprehend only a causal line of reasoning. When we attempt to explain why Hashem created the world, we have to conclude that it was to provide good for all His creations. Hashem "searched" for someone on whom to bestow this good, and because no one existed yet, He had to create the world. He began with the ministering angels, continued with vegetation, insects, and the rest of creation and ended with the making of man. "Hashem is good to all, His mercies are on all His works."[22] Each element of creation serves a purpose and can receive Hashem's goodness.

The Almighty acts in kindness towards the entire creation. Clearly, the main objects of His *chessed* are human beings, and first and foremost among them the Jewish nation, who received the Torah. Hashem's *chessed*, however, extends to the rest of creation as well, each according to his level. A non-Jew has a chance to acquire a place in the World to Come through strict observance of the seven Noachide laws. He could even convert to Judaism. The ministering angels have their own source of merit, while the animals and the rest of the world deserve to be objects of Hashem's *chessed* for their role in benefiting the righteous.[23] The entire world was created in order to serve the *tzaddikim*, and we find that even stones proclaimed: "Upon me shall the righteous one lay his head."[24] Indeed they were all amalgamated into one, in order to have that privilege.

The stone benefited by having Yaakov place his head on it, while man for his part, has the opportunity to enter the Next World and bask in the radiance of the Divine Presence. In fact, every day we pray in *Uva LeZion*, "May it be Your will, Hashem, our God, and the God of our forefathers, that we observe Your decrees in this world, and merit to live and see and inherit goodness and blessing in the years of Messianic times and for life in the World to Come." In *Birkas HaMazon* as well, we recite, "The Compassionate One! May He make us worthy of the days of the *Moshiach* and life in the World to Come."

This raises a question. The Mishna instructs us, "Be not like servants who serve their master for the sake of receiving a reward."[25] Do we have the right to pray for life in the Next World? Let us discuss one of several answers to this question.

There are two possible reasons for accepting a gift:

1) The present is to my liking and I am happy to receive it.

2) The giver wishes to honor me. By accepting his gift I am demonstrating respect for him, for if I do not accept it, he will be insulted.

If I subscribe to the first reason, I am simply a taker, whereas in the second, my taking actually amounts to giving. We find something similar in Gemara *Kiddushin*.[26] If a woman marries a very important person, *kiddushin* would be binding if, instead of the usual method of the *chosson's* giving something to the *kalla*, she presented her husband with a gift which he would accept, assuming that her pleasure at his acceptance of her gift can be valued at a *perutah* or more.

When Taking Is Actually Giving

Later in the Chumash, we read that Avraham Avinu accepted gifts from the kings of Egypt and the Plishtim,[27] but not from the king of Sodom.[28] Avraham felt that the kings of Egypt and the Plishtim were truly honored to bestow a gift upon him, but Chazal tell us that the king of Sodom did not consider it an honor to give a gift to Avraham.[29] He maintained that he was as righteous as Avraham, claiming, "There is no difference between us for we are equals." Accordingly, if Avraham accepted these gifts, he would not be classified as a giver, but a taker, since he would not have given any honor to the king. Thus Avraham refused to accept "as much as a thread to a shoelace."[30] We accept Hashem's gifts in order to fulfill His wish of providing good to the world and thus ensure that His will fills the world.

We constantly bless Hashem: *"Baruch Ata Hashem"* – "Blessed are You, Hashem." What can we possibly bless Him with? Longevity?

Does He not live for eternity? Can we bless Him with health or wealth? That is absurd! What we can do is give Him the blessing that His will fill the entire world, which was His goal in creating the world. When we say that we wish to "inherit goodness and blessing,"[31] we are requesting that we and the other creations fulfill His will. Man's task is thus to perform acts of *chessed*, to be a giver in the spiritual as well as the material sense.

Seeking Acts Of *Chessed*

Those of us in Yeshiva are bound by the schedule, so we do not have the opportunity to go in search of recipients of *chessed*. Actually, even the Yeshiva presents opportunities for *chessed*. Rav Sholom Schwadron zt"l used to say that there are many acts of *chessed*, which even a non-Jew could do, which can help us to acquire a share in the World to Come. For example, if someone asks us what time it is, we can simply answer "Eleven o'clock," or we can also have in mind to fulfill Hashem's commandment of "And go in His ways,"[32] as well as "You shall love your fellow man as yourself."[33] If one takes care to give the precise time, then perhaps he also fulfills the command to "Distance yourself from a false word."[34] So many *mitzvos* can be fulfilled simply by informing someone of the time. One should not however spend too long in contemplation and recitation of "*leShem yichud*," for by then, the time will have changed, and the person asking wishes to know the time now!

We must work on being aware that we are fulfilling acts of *chessed* in our daily lives. When performing routine acts for one's parents, wife or children, one should be conscious of the fact that he is performing *chessed* as Hashem does. Rav Sholom Schwadron zt"l once related that when his children were young, one of them took ill. He suggested to his wife that they move the healthy children temporarily to the grandmother's house, to prevent them from being infected. On the way to the grandmother's house, he met one of his *rebbeim* who asked him where he was headed. Rav Sholom explained that one of the children was sick and he was bringing the healthy ones to the grandmother. The Rav asked him again, "Where are you going?" Rav Sholom thought that the Rav had not understood him the first time and explained in greater detail. The Rav repeated the question, in response to which Rav Sholom provided an even more detailed explanation. After a number of such exchanges, the Rav stopped him, and said: "The big animals also lead their young ones." That is, even animals care for their offspring. "What you should have said," he explained to Rav Sholom, "is 'I am going to the grandmother's house because Hashem commanded me to care for the health of my children, and I am taking them in order to fulfill Hashem's wish!'"

Our task in this world is to seek ways to emulate the Almighty's trait of *chessed* through our actions.

Notes

1   *Bereishis* 1:1

2   *Mishle* 8:22

3   *Yirmiyahu* 2:3

4   Rashi, *Bereishis* 1:1.

5   *Zohar*

6   *Micha* 7:18

7   *Tehillim* 89:3

8   *Pirke Avos* 1:2

9   *Yeshayahu* 55:9

10   *Mishle* 8:30

11   Ibid. 22

12   See *Zohar* 161:2.

13   See *Yalkut Shimoni Shir HaShirim* 988.

14   *Zevachim* 116a

15   *Iyov* 19:26

16   *Koheles* 7:29

17   This point is discussed further in *Sicha* II on *Lech Lecha*.

18   *Nehemiah* 9:8

19   Chapter 1

20   *Bereishis* 22:12

21   *Berachos* 21a

22   *Tehillim* 145:9

23   For an elaboration of this idea see Chapter 1 of *Mesilas Yesharim*.

24   Rashi, *Bereishis* 28:11.

25   *Pirke Avos* 1:3

26   *Kiddushin* 7a

27   See *Bereishis* 12:16 and 20:14.

28   See *Bereishis* 14:22-23.

29   See *Bereishis Rabba* 43:5.

30   *Bereishis* 14:23

31   *Uva LeZion*

32   *Devarim* 28:9

"Be Like Him"

ויאמר אלקים נעשה אדם בצלמנו כדמותנו ... ויברא אלקים את
האדם בצלמו בצלם אלקים ברא אותו

*"And God said: 'let us make Man in Our image as Our
likeness... and God Created Man in His image, in the image
of God He created him."*[1]

How To Be A *Tzelem Elokim*
We recite daily in *Birkos Ha'Shachar*:

יהי רצון מלפניך ה' אלקי ואלקי אבתי שתצילני היום ובכל יום מעזי פנים
...בין שהוא בן ברית ובין שאינו בן ברית...לעולם יהא אדם

*"May it be Your will Hashem, my God and the God of my forefathers,
that You rescue me today and every day from brazen men and from bra-
zenness... whether he is a member of the covenant or whether he is not a
member of the covenant... always be a person."*

The Rav (HaGaon HaRav Shlomo Zalman Auerbach zt"l) used to
quote this *tefillah* and explain that before one worries about the dis-
tinctions between people, one must first and foremost be a *mentsch*.

Man's task in this world is to cleave to Hashem and emulate His ways. Man was created *betzelem Elokim*, in the image of God, and our mission is to work on completing this *tzelem*. This means that our actions must display this Godly image.

The introductory section of the *Tomer Devorah* written by Rav Moshe Cordovero is based on the Thirteen Attributes of Hashem outlined in the book of *Micha*:

מי קל כמוך נשא עון ועובר על פשע

"Who is a God like You, Who pardons iniquity and overlooks transgression?"[2]

Before he explains how man can cleave to these attributes, he prefaces it by saying that man's obligation to do so stems from his being created in Hashem's image.

As the Jews crossed the Yam Suf, they declared: זה קלי ואנוהו – "This is my God and I will beautify Him."[3] The Gemara cites two interpretations of how to beautify Hashem. *Tanna Kamma* is of the opinion that this refers to having beautiful mitzvah-objects such as *tzitzis, tefillin, Sefer Torah*, etc. while Abba Shaul maintains that the Torah is teaching us to emulate the ways of Hashem: "Be like Him: just as God is gracious and compassionate, you also should be gracious and compassionate."[4] The *Tomer Devorah* clarifies that these two views are not contradictory. Abba Shaul is suggesting a different way of "beautifying Him." Beauty manifests itself in character as well as physical appearance.

Hashem only gives; He has no reason to take, for there is nothing which He lacks. One who only takes from others distances himself from Hashem. On the other hand, the more one gives, the closer one comes to Hashem. Man by his very nature is a taker in this world. From the minute a person is born, he has needs: air, milk, clothing, and a home. Receiving these necessities distances us from Hashem. Our task is to give as much as we can in order to come as close as possible.

Taking In Order To Give

HaRav Sholom Schwadron zt"l, the famous *maggid*, once gave a parable to explain the concept of giving. Two store owners in the same town sell the identical merchandise. The first wishes to give to the Jewish community by providing them with *challos*, meat, fish, etc. If he just gave away all his stock, declaring: "Go, buy and eat, go and buy wine and milk without money and without price,"[5] his supply would soon be depleted and he would not have the means to replenish it. In addition, if he could not feed himself and his family, he would be unable to continue serving others. He therefore has no choice but to charge for his products. The other store owner's only interest is to make a profit. Of course, he knows that if he were simply to hang up a sign saying, "Money can be deposited here," he would not have much success in reaching his goal. He therefore has no choice but to provide goods in exchange for the money he takes.

Both stores appear to operate in the same way. Yet the first man's desire is to give to others – he takes in order to give and is drawing nearer to Hashem by emulating His ways of giving. The second merchant, on the other hand, is only interested in taking from others – he gives in order to take. Such a person is distancing himself from Hashem, for he is operating in a way that is contrary to Hashem's *middos*.

One may regard studying in Yeshiva in a similar manner: A student may come to the Yeshiva with the sole aim of availing himself of the Yeshiva's meals three times a day. He realizes that if he were to appear only in the dining room and not in the *beis midrash*, in no time at all he would be expelled. He therefore decides that it is in his best interest to learn a bit as well. Such a person transforms the Torah into "a spade with which to dig" – for food.[6] Let's take a look at another young man: His entire purpose in life is to learn as much Torah as possible, yet it is obvious to him that without food or a *kollel* stipend he would not be able to continue in his quest. In his case, his food or the stipend become a "spade with which to dig" – for the Torah. A person's task is to emulate Hashem to the greatest extent possible – Hashem only gives, He does not take anything. Although a human being is required to be a taker as well, he should do his utmost to ensure that the taking is in order to give and not that he gives in order to take.

The Complete *Tzelem Elokim* – Man And Woman

ויאמר אלקים נעשה אדם בצלמנו כדמותנו... ויברא אלקים את האדם
בצלמו בצלם אלקים ברא אותו.

*"And God said: 'let us make Man in Our image as Our likeness …
And God created Man in His image, in the image of God He created him,
male and female He created them."*[7]

זה ספר תולדות האדם ביום ברא אלקים אדם בדמות אלקים
עשה אתו זכר ונקבה בראם ויברך אתם ויקרא את שמם אדם ביום הבראם

*"This is the account of the descendants of Adam – on the day of God's
creating of Man, He made him in the likeness of God. He created them
male and female, He blessed them and called their name Man on the day
they were created."*[8]

It is only man and woman together who are referred to as 'Adam' – Man. They are the complete *Tzelem Elokim*. The love between man and woman, if one can speak in such terms, symbolizes the love between Hashem and the Jewish nation. *Shir HaShirim*, which describes the love between Hashem and His people, is written in the form of an allegory of the love between a man and a woman.

Man and wife can cement their relationship only when each is interested in giving more and more to the other. My Rebbe, HaRav Dessler zt"l, used to counsel *chassonim* and *kallos* on the secrets of a long-lasting relationship: to give and to give and to give to each other. The same can be said of the relationship between Hashem and the Jewish people. Hashem gives without end. Our task is to do our utmost to fulfill Hashem's wishes. Giving to others and doing as Hashem wishes serves to strengthen this union. Otherwise, God forbid, the ties will be severed.

Avraham Avinu was first and foremost good to his wife. We read how he tried to come to the aid of the people of Sodom. He even

invited three Arabs into his home. (I would not recommend doing that today, for who could guarantee that they really are angels?)
Love for his wife, however, came before Sodom. The story is told of
a young man who saw a woman carrying two heavy baskets. Noting
her obvious difficulty, he ran to assist her, feeling proud of himself
for his tremendous act of *chessed*. As he got closer, he realized that
it was "only" his wife and he was very disappointed to have lost out
on such a mitzvah. Perhaps he then left her to fend for herself. In
a similar vein, Rav Nosson Zvi Finkel, the Alter from Slobodka,
was once having a talk with a young married man. In the course
of the conversation, he asked him whether he helped out at home
on *erev Shabbos*. The man responded: "What kind of a question is
that! Does it not say in the *Shulchan Aruch* that we are obligated to
involve ourselves with *Shabbos* preparations?" The Alter from Slobodka responded, "Would you not have done your share had it not
been dictated in the *Shulchan Aruch*? If a woman works so hard on
your behalf, is it not natural that you would want to help her? " Before studying the *Shulchan Aruch*, one must first and foremost be a
mentsch!

Becoming A Vessel For Receiving The Torah

HaRav Chaim Vital asks, "Why does the Torah not com-
mand us about *middos* – character traits?"[9] He answers that *middos*
are the major prerequisite for observance of the 613 *mitzvos*, and
a man should be imbued with the proper *middos* before he even
begins to approach mitzvah observance. The well-known adage:
דרך ארץ קדמה לתורה[10] teaches us that without proper *middos*, one
cannot receive the Torah. I believe Rav Chaim Vital's insight has
a corollary as well. It is true that a person must have good *middos*
before he approaches Torah and mitzvah observance, but the Torah
also serves to develop our *middos* further. It is impossible to attain a
high level of *middos* unless we are occupied with Torah.

In this world, vessels are made from earthenware, metal, or wood.
In the Next World, they are made from our souls. One who enters
the Next World devoid of good *middos* (assuming one who lacks
these *middos* even has the chance to enter the Next World) will not

have anything to do there. Only good character can serve as a vessel to absorb the Godly light for the soul. Entering the Next World without good character can be compared to someone who tries to carry precious diamonds in a bag that has holes at the bottom. The only way to create a proper vessel is to work on oneself. The more one works on his character, the greater this vessel grows.

We can learn from Avraham Avinu and Moshe Rabenu that positive character traits and especially humility are necessary for receiving the Torah. Avraham knew the entire Torah because he considered himself as 'dust and ash.'[11] It was Moshe Rabenu, the humblest of all men, who had the merit of bringing the Torah down to the Jewish people. The more we feel that we are 'dust and ash,' the less we allow our own selves, our egos, to get in the way and the less separation there is between ourselves and the Torah, the more Torah we will be able to receive in this world.

Someone with a true desire for Torah will not sit and ponder whether learning Torah is worth his while. Adam HaRishon was forbidden to eat from the עץ הדעת טוב ורע – "the Tree of Knowledge of good and bad."[12] Would it have been so terrible if Adam and man in general had known how to differentiate between good and bad? Does Hashem wish us all to remain ignorant of the ways of the world? The Rambam explains that before Adam's sin, man was able to distinguish between truth and falsehood. After the sin, man became calculating – he began to make decisions based on what was good and bad for him.

The greatness of Avraham Avinu was that he did not make such calculations: "You found his heart faithful before You."[13] Of Moshe Rabenu too, Hashem Himself testifies, "In My entire House he is the trusted one,"[14] He does what Hashem wishes and not necessarily what is good for him. This is how one becomes a vessel for receiving the Torah. We may not be on the level of our forefathers, but our goal must be to come as close to that level as possible. If this is truly our goal, we can merit receiving the Torah and the Godly light of the Next World.

Notes

1   *Bereishis* 1:26-27

2   *Micha* 7:18

3   *Shemos* 15:2

4   *Shabbos* 133b

5   *Yeshayahu* 55:1

6   *Avos* 4:5

7   *Bereishis* 1:26-27

8   *Bereishis* 5:1-2

9   See *Shaarei Kedusha, Chelek* 1, *Shaar* 2.

10   *Vayikra Rabba* 9:3

11   *Bereishis* 18:27

12   *Bereishis* 2:9

13   *Nehemiah* 9:8

14   *Bamidbar* 12:7

Parshas Noach

"*The World Is Built On Kindness*"

"Their Sentence Was Sealed On Account Of Robbery"

In *Parshas Bereishis* we discussed the fact that one of the pillars on which the world stands is *chessed* and that *chessed* is necessary to sustain the world. Yet unfortunately, not long after the creation, we read about the sinful behavior of the generation of the Flood: "Hashem saw that the wickedness of Man was great upon the earth and that every product of the thoughts of his heart was but evil always"[1]... "And the earth had become corrupt before God and the earth had become filled with robbery."[2]

In response, Hashem decides to destroy the world. Chazal tell us that, despite their licentious behavior and idol worship, "their sentence was sealed only on account of robbery."[3] Is a non-Jew not liable for the death penalty for violating any of the Noachide laws? Furthermore, if we examine our own legal system and compare the punishments for various sins, we will find that the punishment for robbery is far less than for other transgressions: והשיב את הגזלה – "He shall return the stolen object."[4] This does not seem so severe; a thief must return what he has taken. Perhaps one incurs *malkus*, the general penalty of lashes administered by *beis din*, for violation of Torah laws in the form of a לאו[5], but there is certainly no death penalty for robbery. It appears therefore that robbery is a relatively minor offense compared to the many other terrible acts of that generation. Why did robbery seal their judgment?

Robbery Is The Antithesis Of *Chessed*

It would appear to me that the reason is that Hashem acts with His creatures מדה כנגד מדה – "measure for measure."[6] As long as a person does not steal, there is still room for Hashem's Attributes of *Rachamim* – Mercy and *Chessed* to intercede and to find something favorable to say about this individual. With other sins, even if from the perspective of justice the person deserves punishment, the Attribute of *Chessed* works to make Hashem slow to anger and thus the person is not punished so severely. Robbery, however, is the antithesis of *chessed*. *Chessed* implies giving something that one has no obligation to give, while robbery has the opposite implication – taking that which is not rightfully yours. Because Hashem acts "measure for measure," when a person steals, the Attribute of *Chessed* cannot intercede. The judgment of that generation was sealed on account of the robbery that was so widespread that it blocked the intercession of *Chessed*, and this is what finally brought about the Flood.

Noach Preserved The World Through Kindness

How did Hashem preserve the world despite the decree to destroy it? He took Noach and his family, placed them inside the ark, and gave them the task of spending one full year involved in acts of *chessed*. עולם חסד יבנה – "the world is built on kindness."[7] Only in this way could they create the world anew. I have always marveled at the incredible acts of *chessed* Noach and his family performed. That year in the ark must have been exceedingly difficult. The *midrash* tells us that for that entire year they did not sleep.[8] It is clear why they were unable to sleep. They were running a hotel which employed only eight waiters – Noach, his wife, his three sons, and their wives – to serve thousands of guests! Each guest had his own dietary requirements – this one ate meat, that one's food was dairy, while the third ate only parve. In addition, each guest demanded his meal at a different time. Some ate before *Tikkun Chatzos*, some after. There were no specific opening hours for the dining room. Food was served twenty-four hours a day! One cannot begin to describe the difficult year Noach and his family experienced in the ark.

It was only recently that I realized an added dimension to their *chessed*. Not only did they act this way towards thousands of animals – lions, tigers, elephants, and others – twenty-four hours a day, but their *chessed* extended to human beings too. Which human beings? Was the world not destroyed except for them? They performed acts of *chessed* towards each other as well. When Noach took upon himself to feed the lion, it meant that his wife did not have to. When his wife decided to feed the tiger, Shem was absolved from such an obligation. Not only did Noach lighten the burden of his wife by feeding the lion, but he spared her bodily harm. We know that Noach was bitten by the lion for arriving late with its food.[9] If it had been his wife who was late, she would have been hurt. Throughout the time in the ark, in addition to caring for the animals, they performed *chessed* with each other. "The world is built on kindness." The world had been recreated with *chessed* as its foundation.

When Noach emerged from the ark, he brought offerings to Hashem. In response to these offerings, Hashem promised never to bring another Flood to the world. Noach thus managed to prevent thousands of Floods. How many Floods did Noach prevent? Every time we see a rainbow in the sky, it is a sign that there should have been a Flood![10] The offerings Noach brought were but another example of the tremendous *chessed* that he did for the world.

Avraham Vs. Noach

Noach is introduced to us as a *tzaddik*:

אלה תודות נח נח איש צדיק תמים היה בדרתיו את האלקים התהלך נח

"These were the offspring of Noach – Noach was a righteous man, perfect in his generations; Noach walked with God."[11]

---

10   There were generations of *tzaddikim* in which no rainbows ever appeared, for their own merit prevented a flood. See Rashi *Kesubos* 67b.

Chazal discuss the phrase, "in his generations." Some Sages maintain that the phrase is in praise of Noach. If he was righteous even in his corrupt generation, how much more righteous would he have been if he had lived at the time of Avraham Avinu and been influenced by him. According to others, however, it is critical of him. Only in his generation, compared with the extremely wicked people of his era, was he considered a *tzaddik*. If he had lived at the time of Avraham Avinu, his righteousness would have been insignificant. Let us see in what way Noach's *chessed* differed from Avraham's.

Avraham Avinu was known as the pillar of *chessed*. While Noach performed incredible acts of *chessed*, Avraham's ways were even greater, as we learn from Chazal. "The Attribute of *Chessed* said, 'So long as Avraham was in this world, I did not have to perform my job, for Avraham took my place.'"[12] Avraham Avinu was the personification of *chessed* in this world. Noach sacrificed himself for a whole year by feeding the entire creation, yet he gave them only what they needed – meat or hay, each animal in accordance with its habits. Avraham Avinu not only fed the creations, but he created them himself! What do we mean? He took the poor, downtrodden people who were destined to live a very short life (in this world only) and provided them with eternal life through the Torah that he taught them and the *yiras Shamayim* that he instilled in them.

The Torah describes Avraham's and Sarah's work as "the souls that they had made in Charan."[13] Rashi explains, "For they took them in under the wings of the Divine Presence. Avraham would convert the men and Sarah would convert the women, and Scripture considers them as if they made them."[14] In addition to providing for their physical needs, "He took cream and milk and the calf which he had prepared and placed these before them,"[15] he taught them to acknowledge the Creator after Nimrod had encouraged idol worship among them and the Name of God had been forgotten. The Torah relates that Avraham "planted an *eshel* in Be'er Sheva, and there he proclaimed the Name of Hashem, God of the Universe."[16] Rashi offers two interpretations for the word *eshel* – 'an orchard' or 'an inn for guests.' The letters אשל – *eshel* – stand for לינה ,שתיה ,אכילה – eating, drinking, lodging. "After they ate and drank, Avraham would say to them, 'Bless Him of Whose you have eaten. Do you believe that you have eaten of that which is mine? Of that which belongs to Him Who spoke and brought the universe into being you have eaten.'" Avraham provided his guests not only with physical sustenance but with spirituality and life in the Next World. What greater *chessed* can one perform with his fellow man? It is for this reason that Avraham is referred to as the pillar of *chessed*. It may be true that Noach taught Torah too, but he never thought of announcing it to the world, the way Avraham Avinu did.

The Jewish People Are Children Of Avraham

As we mentioned above, the world exists today in the merit of Noach, whose offerings have prevented thousands of floods. Even so, the ancestry of the Jewish people is not traced to Noach, but to Avraham Avinu. The other nations are all referred to as children of Noach; not so the Jewish people. In fact the Mishna tells us that if one were to vow that he would not benefit from *Bnei Noach*, he would be forbidden to benefit from a gentile, but permitted to benefit from a Jew[17]. The Gemara goes on to ask, "Do not the Jewish people also descend from Noach?" The Gemara answers "Once Avraham Avinu was singled out by God from the rest of humanity and endowed with a special sanctity, Jews are referred to by his name."[18]

It may be through the merit of Noach that the world exists. In fact the first remembrance we mention in *Zichronos* on Rosh Hashana is "Hashem remembered Noach,"[19] yet when Avraham Avinu was chosen, the Jewish people ascended to an even higher level. We are descended from Avraham, Yitzchak, and Yaakov rather than Noach, because Avraham Avinu spread the message of faith throughout the world. Noach was a believer, yet he kept that belief to himself. If Noach were to be asked whether there was a Creator, he would answer with an emphatic 'Yes!' He would go on to explain that there is certainly justice in this world and there is a Judge. Chazal tell us that Noach spent one hundred and twenty years rebuking his generation. "They would ask him 'Of what use is this (ark) to you?' He would say to them, 'In the future, the Holy One, Blessed is He, is going to bring a flood upon the world.'"[20] Noach certainly tried hard to rebuke them and to cause them to repent, yet he did not travel from city to city announcing, "There is justice and there is a Judge and there will be a great flood." He stayed at home.

Spreading The Message – To Whom?

Avraham, on the other hand went from city to city, kingdom to kingdom trying to spread the idea of belief in Hashem.[21] The task of the Jewish people is to follow in Avraham Avinu's footsteps and spread his message of faith. "You are My witnesses – the word of Hashem."[22] We must announce to the world that there is a Creator. Our actions alone, by following in the path of Avraham Avinu, can spread the word of Hashem. If we are not fortunate and our actions alone do not succeed in spreading the word, we are still witnesses that there is a God in this world. The other nations' hatred for us is testimony that we are on Hashem's side. When the entire world, with the exception of those few who can be classified as righteous gentiles, is trying to uproot us, we are still fulfilling, "You are my witnesses – the word of Hashem." Given that a witness may not conceal his testimony, we are obliged to publicize Hashem's uniqueness and not wait until the other nations hate us. They do hate us, but we need not wait to see it. We must stand up and spread the message of faith. Clearly, the place to begin is not with the other nations. We must begin with our own people. There are in fact many Jews today involved in spreading the message of observing the seven Noachide Laws to non-Jews. I am of the opinion that we must begin by spreading the message of Torah to our fellow Jews before we try to change the other nations.

Distinguishing Marks Of A Jew

Not everyone has it in him to spread the message successfully to the secular population, but we must involve ourselves to the best of our ability in this pursuit. The very fact that they see us wearing *kippot* is already a dissemination of faith. I must point out that although removal of the *kippah* is permitted under certain circumstances such as bathing or having a haircut, one may not do so to give the appearance of a secular Jew. Of course, life-threatening circumstances are an exception. The *poskim*, for example, permitted those involved in *Peilim* to dress up in secular clothing in their attempt to save children from missionaries and secular *kibbutzim*. This can truly be considered as saving lives. Similarly, one working among gentiles may find it dangerous to reveal his faith. In that case he certainly may remove his *kippah*. In other circumstances, dressing up as a secular Jew is a very serious offense. "You are my witnesses." A Jew's actions must be testimony to his beliefs. Wearing a *kippah* is not such a great obligation – perhaps it is nothing more than a nice custom. Certainly there are much more serious *mitzvos* that one can violate. If, however, one removes it with the intention of appearing *chiloni*, he has committed a terrible sin.

It is well-known that when certain youngsters go to the movies, God forbid, they remove their *kippot* in order not to cause a *chillul Hashem*. They are mistaken. This is a far greater *chillul Hashem*. By going to the theater they have perhaps violated one commandment; by removing their *kippot* they give the appearance of violating all six hundred and thirteen *mitzvos*! If one can control himself and not go to the theater, that would be the best solution. But to go and then in addition to remove one's *kippah* is a very serious offense. Wishing to appear as a *chiloni*, borders on *yehareg ve'al yaavor*, and is permitted only when the situation is life-threatening. We are all witnesses for Hashem – "All who see them will recognize them, that they are the seed that Hashem has blessed."[23]

The Rambam writes,[24] "One may not follow the ways of the other nations nor even imitate them ... A Jew should be distinguishable from them and it should be clear from his clothing and other actions, just as he is distinguishable from them in his ideas, and it says: 'And I have separated you from the peoples to be Mine.'"[25] It is not only his outlook on life that separates Jew from gentile; his behavior and appearance are indicative of who he is as well. If one wears a particular coat because he is cold, or something light because it is a hot summer day, that is fine. However, donning a specific article of clothing in order to look like the non-Jews is not appropriate. This is why many people wear *shtreimels* or the like, for today the gentiles do not dress in this manner and we must be distinguishable from the other nations. The Yemenites, in fact refer to the *peyos* (sideburns) as *simanim* – 'signs'. The *peyos* distinguish Jews from others.

We bless Hashem weekly in *havdalah*:

המבדיל בין קדש לחול בין אור לחשך בין ישראל לעמים בין יום השביעי
לששת ימי המעשה

"Who distinguishes between sacred and secular, between light and darkness, between Israel and the other nations, between the Seventh Day and the six days of labor."

People who do not understand the difference between sacred and secular, and do not distinguish between the Seventh Day and the six days of labor, do not distinguish between Israel and the other nations either. It is clear that they do not distinguish between light and darkness – they are blind to the world around them. Unfortunately this describes many of today's leaders. We must pray that Hashem replace them with leaders who will lead us to Torah, *yiras Shamayim*, and the fulfillment of *mitzvos*.

Rather than giving Jerusalem to the Arabs, may we merit a Jerusalem with the rebuilding of the *Beis HaMikdash* speedily in our day. Amen.

Notes

1   *Bereishis* 6:5

2   Ibid. 11

3   Rashi, *Bereishis* 6:13

4   *Vayikra* 5:23.

5   See *Kovetz Shiurim*, HaGaon HaRav Elchanan Wasserman zt"l, on *Baba Basra*; note 5.

6   *Shabbos* 105b

7   *Tehillim* 89:3

8   See *Tanchuma Parshas Noach* note 9.

9   See Rashi *Bereishis* 7:23.

11 *Bereishis* 6:9-10

12 *Sefer HaBahir* page 86, note 191.

13 *Bereishis* 12:5

14 Rashi, ibid.

15 *Bereishis* 18:8

16 *Bereishis* 21:33

17 See *Nedarim* 31a.

18 Ibid.

19 *Bereishis* 8:1

20 Rashi, *Bereishis* 6:14.

21 See Rambam, *Hilchos Avoda Zara* 1:3.

22 *Yeshayahu* 43:10

23 *Yeshayahu* 61:9

24 *Hilchos Avoda Zara* 11:1

25 *Vayikra* 20:26

"For In The Image Of God He Made Man"

שופך דם האדם באדם דמו ישפך
כי בצלם אלקים עשה את האדם

*"Whoever sheds the blood of man, by man shall his blood be
shed, for in the image of God He made man."[1]*

All Are Created In God's Image

Chazal offer several interpretations for this verse and they derive
many *halachos* from it.[2] According to the *pshat*, however, the Torah
is informing us that whoever spills the blood of his fellow human
being will be subject to the death penalty at the hands of man, in
the form of the *beis din*. Although the previous *pasuk*: "But of man,
of every man for that of his brother I will demand the soul of man,"[3]
implies that Hashem, Himself, demands that the murderer pay for
the victim's blood with his life, *beis din* may not rely on this and is
commanded to punish the murderer.

Who is this man created in the image of Hashem? I believe there
are three possible people the *pasuk* could be referring to. Firstly, it
could be the murder victim. Like any other human being, he was

created in God's image. By his action, the murderer has killed an image of Hashem, and has thus detracted from Hashem's image. Just as destroying an image of a human king is viewed as an act of treason against the king's sovereignty and is punishable by death, so too murdering a human being is the destruction of the likeness of The King of kings, so to speak, and is a rebellion against the Kingdom of Heaven, which incurs the death penalty.

This explanation presents a difficulty. One of the foundations of our faith is that no person can possibly harm another of his own volition. Only the Creator has the power to do so. If the murderer succeeds in killing his victim, it signifies that there was a Heavenly decree that the victim must die. In a similar vein, our Sages have an innovative understanding of this *pasuk*: "If you build a new house, you shall make a fence for your roof, so that you will not place blood in your house if a fallen one falls from it."[4] Chazal are teaching here: "The victim deserved to fall from the time of the six days of creation, for indeed he has not yet fallen and Scripture calls him 'a fallen one.'"[5] If someone fell, it would not be because the owner of the house had failed to place a fence around the roof, but rather because that person was destined to fall. Had it not been from this roof, he would have fallen from somewhere else. Despite this, from our perspective we must ensure that it is not our roof he falls from. We are therefore commanded to take the necessary precautions and construct a fence. If it is so decreed, Hashem will find another roof for him to fall from.

The Prayer Of The Robber

A robber was once asked what he prays for on Yom Kippur. He answered: "I pray that if it is decreed that someone be the victim of a robbery, may it come about through me and not through someone else." This is clearly not how we should act; we should pray that we not be responsible for any calamity that befalls someone else. Not only must we pray for this but we must take action as well, by constructing a protective fence around our roof. The fact remains, however, that we do not have the power to harm another. If someone is harmed it is only because it was ordained by Heaven. Yosef told his brothers: "It was not you who sent me here, but Hashem."[6] You threw me into the pit and sold me into slavery, because it was Hashem's will. If you had not done it, someone else would have.

Give Credit Where Credit Is Due

Obviously we can make such statements only when we are wronged. If someone does something good for us, we should not say to them, "You were not responsible for this good deed; it was ordained by Heaven." This is how some commentators explain Lavan and Besuel's words when they attributed the *shidduch* between Yitzchak and Rivka to Hashem: "The matter stemmed from Hashem."[7] They feared that Eliezer the *shadchan* would demand a hefty fee, so they conveniently gave Hashem all the credit, thus absolving themselves of any obligation to pay Eliezer. Good things do come from Hashem, but we must give credit to the person who was instrumental in facilitating them. We learn that Moshe Rabenu was grateful even to the river and the sand that had protected him.[8] Moshe told Yisro's daughters that it was not he who rescued them from the shepherds, but the Egyptian whom he had killed. After killing the Egyptian, he was forced to flee from Egypt to Midian and thus was present at the well, so the Egyptian was ultimately responsible for their rescue.[9] The evil Egyptian had no intention of saving Yisro's daughters and surely did not even know who they were. Nevertheless, Moshe told them that they must recognize the source of their rescue. To sum up, we must acknowledge that good comes from Hashem, yet at the same time we must also give credit to His human 'instruments.' When it comes to bad things, however, we should not hold the perpetrator responsible, but rather attribute it all to a Heavenly decree. If this is correct, what right do we have to punish the murderer, if the victim was destined to die anyway?

We need to understand the verse differently. My father zt"l suggested that the 'man' referred to in the *pasuk* is not the victim but the judge. From where does a human being have the authority to judge his fellow man in such a harsh manner? Because "in the image of God, He made man." Man was created in the image of God and was thus given God's ability to judge. The Torah uses the expression *tzelem Elokim* while, as we know, the name Elokim connotes the Attribute of Justice.

The Murderer Has Killed Himself

With all due respect to my father zt"l, perhaps we can offer an additional interpretation of the *pasuk*. "For in the image of God, He made man" refers to the murderer himself! When man murders, he destroys his own Godly image and it is for this that he is punished. In what way does a murderer destroy his Godly image? The Tomer Devora teaches us that man is *tzelem Elokim* in body as well as in mind. One who is similar only in body mocks this image. Man's task in this world, is to 'shape' himself as closely as possible after His Creator. In other words, we are required to emulate the Almighty by our actions as much as possible.

When the Jewish people were crossing Yam Suf, they declared: זה קלי ואנוהו – "This is my God and I will beautify Him."[10] In *Sicha* II for *Parshas Bereishis* we cited a Baraisa which interprets this verse as, "Beautify yourself before Him in fulfillment of Commandments."[11] The Baraisa cites examples of how one beautifies oneself before Hashem: "Make before Him a beautiful *sukkah*, a beautiful *lulav*, and a beautiful *shofar*, beautiful *tzitzis* and a beautiful Torah scroll."[12] Onkelos in fact interprets the *pasuk* to mean, "This is my God and I will build Him a Sanctuary." He analyzes the word 'anvehu' as coming from the same root as 'naveh' – 'a dwelling place.'

Hashem's Sanctuary has to be beautiful. Our souls too must be beautiful, in keeping with the interpretation of this *pasuk* offered by Abba Shaul: '*Ve-anvehu*' – '*hevei domeh lo*' – 'Be like Him.' According to this explanation, '*ve-anvehu*' comes from '*ani vehu*' – 'me and Him.'[13] How can one emulate Hashem? "Just as God is gracious and compassionate, you should also be gracious and compassionate."[14] Material things can be made beautiful by adding gold and silver, while a person can develop a beautiful soul by acting in the image of Hashem. Just as the physical *Mishkan* must be a place which houses the physical Torah, our soul too must be a place which houses the spiritual Torah.

In *Moreh Nevuchim*, we learn that only four people reached the level of complete devotion to Hashem – Moshe Rabenu and our three forefathers. Their thoughts were constantly with Hashem, whether they were involved in *mitzvos* or whether they were involved in caring for their flocks. While it is highly unlikely that we could reach such a level of perfection, each of us on our own level must become as close as we can to Hashem, by emulating His attributes, and by cleaving to *talmidei chachamim*. The murderer did the opposite of this; he totally destroyed his Godly image and for this he is punished.

We mentioned earlier the concept of giving credit where credit is due. If someone does something good even without intention, he is rewarded for it. How much more so, then, when a person intends to do good. Reward is commensurate with the effort invested:

The Torah relates at the end of *Parshas Noach*:

וישת מן היין וישכר ויתגל בתוך אהלה.

וירא חם אבי כנען את ערות אביו ויגד לשני אחיו בחוץ.

ויקח שם ויפת את השמלה וישימו על שכם שניהם וילכו

אחורנית ויכסו את ערות אביהם ופניהם אחרנית וערות אביהם לא ראו

"He (Noach) drank of the wine and became drunk, and he uncovered himself within his tent. And Ham, the father of Canaan, saw his father's nakedness and told his two brothers outside. And Shem and Yefes took a garment, laid it upon both their shoulders, and they walked backwards, and covered their father's nakedness. Their faces were turned backward, and they saw not their father's nakedness."[5]

Rashi comments that the description of Shem and Yefes taking the garment is described by the singular ויקח rather than the plural ויקחו – "This teaches us about Shem that he exerted effort in the fulfillment of the commandment more than did Yefes." They acted together, yet in the Heavens it was clear that Shem put "more of his heart" into the act. As reward for their action, Shem merited the mitzvah of *tzitzis*, for the fulfillment of which he and his descendants were granted a share in the World to Come, while Yefes was rewarded with burial rights for his descendants who were killed in the war of *Gog u'Magog*. What a vast difference extra effort makes!

Exerting Effort

The same idea applies to learning Torah. Chazal cite the *pasuk*, "Then you will return and see the difference between the righteous and the wicked, between one who serves Hashem and one who does not serve Him."[16] They expound: "He that serves Hashem and He that does not serve Him are both perfectly righteous; but he who reviewed what he learned one hundred times cannot be compared to him who reviewed what he learned one hundred and one times."[17] Relative to one who has reviewed his learning one hundred and one times, one who has reviewed it "only" one hundred times is not considered a servant of Hashem because he did not exert sufficient effort in his Torah study.

The *pasuk* states "And it was this matter that he (Yeravam ben Nevat) raised a hand against the king: Shlomo had built up the Millo and closed up the breach of the City of David his father."[18] Chazal elaborate on Yeravam's rebuke of Shlomo: "Your father David made breaches in the wall so that Israel might come up to Yerushalayim for the festivals and enter the city with ease. You, on the other hand, closed up the breaches in order to levy a toll for Pharaoh's daughter."[19] Chazal add: "Why did Yeravam merit kingship? Because he rebuked Shlomo HaMelech. Why was he subsequently punished? Because he rebuked in public." It was one and the same action which merited him the kingship and lost it for him. Hashem's judgment is so precise that a person is judged for the positive and negative aspects of every act.

The concluding *pasuk* of the book of *Koheles* is: "For God will judge every deed – even everything hidden – whether good or evil."[20] They said in the academy of Rav Yannai, "This refers to one who gives charity to a poor person in public, as in the incident that occurred with Rav Yannai. He saw a certain man who gave a small coin to a poor person in public. Rav Yannai said to him, 'It would have been better if you had not given him the charity than what you have done now; for you have given him charity in public and embarrassed him.'"[21] We see that a person can be judged negatively even when doing a good deed.

Another Gemara relates, "Two patients were confined to a sick bed with the identical illness, or similarly, two suspects came before a tribunal with the identical case against them. This patient recovered and was able to leave his bed whereas that patient was not able to leave his bed. This suspect was spared from capital punishment, whereas that one was not spared. Why did this one merit leaving his sick bed, while that one did not merit leaving his? Why was this suspect spared from capital punishment, while the other one was not spared? This one prayed for relief and was answered, while that one prayed and was not answered. Why was this one answered and that one not answered? Because this one prayed a complete prayer, so he was answered, but that one did not pray a complete prayer, so he was not answered."[22] If a person puts more of his heart into his prayers it can greatly affect Hashem's response.

The Gemara teaches us, "The non-essentials of a mitzvah prevent disaster, for the wave-offering is non-essential (Rashi: – One can achieve atonement without it), and wards off the bad spirits."[23] Nevertheless, one must first be concerned with the details of the mitzvah itself before worrying about the non-essentials. Being precise in details of *mitzvos* is of primary importance. There is no value to non-essentials or even placing one's heart in a mitzvah without strict observance of its details. Eating less than a *kezayis* of matzah on Pesach serves no purpose.

There is a discussion as to whether beautifying a mitzvah (*noi mitzvah*, which we discussed above) is viewed as one of the details of a mitzvah. If we consider *noi mitzvah* as part of the mitzvah, then one who has performed a mitzvah without *hiddur* has not fulfilled the mitzvah. However, the Rav (HaGaon HaRav Shlomo Zalman Auerbach) zt"l, ruled that although a person who has not beautified the mitzvah has not fulfilled the commandment "*Ve-anvehu*" – "I will beautify Him,"[24] he has fulfilled the mitzvah itself.

From the *Mesilas Yesharim*, it appears that beautifying a mitzvah is a fulfillment of the mitzvah to fear Hashem. Based on this, we can conclude that if a person does not take care to purchase a beautiful *lulav*, he will have the mitzvah of *lulav*, but not of fearing Hashem.

Our task in this world is to fulfill both interpretations of זה קלי ואנוהו. We must put as much effort as we can into beautifying our *mitzvos*, and we must also try as much as is humanly possible to emulate Hashem and to be the best *tzelem Elokim* we possibly can.

Notes

1   *Bereishis* 9:6

2   See *Sanhedrin* 57b and 72b.

3   *Bereishis* 9:5

4   *Devarim* 22:8

5   *Shabbos* 32a

6   *Bereishis* 45:8

7   *Bereishis* 24:50

8   See Rashi, *Shemos* 17:19 and 8:12.

9   See *Shemos Rabba* 1:32.

10   *Shemos* 5:2

11   *Shabbos* 133b

12   Ibid.

13   See Rashi there.

14   *Shabbos* 133b

15   *Bereishis* 9:21-23

16 *Malachi* 3:18

17 *Chagiga* 9b

18 *Melachim* I 11:27

19 *Sanhedrin* 101b

20 *Koheles* 12:14

21 *Chagiga* 5a

22 *Rosh Hashana* 18a

23 *Sukkah* 38a

24 *Shemos* 15:2.

Parshas Lech Lecha

The Heritage Of Eretz Yisrael

Gifts With Strings Attached

Picture this scenario: a friend comes along and gives you a gift. You're grateful and happy. But then he comes back and says, "By the way, the gift has strings attached. I want you to do such and such in return." A while later he comes back with still more demands. By now you're not looking so happy …

At first glance, this is how Hashem appears to be acting with Avraham Avinu in our *parsha*. Hashem promises Avraham לזרעך נתתי את הארץ הזאת. "I have given this land to your descendants."[1] Later on, He seems to make acquiring the Land contingent on the mitzvah of *bris milah*.

ואתה את בריתי תשמר אתה וזרעך אחריך לדרתם – "And as for you, you shall keep My covenant – you and your offspring after you throughout the generations."[2] As we read on, we notice that even *bris milah* is not sufficient. Receiving *Eretz Yisrael* depends on observance of all 613 *mitzvos*!

Our analysis that Hashem is making this gift conditional is clearly incorrect. We need to find another way to explain the sequence of events. A better comparison would be if the friend offered us a plot of land to tend. The following day he informs us that the land is unsuitable for growing wheat, but would be more productive if we were to plant an orchard. The friend then teaches us how to plant and maintain an orchard – we need to fertilize the soil, then plant the seedlings, give them lots of water, and take good care of them. The giver in this case is not setting conditions, but is teaching us how to make best use of the gift he has given us. Not only would we not have any complaints against him; we would even feel grateful to the friend for his advice as well as for the gift.

Similarly, Hashem promised *Eretz Yisrael* to Avraham Avinu and then taught him how to keep the Land, warning him that without *bris milah*, he would not be able to take possession of it. Receiving the Land and remaining in it are conditional on fulfillment of *bris milah*, as well as the rest of the 613 *mitzvos*. The Land spat out the Canaanites. It could, *Hashem yerachem*, spit you out too, if you do not keep the *mitzvos*. In *Birkas Ha'Mazon* we describe this precious Land as ארץ חמדה טובה ורחבה – "a desirable, good, and spacious land." We also thank Hashem for the בריתך שחתמת בבשרנו – "Your covenant which You sealed with our flesh," as well as תורתך שלמדתנו – "Your Torah which You taught us." The "desirable, good, and spacious land" cannot be ours unless we keep "the covenant which You sealed with our flesh," and the "Torah which You taught us." Any attempt to settle the Land without fulfilling these conditions will be unsuccessful.

During the reign of the wicked king Achaz over Yehuda, Hoshea ben Elah ruled as the last king of Israel. *Am Yisrael* sinned terribly, worshipping idols and doing wicked things to anger Hashem. Hashem sent them into exile to Assyria. Sancheriv, king of Assyria, brought in foreigners from Bavel, Kutta and elsewhere to occupy the now desolate cities of Samaria. These nations continued worshipping their idols as they had in their countries of origin. As punishment, Hashem afflicted them with a plague of lions until they learned "the laws of the God of the land"[3] – that the Land cannot tolerate *avoda zara*. Settling the Land successfully requires observance of Torah and *mitzvos*. There are many countries throughout the world, many far vaster than *Eretz Yisrael*. What makes this Land so special is that it is the "Land that Hashem, your God, seeks out; the eyes of Hashem, your God, are always upon it."[4] Hashem did not give us the gift of *Eretz Yisrael* and then demand something in exchange for it, God forbid. We can only retain possession of a Land so saturated with spirituality by observing the covenant of *bris milah* and all the other *mitzvos*. A person can reside in Canada or Switzerland without fulfilling *mitzvos*, but he cannot live in *Eretz Yisrael* under those conditions. This is what Hashem taught Avraham Avinu and later the rest of the nation at Har Sinai and then at Har Grizim and Har Eival.

Only One Treaty

Today we are witness to the Land's being taken from us, *Hashem yerachem*. Many good Jews are fighting against the so-called "peace treaties" and trying to save the Holy Land. At the same time, however, some of these same people are part of a movement calling for a new 'social contract' which would involve compromising observance of *mitzvos* in *Eretz Yisrael*. The only treaty we know is the one we made with Hashem at Har Sinai and reiterated at Har Grizim and on Arvos Moav. This is the only contract which gives us any right to the Land! The only alternative would be a Palestinian treaty, which we certainly do not desire. There can be no other treaty! What right do we have to enter into an agreement permitting secular Jews to travel on *Shabbos*?

The Chafetz Chaim once tried to persuade store owners to close their businesses on *Shabbos*. As always, the Chafetz Chaim spoke with the utmost sincerity. דברים היוצאים מן הלב נכנסים אל הלב – "Words that emanate from the heart enter the heart." The businessmen listened and agreed to keep their stores closed on *Shabbos*. However, a number of the store owners claimed that they needed a few more weeks to organize their businesses, after which they would close on *Shabbos*. The Chafetz Chaim gently responded, "*Kinderlach*, if the *Shabbos* were mine, I would allow you to keep your stores open with pleasure. However the *Shabbos* is not mine. It belongs to Hashem; He gave it to us. Do I have any right to permit you to desecrate it?" Does anyone think for a moment that the Mishna Brura is a series of *chumros* which the Chafetz Chaim fabricated? His rulings are based on the Gemara and the later authorities; he did not make his own decisions to permit that which is forbidden. Certainly we too have no right to permit *Shabbos* desecration. Many places of entertainment in Tel Aviv may already be open on *Shabbos*, but for religious Jews to give their stamp of approval? That is a disgrace! Even if all the religious parties decided to vote in favor of this social contract, it would still have no meaning.

The only treaty we know is the one between us and the Almighty. Our job is to help each other to fulfill our end of the bargain. כל ישראל ערבים זה לזה – "All Jews are responsible for one another."[5] It is forbidden for any religious or non-religious Jew to desecrate the *Shabbos*. If we are unable to persuade our secular brethren to keep *Shabbos*, if we are unable to put enough effort into bringing them closer to *Shabbos* and Torah – and in my opinion more time should be spent on this – we should at least not give our stamp of approval to *Shabbos* desecration. Our task is to demonstrate to the secular Jews what *Shabbos* is – to teach them about the sanctity of *Shabbos*. No treaty can ever permit *chillul Shabbos*. We cannot burn the candle at both ends – on the one hand to oppose a treaty with the Palestinians calling for giving them parts of *Eretz Yisrael*, such as the treaty signed at Wye (what an appropriate name – "oy vye!"), while at the same time to support a treaty violating the very purpose of our being in this Land!

Who Was Avram?

I have difficulty with another section of the *parsha* – the opening *pasuk*. The *parsha* begins:

ויאמר ה' אל אברם לך לך מארצך וממולדתך
ומבית אביך אל הארץ אשר אראך

"Hashem said to Avram, 'Go for yourself from your land, from your relatives and from your father's house to the land that I will show you.'"[6]

Who was Avram and why was he chosen? Until this point, the Torah has provided us with little background information on the future father of the Jewish nation.

It is only from our Oral Tradition that we know that Avraham Avinu recognized his Creator at age three and broke his father's idols, that he sanctified Hashem's Name in Ur Kasdim, and tried to convince others to serve Hashem. The incident in Ur Kasdim is alluded to later when Hashem said: אני ה' אשר הוצאתיך מאור כשדים "I am Hashem Who brought you out of Ur Kasdim,"[7] yet we find no reference at all to the other incidents.

A simple reading of the end of *Parshas Noach* and the beginning of *Parshas Lech Lecha* implies that it was through Terach's merit that Avraham was chosen to make the journey to Eretz Yisrael. Although a week separates the readings of *Parshas Noach* and *Parshas Lech Lecha*, in the Torah itself the words are contiguous. At the end of *Parshas Noach* we read: ויקח תרח את אברם בנו...ללכת ארצה כנען "Terach took his son Avram … to go to the land of Canaan."[8] Terach was unable to complete the journey and then *Parshas Lech Lecha* begins, "Hashem said to Avram, 'Go for yourself from your land, from your relatives and from your father's house to the land that I will show you.'"[9] It seems that Terach and Avraham set out together on a journey, but Terach died on the way and Avraham completed the journey without his father. We are not told anything about Avraham prior to the Divine Revelation he received. At this point the Torah begins to relate some of Avraham's great deeds and the immense trials of faith he underwent, but from the way the *parsha* begins, it appears as if Hashem had no special reason for choosing Avraham – He could just as well have revealed Himself to someone else.

Hashem Chooses Avraham

Clearly the Torah is trying to teach us a lesson. The Torah is emphasizing that indeed Hashem could have chosen someone else. As we recite in the Pesach Haggadah, "Yehoshua said to the entire nation, 'Thus said Hashem the God of Israel: your forefathers, Terach, the father of Avraham and the father of Nahor, always dwelt beyond the river, and they served other gods, but I took your forefather Avraham from beyond the river and led him throughout all the land of Canaan.'"[10] Is this all Yehoshua can say about Avraham Avinu? Why does he ignore the fact that Avraham recognized his Creator at a tender age? It appears as if Avraham was an idol worshipper, and suddenly, for no apparent reason, Hashem whisked him away, "beyond the river and led him throughout all the land of Canaan." Apparently the relationship between Hashem and Avraham did not begin with Avraham's recognizing the existence of a Creator, but rather with Hashem having chosen Avraham.

In fact, we recite every morning:

אתה הוא ה' האלקים אשר בחרת באברם והוצאתו מאור כשדים

"You are Hashem the God, Who selected Avram and brought him out of Ur Kasdim."[11]

There, however, the *pasuk* concludes:

ומצאת את לבבו נאמן לפניך

"You found his heart faithful before You."[12]

Nevertheless, it does appear as if Hashem chose Avram and brought him out of Ur Kasdim before He found his heart faithful. It is well-known that Avraham recognized the existence of the Creator on his own, that he allowed himself to be thrown into the furnace rather than renounce his beliefs and that he spread the message of *emunah* and *chessed*. Why are these not mentioned? Why are we given the impression that these reasons were not factors in Hashem's decision to choose Avraham?

The Torah is teaching us that although Avraham had many merits, which it goes on to relate, such as the *Akeida*, the Creator's choice preceded all this. Avraham was created with qualities such as a great heart and mind, but it was left up to him which path he would choose. Perhaps Nimrod and others had similar qualities, yet they chose a different path. It was because Avraham chose to follow Hashem that ומצאת את לבבו נאמן לפניך. Hashem, however, had chosen Avraham even before Avraham chose to follow the ways of Hashem. Out of all the idol worshippers of the generation, he was chosen to make the journey to the land of Canaan. The *pasuk* states: מי יתן טהור מטמא לא אחד – "Who can produce purity from impurity? No one!"[13] One example that Chazal bring to clarify this *pasuk* is that of Avraham being taken from the idol worshipping home of Terach and brought to *Eretz Yisrael* to serve Hashem.[14]

What point am I trying to make? Man has free choice and if he chooses the good path, he will be duly rewarded. The Rambam teaches us, in *Hilchos Teshuva*, that the idea of free choice is one of the foundations of our faith. Every person has the ability to become as great a *tzaddik* as Moshe Rabenu (though not as great a prophet) or as evil as Pharaoh. There is, however, a higher world where things are preordained.

A World Of Illusion

Our physical world is one of choices, and every move we make is based on our decision about which path to follow. In relation to the upper worlds of Absolute Truth, we are living in a world of illusion. If a child dreams that he lost his toy car, it is only a dream and not reality. He might have cried himself to sleep over the loss of his car, only to awaken in the morning to find it safely tucked under his pillow. What is the dream? That the car was lost. What is reality? That the car was not lost. Can we call this reality? Is the car really a car? Is it not just a piece of plastic with rubber wheels that can be rolled back and forth! What the child perceives as reality is only an illusion. In the adult world, it appears to us that the adult is driving the car. The truth is that neither the car nor the driver is in control. Hashem runs the world and in a sense even the adult's car is imaginary.

From the perspective of the world we live in, our decisions are based on free choice. However, from the perspective of the higher worlds, it is all imaginary. Hashem decreed that Avraham will be Avraham, Yitzchak will be Yitzchak, and Yaakov will be Yaakov. In our world it appears to us as if we have free choice to decide how to live our lives, and we must live according to this illusion. It is forbidden for us to act upon what we think has been decided.

Likewise, we are all well aware that כל דעביד רחמנא לטב עביד "Whatever the Merciful One does, He does for the best."[15] Chazal tell us: "The World to Come is unlike this world; in this world, on good news one says ברוך הטוב והמטיב – 'Blessed Who is good and does good,' and on bad news one says ברוך דיין האמת – 'Blessed is the

True Judge.' In the World to Come, there will be only one blessing, 'Who is good and does good.'"[16] In the upper worlds, everything is viewed as being for the good. In this world, however, when a tragedy occurs, God forbid, we must recite ברוך דיין האמת. We are forbidden to rationalize that since we know everything Hashem does is for the good, we should recite the *beracha* of ברוך הטוב והמטיב. We live in an illusory world and we must act accordingly.

The Gemara[17] quotes a curious statement: "As they were about to enter the *pardes*, Rebbi Akiva told his colleagues, '"When you arrive at the stones of pure marble do not say 'Water, water!' Calling marble 'water' would be a lie and 'One who tells lies shall not be established before my eyes.'"[18]

Judgment And *Chessed*

What does this mean? Is it not obvious that marble should not be mistaken for water? Must Rebbi Akiva quote a *pasuk* to justify why his colleagues should not speak such nonsense when they enter the *pardes*? There are obviously deeper meanings behind this Gemara. As far as we are able to comprehend something so profound, the intention is that marble refers to strength, to the harsh Attribute of Judgment. The Attribute of Judgment, however, stems from the Attribute of *Chessed*. Water represents *chessed*. Judgment is really all *chessed* and even when we experience some of the harsh judgment of this world, we realize that it is all for the good: "Whatever the Merciful One does, He does for the best."[19] Perhaps, Rebbi Akiva thought, they may only see the good in whatever happens to them. Rebbi Akiva therefore tells them that in this world we cannot refer to judgment as *chessed*. When we arrive in the Next World we will recite *hatov vehameitiv* for what appears to be a harsh judgment, but in this world we may not, because we are unable truly to perceive it as such.

The above Gemara refers to the same Rebbi Akiva who laughed when he witnessed foxes emerging from *Har HaBayis*, because he knew that this fulfillment of the first half of Zecharia's prophecy assured the ultimate fulfillment of the second half: "Old men and women will once again sit in the streets of Yerushalayim!"[20] At the same time, however, Rebbi Akiva tore his clothing together with the other sages in mourning for the *Har HaBayis* which now lay desolate. We are not permitted to rejoice at the site of the destruction and say "I know the *Beis HaMikdash* will soon be rebuilt." We have to tear our clothes when we approach the site of the desolation. We know that Zecharia's prophecy will be fulfilled eventually, but in the meantime, there is destruction! When one receives bad news, he must express what he feels and that is ברוך דיין האמת! We know that there is a World above this World of Choice, but we must act according to the illusory world we live in.

In *halacha* we find many areas in which appearances are significant even when they contradict reality. Let me cite one example: there is a discussion in the Gemara about the direction in which one must pray. We follow the opinion that we must always face Yerushalayim whether we are standing to the east, west, north, or south. Another opinion states: "the Divine Presence is in the west."[21] Were we to follow this view, no matter where one is in the world, he would be obliged to pray facing west. Just as at Har Sinai and in the *Mishkan*, the *Shechina* was in the west, it always remains in the west. If so, what would we be facing when we face west? Someone in Yerushalayim would be facing more or less towards Beit Shemesh or Ramle, yet if a Jew in the United States were to pray towards Ramle, he would be facing east, not west! For him the Divine Presence cannot be in Ramle because that is towards the east. Where is the *Shechina*? Is it west of Tel Aviv? Is it in the Mediterranean? This also cannot be, because for a Jew in America, the Mediterranean is to his east!

The answer is that it all depends on a person's perspective. Beit Shemesh is to my west, while west of Tel Aviv is Greece, and west for most Americans refers to Los Angeles. West changes with a person's perspective. Each person can say that to him, the *Shechina* resides to his west even though this may be to someone else's east. According to this opinion (which we do not follow) the *halacha* is that you must pray to your west while another person must pray to his west even if this means that you are each facing towards a different place.

Earning Our Share In The World To Come

We do not live in a world of absolute knowledge of Hashem. We live in our illusory world of choice. We must make the best choices based on the information we have, even if we know that another world exists. That is the world of Absolute Truth, in which Hashem took Avraham out of the house of idol worship for reasons we do not know, the world which "all of Israel have a share of."[22] We may be aware of the other world's existence, but we are not permitted to act on this knowledge. We must strive to reserve for ourselves a place in the Next World by making the correct choices. We mention זכות אבות – the merit of our forefathers, at every opportunity, but we must earn our share of the Next World on our own merit, not on the merit of our fathers and not because we rely on the promise that "Every Jew has a share in the World to Come."[23]

A Jew may ask, "Why should I bother to learn Torah and fulfill *mitzvos*, if in any event every Jew has a share in the World to Come? So, I might not be given a front row seat along with the other *tzaddikim* in Gan Eden and I probably will not eat from the head of the *liviasan*; perhaps I will get the tail. It is sufficient to know that I have a share in the Next World!" The Chafetz Chaim explained the answer to this with an analogy. There was once a rich factory owner who gave very generously to charity. He instructed his treasurer that every Rosh Chodesh, when he gave out the salaries, he should set aside money for the poor – each portion based on what the owner determined. One Rosh Chodesh, the owner came to see how his business was operating and to observe the allocation of the monies. When the workers came to receive their salaries, they appeared before him and introduced themselves according to their occupations – one was an engineer, one an electrician, one a handyman, and so on. One man was left standing there. The owner went over to him, shook his hand, and asked him what work he did. He answered that his function is to receive a salary. The nearby crowd burst out laughing, but the poor fellow was acutely embarrassed.

The Chafetz Chaim explained that this is how a Jew will feel if he enters the Next World bare of *mitzvos*, relying solely on the fact that every Jew has a share in the World to Come. He will be embarrassed and everyone will laugh at him. Worse than that is the fact that in this world, someone who receives a paycheck without working for it suffers some embarrassment, goes home, and the embarrassment passes. In the Next World, the embarrassment is eternal. We must arrive in the Next World, not only because every Jew has a share in the World to Come, in the same way as Hashem chose Avraham even before Avraham demonstrated his righteousness, but through making the right choices in life. This applies to every Jew.

Become An Executive!

I can think of another potential cause for laughter. What would happen if the factory employed a person as a janitor, when he had all the necessary skills and qualifications to become a manager? When his turn comes and the owner asks him what he does, he will be very embarrassed to answer that he sweeps floors. You could have been a high ranking executive! Why are you sweeping floors? In this case, he earned his salary, but he had the qualifications to earn much more. If we are blessed with the ability to become managers, it is forbidden for us to sweep floors! Every one of us here in the Yeshiva has the ability to become a high ranking "executive." *Tosafos*[24] write that it is only natural for someone who sets out to learn Torah to become great. Obviously it requires hard work on his part, but the potential exists within anyone who sets out to learn.

Many years ago I was sitting with my Rebbe, HaRav Nachum Pertzovitz zt"l in Yeshivas Mir, when a student approached him to seek his counsel. This young man was troubled by the fact that he had already spent five years in the Yeshiva and did not feel that he had seen positive results from his learning. The student asked, "Do Chazal not teach us that a person who has learned for five years and has not seen *siman bracha* will probably never see it?"[25] He wondered if perhaps the time had come to leave the Yeshiva. Rav Nachum answered that the Gemara refers to a person who has spent his time learning; a person who has not learned cannot hope to see any *siman bracha*!

When the *Tosafos* state that a person who sets out to learn generally does see a *siman bracha*, the condition is that he must expend great effort and not rely on the merit of his forefathers. The fact that he is descended from Avraham Avinu and that his grandfather was the Rav of the community is not enough. One must strive to achieve his own greatness irrespective of who his grandfather may have been.

This requirement is incumbent on every Yeshiva student, but we in Yerushalayim have an even greater obligation. Interestingly, the first Talmud Torah as we know it was founded in the time of the Talmud. The Gemara[26] states, "The sages enacted that teachers of children[27] be appointed in Yerushalayim. Which verse were they expounding? 'For Torah shall go forth from Zion and the word of God from Jerusalem.'"[28]

We can learn from here that Yerushalayim is the place best suited for anyone to learn Torah. Baruch Hashem, we merited receiving an education in our youth and are not beginning now with *Aleph Beis*. The location of our Yeshiva, overlooking the *Kosel HaMaarovi*, is more suited for growth than any other Yeshiva on earth – it is our choice whether to become executives or to sweep floors. Hashem knows what will become of us, but we must make our own decisions and choices.

Many feel that we need religious doctors and engineers. Certainly that would be great, but we must keep in mind that doctors and engineers can come from the secular public while only a religious Jew can become a Torah giant! Only Yeshiva students can become *gedolei Torah*.

Growing In Torah

Our obligation is, to toil, to spend many hours in Torah study and to become great. There are two types of *bitul Torah*. There is quantitative *bitul Torah*, where a person does not utilize his time properly in order to learn as much as he can, and what the *Acharonim* refer to as qualitative *bitul Torah*; if one had the opportunity to study the Gemara, *Rishonim*, and *Acharonim* but he instead elected to study *Ein Yaakov*. A person who could have learned much more deeply but

---

27   This enactment was abolished when it became clear that only older children were being sent, while the younger the child was, the greater benefit there was to his learning.

satisfied himself with Gemara and Rashi is guilty of qualitative *bitul Torah*. Obviously, one is not expected to do more than he is capable of, but a Jew who could do more is guilty of *bitul Torah* if he spends his time studying only simpler texts.

We must all strive to be great, to grow in Torah in all the forty-eight ways in which the Torah is acquired, but first and foremost by learning. We must concentrate hard when we *daven*. והאר עינינו בתורתך ודבק לבנו במצותיך – "Enlighten our eyes with Your Torah and let our hearts cleave to Your *mitzvos*." and חננו מאתך דעה בינה והשכל – "Endow us graciously from Yourself with wisdom, insight, and discernment."[29] We must pray that Hashem grant us the wisdom of the Torah.

The Chafetz Chaim used to wonder how a Jew can beseech Hashem for דעה בינה והשכל and ask והאר עינינו בתורתך and yet not open a sefer after *davening* to check if his prayers were answered!

We must *daven*, learn, and follow in the footsteps of Avraham Avinu by performing many acts of *chessed*. A *bachur* need not look outside the Yeshiva for *chessed* opportunities, for there are many opportunities inside as well. A veteran *talmid* can help a new *talmid* get settled. If you understand the Gemara, you can help someone who is having difficulty. In the same way that Avraham Avinu merited receiving the Land of Israel through Torah, *avodah*, and *gemilus chassadim*, we too can merit receiving the Torah and *Eretz Yisrael*. The *pasuk* states "And He gave them the lands of nations, and they inherited the toil of regimes, so that they might safeguard His statutes and observe His teachings."[30] If we strengthen our Torah, *avodah*, and *gemilus chassadim*, then we will merit receiving the gift Hashem promised to Avraham, Yitzchak, and Yaakov.

Perhaps one area which warrants special emphasis is "*Oneg Shabbos*" – "delighting in the *Shabbos*." Why do I single out this mitzvah? The Gemara states, "Whoever delights in the *Shabbos* is granted a נחלה, a heritage – without troubles."[31] If today all we see is "troubles without the נחלה – the land," then perhaps the way to remedy the situation is to delight in the *Shabbos*, which promises us "heritage – without

---

29 חכמה בינה ודעת in Nusach Sefard.

troubles." Then we will truly deserve to receive "the heritage of your forefather Yaakov,"[32] and merit seeing the total redemption speedily in our days, Amen.

Notes

1   *Bereishis* 15:18

2   *Bereishis* 17:9

3   *Melachim* II 17:27

4   *Devarim* 11:12

5   *Shevuos* 39a

6   *Bereishis* 12:1

7   *Bereishis* 15:7

8   *Bereishis* 11:31

9   *Bereishis* 12:1

10   *Yehoshua* 24:2-3

11   *Nehemiah* 9:7

12   Ibid. 8

13   *Iyov* 14:4

14   See *Bamidbar Rabba, Parsha* 19.

15   *Berachos* 60b

16   *Pesachim* 50a

17   *Chagiga* 14b

18 *Tehillim* 101:7

19 *Berachos* 60b

20 *Zecharia* 8:4

21 *Baba Basra* 25a

22 *Sanhedrin* Perek 10, Mishna 1

23 *Sanhedrin* 90a

24 *Kesubos* 63a

25 See *Chullin* 24a.

26 *Baba Basra* 21a

28 *Yeshayahu* 2:3

30 *Tehillim* 105:44-45

31 *Shabbos* 118a

32 *Yeshayahu* 58:14

The Making Of A Soul

ויקח אברם את שרי אשתו ואת לוט בן אחיו ואת כל רכושם
אשר רכשו ואת הנפש אשר עשו בחרן ויצאו ללכת ארצה כנען
ויבאו ארצה כנען.

*"Avram took his wife Sarai and Lot, his brother's son, and all
their wealth that they had amassed, and the souls they made
in Haran; and they left to go to the land of Canaan."*[1]

"The Souls They Made In Haran"

What is the meaning of "the souls they made?" How does one
go about making a soul? Onkelos interprets this "soul industry" as
וית נפשתא דשעבידו לאורייתא – "the souls that were subjugated to
the Torah by the influence of Avraham and Sarah". In the words of
Rashi:

אברהם מגייר את האנשים ושרה מגיירת הנשים
ומעלה עליהם הכתוב כאילו עשאום.

*"Avraham would convert the men, and Sarah would convert the wom-
en, and Scripture considers them as if they made them."*

What defines a person's soul? We recite daily in *Krias Shema*: ואהבת את ה' אלקיך בכל לבבך ובכל נפשך ובכל מאדך. – "You shall love Hashem, your God, with all your heart, with all your soul, and with all your resources."[2] Chazal tell us, ובכל נפשך – אפילו הוא נוטל את נפשך –"With all your soul, 'even if he takes your soul.'"[3] What about a person who, Baruch Hashem, is not called upon to give up his life in order to sanctify Hashem's Name? How does he love Hashem בכל נפשך – "with all his soul?" When Avraham Avinu approached the people of Cheis, wishing to purchase a plot of land in which to bury his wife Sarah, he said: "אם יש את נפשכם לקבר את מתי מלפני" Some of the commentaries[4] interpret this request to mean "If it is truly your will to bury my dead before me." In this context the word נפש refers to a person's will and desire and we would thus explain the Torah's command to love Hashem בכל נפשך as referring to loving Hashem with our entire will.

When Avraham and Sarah made souls in Haran, they 'made their will' for them; they transformed them, so that they no longer desired to follow the dictates of their *yetzer hara*, but began to follow the true desire of their soul to serve Hashem. This is how they "made souls." The people may not have been Jewish, but even non-Jews possess an innate desire to serve Hashem. *Halacha* mandates that if they express a sincere desire, we should convert them, or at least influence them to accept upon themselves the seven Noachide laws.

Although total devotion to Torah is referred to as שעבוד and the person devoted to Torah is called an עבד ה' – "a servant of Hashem," in reality it is the ultimate freedom of which a person is capable. The Baraisa teaches us: אין בן חורין אלא מי שעוסק בתורה. – "The only free man is one who is involved in Torah."[5] In the words of Rabbi Yehuda HaLevi: עבדי הזמן – עבדי עבדים הם, עבד ה' – הוא לבד חפשי – "Slaves to their time – are truly enslaved, a slave to Hashem – he alone is free."

We recite in the evening *berachos* of *Krias Shema*: המכה בעברתו כל בכורי מצרים ויוצא את עמו ישראל מתוכם לחרות עולם – "Who struck with His anger at the firstborn of Egypt and removed His nation from their midst to eternal freedom."

In what sense did we emerge from the bondage of Egypt to eternal freedom? Did Hashem not simply remove us from the bondage of Egypt and make us His servants, *lehavdil*? We can learn from here that being a servant of Hashem is in fact "eternal freedom."

We may ask in what way a servant of Hashem has achieved eternal freedom. Are there not many more demands placed on an עבד ה' than on a slave of Pharaoh? We were only slaves to Pharaoh for six days a week,[6] and we were given some semblance of freedom at night in order to sleep.[7] A true עבד ה' serves Hashem day and night. His every move is subject to the laws of the Torah twenty-four hours a day, seven days a week! *Halacha* dictates how we must sleep at night,[8] how we must arise in the morning,[9] how we must wash our hands,[10] how we get dressed,[11] how and what we must eat, and much, much more. It is true that after all is said and done, we would rather be servants of Hashem than of Pharaoh, but can we truly classify this as eternal freedom?

In order to answer this question, let us first try to understand the distinction between a slave and a free man. A slave is subject to the will of his master. Even if the master is kind and considerate, and does not overburden the slave with hard labor the way Pharaoh did, in the final analysis, it is the master who determines the course of the slave's life, not the slave himself. A free man, on the other hand, dictates his own path in life and is not subjugated to the whims of anyone else. Accordingly, we can say that one who follows the dictates of his *yetzer hara* is nothing more than a slave. He may consider himself free, but in truth he is a slave. Why? Because the wish of my *yetzer hara* is not necessarily my wish. My *yetzer hara* is not me, but another entity outside of me. It is my soul, the Godliness in me, which is my true self. What my soul wants is the opposite of what my *yetzer hara* wants. Therefore, if I allow my *yetzer hara* to dictate my life, I am nothing more than a slave to it, and it is my master. When I follow the needs and desires of my soul, the true me, then I am truly a free man, in complete control of my actions.

The *Yetzer Hara's* Masquerade

The *Chovos HaLevavos*[12] writes that a person must realize that the *yetzer hara* is his biggest enemy. "When you are asleep, he is awake. (You may not notice him, but he is eagerly waiting to trip you up.) You may try to ignore him, but he is certainly not ignoring you. He gives the outward appearance of being your good friend as if he loves you; in truth he is your biggest enemy who is only masquerading as your friend."

In my humble opinion, this idea posited by the *Chovos HaLevavos* can be extended. Let us use the following analogy – a man undertakes a mission to spy on another nation, for example, Syria. In his attempt to uncover Syrian military secrets, the spy disguises himself as a good friend of the Syrian President or the Chief of Staff.

The spy may succeed in convincing the president that he is indeed his good friend, yet he will never succeed in convincing him that he (the spy) is the real President of Syria. The *yetzer hara*, however, has far more sophisticated methods – he not only disguises himself as your good friend, but he disguises himself as you! He persuades you that he is you and that what is good for him is good for you. In reality what he wants is the polar opposite of what you want. What does the *yetzer hara* truly desire? He wishes to remove you from the world; not only from the Next World, but from this world as well.

Chazal debate what would happen if we were to leave a goat or a small lamb beside a snake or scorpion. They conclude that it would come to no harm, for instinct teaches animals to beware of anything dangerous. However, if we left a baby, God forbid, in the same place, the curious baby would try to touch the snake or scorpion. Similarly, if we were to leave a goat or lamb near an open pit, the animal would instinctively be careful not to stand too close to the edge. On the other hand, if we were to leave a baby near an open pit, heaven forbid what would result!

What accounts for this distinction? כי יצר לב האדם רע מנעריו – "Because man's inclination is evil from his youth."[13] "From the time that he stirs to leave his mother's body, the urge to do evil is put in him."[14] At this young age, the *yetzer hara* is already pushing him into acting in a way that places his life in danger. The *yetzer hara* has no desire to kill the lamb, only the baby. This is part of his plan to remove him not only from the Next World but from this world as well.

How many people do we know who continue to smoke although they are fully aware of the dangers? Who does not know the damage drugs can cause, yet people continue to use them? Why? This is the *yetzer hara*'s attempt to hasten man's departure from this world. If he does not succeed, he tries to at least make sure that we do not enter the Next World. The *yetzer hara* is our biggest enemy, and we should constantly be on our guard not to mistake his identity for our own.

Spiritual Delicacies

While the *yetzer hara* tries to ensnare us in sin, our souls aspire to the opposite. All souls originate from under the Throne of Glory,[15] especially Jewish souls, which were carved in a lofty and holy place, and therefore have no interest in the ambitions of the *yetzer hara*. Chazal use the following parable to interpret the *pasuk*, וגם הנפש לא תמלא – "His wants are never satisfied."[16]

There was once a simple villager who married a princess. He would shower her with all the gifts this world has to offer, yet they meant nothing to her. Why? Because as the king's daughter, she had grown up cosseted in a sumptuous palace, her every wish catered for. By the same token, if we were to offer our soul all the delicacies of the world, it would be dissatisfied. Our soul came from way up above and has no interest in physical things such as food.[17] A princess who marries a simple villager does not enjoy the country lifestyle. What's in it for her – onions and garlic? In the king's palace she was accustomed to fatted geese, roasted doves, and other royal delicacies.

This is precisely how the soul feels in this world. Our souls were carved from under the Throne of Glory, and are accustomed to spiritual delicacies – Torah and *mitzvos* are their source of nourishment. What do we give them in this world? Fish and meat! What can a soul do with fish and meat? Partaking of food in fulfillment of a mitzvah such as *seudas Shabbos* or perhaps strengthening oneself in order to serve Hashem better, satisfies the soul, but eating for pleasure's sake alone is of no value to the soul, which can be nourished only with spiritual food.

We now know that the *yetzer hara* is not man's self. His soul is his self. We might perhaps have thought that our body is our self, however every month we get a totally new body. Within the space of a month all our cells die off and new ones replace them. We may have a new body, yet we still feel the same self. Therefore our self cannot be our body but it must be our soul.

(However, if this is so, I have difficulty understanding the *beracha* we recite each morning:

אלקי נשמה שנתת בי טהורה היא

"My God, the soul that You placed within me is pure."

What do we mean when we say "the soul that you placed within me?" Is 'me' not the soul itself? How then can we speak of placing the soul within me?)

Tools From The Soul's Toolbox

If the body is not me, then what is it? The body is nothing more than clothing for the self, to house the soul that Hashem sent down to this world. The body provides the tools with which to observe *mitzvos* and perform good deeds. Had it not been for the body, the soul would have no means of carrying out its task in this world.

In addition to the physical body, my soul has other tools to assist it in fulfilling its mission. My mind, for example, is also not my self. It is another tool used to facilitate the soul's work. One of the *Rishonim* defined the mind as המליץ בין האדם ואלוקיו – 'the messenger, the liaison between man and his God.' The intelligence I have been blessed with helps me to know and serve Hashem better. This in no way implies that my mind is me. The only self is my soul.

A person's parents, his wife, and his children are also aids to facilitate his serving Hashem. The Torah commands us that if a man dies without children, God forbid, his brother must fulfill the mitzvah of *yibum* and marry the widow. The deceased's wife was given to him to enable him to father children. Because he did not merit this, his *tikkun* is that his brother will father children through the same woman. Similarly, monetary possessions are also tools to assist us in serving Hashem. When Tzlafchad's daughters came to demand their father's inheritance, their claim was not "Why should our share be diminished?" but rather "Why should the name of our father be omitted from among his family?"[18] When the children inherit the father's possessions and use them to serve Hashem, this is also a *tikkun* for his soul; when there is no heir, this *tikkun* cannot take place. Tzlafchad's daughters desired to provide a *tikkun* for their father's soul by inheriting his share of *Eretz Yisrael*, as well as any other material possessions he had in the desert. Material wealth is therefore also given us to assist us in better serving Hashem. Just as I do not think for a moment that my material possessions are me or that my wife is me, it is clear that my body and my mind are not me either.

Fallen Fruits

All these are tools to help the person achieve his true desire which is to serve Hashem and follow the dictates of the Torah. In *Parshas Haazinu*, Moshe Rabenu refers to the Jewish people as עם נבל.[19] The expression נבל generally has derogatory connotations – implying something vile and despicable. Onkelos interprets this phrase to mean עם דקבילו אורייתא – "the nation that received the Torah." This is very puzzling. Is עם נבל a fitting description for the people who accepted the Torah? Are they not a benevolent and generous nation? They should have been called עם צדיק – 'a righteous nation.' Perhaps the other nations who refused the Torah should be called נבל.

The Vilna Gaon elucidates Onkelos' interpretation. This appellation is based on a *midrash* in which the Torah is referred to as "נובלות חכמה של מעלה". The word נובלות in this case does not refer to things which are vile, but to things which have fallen – "fallen wisdom from above." This may be compared to a fruit tree which is so high that its fruits are out of reach. In the absence of a tall ladder, the only fruits which can be collected and eaten are those which have fallen from the tree onto the ground. Similarly, Godly wisdom is so lofty that man cannot hope to attain it, for "only God understands its way."[20] Hashem brought down to earth some נובלות of his wisdom in the guise of the Torah. The עם נבל who received the Torah refers to the people who received נובלות, which give us some grasp of Hashem's wisdom."[21] Each of us has the opportunity to attain as much of these נובלות as we can, according to our own level. A child in the first grade will comprehend the Torah on his level while a great *talmid chacham* will be able to understand much more. Rebbi Akiva Eiger learned Torah as did Chazal and Moshe Rabenu. In fact they continue to learn Torah in Gan Eden – yet none of them has the ability to fully grasp the totality of the Torah in its perfect state. Only the Almighty Himself can perceive the Torah in all its profundities. "As high as the heavens over the earth, so are My ways higher than your ways and My thoughts higher than your thoughts."[22]

The Torah became נובלות חכמה של מעלה only after Moshe Rabenu brought the Torah down to us. What happened before then? "Avraham Avinu fulfilled the entire Torah before it was given."[23] This applies to the other forefathers as well. How were the forefathers able to fulfill the Torah before it was given to us? Chazal teach us: "Avraham's two kidneys became as two pitchers of water and were flowing with Torah."[24] What does this statement mean? As we know, the Torah is the blueprint for the world. In the well-known words of the *Zohar*, הסתכל באורייתא וברא עלמא – Hashem "looked in the Torah and then created the world."[25] Given that man is a microcosm[26] he represents, from a certain perspective, a reflection of the Torah. As the *pasuk* states: ומבשרי אחזה אלוה – "I can view God from my flesh"[27] – Man himself can look inward and gain some insight into the plan from which the world was created – the Torah. The degree of insight is limited to each person's ability to grasp it.

Intrigues And Biases

Why can we not accomplish what our forefathers did and acquire the Torah on our own? Why was there a need for Moshe Rabenu to bring the Torah down to us? Shlomo HaMelech teaches us: אשר עשה אלקים את האדם ישר והמה בקשו חשבונות רבים "God has made man simple, but they sought many intrigues."[28] When man is straight and simple, everything comes out the way it should. When our desire is to fulfill the will of Hashem, we are able to do so without being taught. The problem is that man is biased in everything he does. When there are other issues and "intrigues" that interfere with our true understanding of the Torah, we cannot perceive its "straight" approach. When we search for what is good for us, we require Moshe Rabenu to inform us of what it is that Hashem wants from us.

If a man is biased by what he wants, he cannot arrive at the truth. A man once asked a merchant what two plus two was. He responded, "It depends if I am buying or selling. If I am purchasing, the answer is three; if I am selling, then it's five." How can a person possibly expect to attain true Godly wisdom with such methods of calculation? Only when a person searches for the right answer, for the truth, regardless of whether he is buying or selling, will he have the ability to arrive at a true understanding of the Torah.

Avraham Avinu and the other forefathers are referred to as ישרים[29]. They were totally straight. Even in a generation of idol worshippers, Avraham Avinu was able to recognize his Creator. Such a person, who seeks only the absolute truth can say מבשרי אחזה אלוה "I can see God from my flesh." We all have the ability to attain the Torah on our own, yet our calculations are not always honest. That is why we needed Moshe Rabenu to bring the Torah down to us. Now our task is to acquire as much of it as we can, each on his own level.

This is what Yeshiva is for. The learning and broader educational goals of the Yeshiva are here to help us to achieve our true desire. In addition, Yeshiva develops our thinking and analytical skills. During *shiur* we learn the *sevaros* of the *Ran* and the *Rosh*, the *Ketzos* and *Nesivos*. This accustoms us to the Torah's thought processes. It goes without saying that success in this area will only come about if the learning is accompanied with *yiras Shamayim*, for without that we cannot attain any true Torah achievement.

Learning How To Think

My esteemed teacher, HaGaon HaRav Chaim Shmuelevitz zt"l used to ask, "When can a man be described as being the *talmid* – a true disciple – of his Rav?" This description implies more than being able to quote how the Rav explained the Gemara on a particular *daf*.

As important as that may be, it is not sufficient reason to confer upon him the designation of *talmid*. A true disciple knows how the Rav would have explained a Gemara that was not studied in the *shiur!* Not only is he able to recall what the Rav said, but he is able to think like the Rav as well. One of the goals of Yeshiva is to teach us how to think, how to analyze Gemaras and sections of the *Shulchan Aruch* that were not studied in the Yeshiva. We must learn how to analyze each paragraph of the *Shulchan Aruch*, to figure out on what it is based, what the difficulties are, and what still requires resolution.

It is told of HaRav Yehoshua Leib Diskin zt"l that when he encountered a new *sefer*, he would pick it up and learn one chapter from it. Then he would be able to infer what the author had to say about all the other subjects addressed in the book. By learning a single chapter he was able to analyze the thought processes of the author!

We know that Shlomo HaMelech "was wiser than all men."[30] Chazal make an interesting observation that he was "even wiser than the fools." Is this supposed to be a compliment? How does calling him wiser than fools show us the extent of his wisdom? Should Chazal not have said "that he was even wiser than all the wise men"? To be wiser than the Rashba, Ramban, Ravina and Rav Ashi, to be more intelligent than Shaul HaMelech and David HaMelech – that is a compliment! What does it take to be wiser than a fool? Are we not all worthy of that distinction? There are many different ways of understanding Chazal's words. One explanation is that it is possible to uncover the thought-process of a wise man. What do I do when I have difficulty understanding the Rashba? I try to analyze it – what it is based on, how he learned the *sugya*, how he understood the Gemara, what was difficult, how he resolved the difficulty. In the final analysis, I can determine how the Rashba thought. On the other hand, the fool's convoluted way of thinking is almost impossible to understand. When asked to name a specific object, he may answer "Wednesday!" Why did he not answer "Thursday"? Who knows! Only Shlomo HaMelech was able to understand this. This is what Chazal meant when they called him "wiser than all men – even the fools."

Avraham Avinu was not satisfied with simply amassing Torah knowledge. He wanted to cleave to Hashem by emulating His ways in his own actions. The Torah must not remain an abstract concept. Avraham involved himself in many acts of *chessed*, among them imparting the Torah he had learned to others. Avraham taught his guests wisdom and introduced them to the idea of a Creator. Can there be a greater *chessed*? His *chessed*, as we know, extended to physical matters as well. He would provide his guests with milk or meat, with lodging and anything else they may have needed.

Emulating Hashem

The prophet Yirmiyahu tells us, "Thus said Hashem: 'Let not the wise man glorify himself with his wisdom, and let not the strong man glorify himself with his strength; let not the rich man glorify himself with his wealth. For only with this may one glorify himself: contemplating and knowing Me, for I am Hashem Who does kindness, justice and righteousness in the land, for in these is My desire, the word of Hashem.'"[31] In other words, wisdom, strength, and wealth are not cause for glory. These are gifts given to us from Hashem to be used to serve Him. When can one glorify himself? "By contemplating and knowing Me." I once heard from a Rosh Yeshiva that when the Tanach uses the verb "to know," it is not simply "knowledge" but connotes a connection, an attachment. When can these gifts of wisdom, strength, and wealth be considered mine? When I "know" Hashem and realize that He is "Hashem Who does kindness, justice, and righteousness in the land," and therefore I conclude that I must emulate His ways and perform acts of kindness, justice, and righteousness. To perform acts of kindness such as making "the souls that they made in Haran" requires wisdom. To carry out justice requires strength, to give to *tzedaka* requires wealth. Only when the wisdom, strength, and wealth we were blessed with are used for such purposes, do we have something to glorify ourselves with. Without them, then there is nothing to be proud of; Hashem gave you a gift which you did not use properly.

We mentioned Avraham Avinu's *chessed* of imparting wisdom to others. He was able to save Lot because it was important to him to carry out justice by waging war against Amrafel and his allies. In the *parsha* Avraham is informed that Lot was taken captive: "ויבא הפליט ויגד לאברם העברי" – "And the fugitive came and told Avram the Ivri."[32] What does the description אברם העברי mean? Chazal explain, כל העולם כולו מעבר אחד והוא מעבר אחד – "The entire world is on one side and he is on the other side."[33] Having to go against the entire world did not deter Avraham Avinu. Nimrod tried to force people to worship *avoda zara* just as Terach and the other fools did – Avraham was uninfluenced, for his only desire was to serve Hashem. This is the simple understanding of the *midrash*.

Why was this particular incident chosen to highlight the vast distance between Avraham and the others? I would like to suggest another understanding of the *midrash*. Who does "the entire world on one side" refer to? The entire world including Avraham himself! He was on the other side of himself! In other words, Avraham had spent his entire life preaching and performing acts of *chessed*. He must now switch to "the other side," to the Attribute of Justice, and wage war and kill the enemies of Hashem. An internal battle raged within Avraham: *chessed* was pulling him in one direction while justice was pulling in the other. This too did not disturb him, for it was Hashem's will that justice be served and that Avraham defeat Amrafel in order to save Lot. If it meant acting totally out of character, then that is what he would do.

Another aspect of Amrafel and his accomplices rendered them especially evil. The Torah describes their battling as "עשו מלחמה" – "They made war"[34] rather than "they fought the war." Chazal explain that they were the ones who invented the art of war, the worst invention in the history of mankind.[35] Although Kayin had already murdered Hevel, as terrible an act as that was, it was a private affair. Amrafel and his accomplices introduced the idea of killing people simply because one nation wishes to conquer another's territory or to depose its king. Think of how many millions have been killed from the days of Amrafel until today. In the Second World War alone, in addition to the tragedy that befell the Jewish nation, I believe thirty million people were killed! Avraham felt compelled to fight this evil.

The will of Hashem alone, and not his own will, not even the ways of *chessed* he had been accustomed to until this point, determined Avraham's course of action. Had those same people been visitors to his home, he would have honored them. When he spotted angels in the guise of Arabs, he rushed out and bowed down to them.[36] But when they come to fight against Hashem and against Lot, in their efforts to uproot the Name of Hashem in this world, *chessed* plays no role – Avraham arms himself with the Attribute of Justice and goes out to war.

Decisions like Avraham Avinu's cannot be based on our intellect alone. We require the guidance of the Torah and its scholars. The goal of Yeshiva extends beyond teaching us Torah; it is that we acquire the ability to become Torah scholars. We must strive to become great scholars, who will be able to guide others along the correct path, the path forged for us by our holy forefathers and Moshe Rabenu.

May following this path bring us eternal life.

Notes

1   *Bereishis* 12:5

2   *Devarim* 6:5

3   *Berachos* 61b

4   Rashi, Ramban, Sforno

5   *Avos* 6:2

6   See *Shemos Rabba* 1:28 where we learn that the Jewish people did not have to work on *Shabbos.*

7   Ibid.12

8   See *Shulchan Aruch, Orach Chaim Siman* 239.

9   See ibid. *Siman* 1

10 Ibid. *Siman* 4

11 Ibid. *Siman* 2

12 *Shaar Yichud Hamaase* 5

13 *Bereishis* 8:21

14 Rashi.

15 See *Zohar, Chelek* 3, 29b.

16 *Koheles* 6:7

17 See *Koheles Rabba* 6:1.

18 *Bamidbar* 27:4

19 *Devarim* 32:6

20 *Iyov* 28:23

21 See introduction to the Gr"a's commentary on *Shulchan Aruch*, written by his grandson.

22 *Yeshayahu* 55:19

23 *Kiddushin* 82a

24 *Bereishis Rabba* 95:3

25 *Zohar Shemos* 161:2

26 See *Tanchuma Pekudei*, Siman 3.

27 *Iyov* 19:26

28 *Koheles* 7:29

29 See *Avoda Zara* 25a.

30 *Melachim* I 5:11

31 *Yirmiyahu* 9:22

32 *Bereishis* 14:13

33 *Bereishis Rabba* 42:8

34 *Bereishis* 14:2

35 See Rashi *Tehillim* 37:16.

36 See *Bereishis* 18:2

Parshas Vayera

True Emunah

ויצא לוט וידבר אל חתניו לקחי בנותיו
ויאמר קומו צאו מן המקום הזה כי משחית ה' את העיר
ויהי כמצחק בעיני חתניו

*"Lot went out and spoke to his sons-in-law and the betrothed
of his daughters and he said, 'Get up and leave this place, for
Hashem is about to destroy the city!' But he seemed like a jester
in the eyes of his sons-in-law."[1]*

"Like A Jester"

His sons-in-law were so convinced that Lot could not be telling
the truth that the only plausible explanation was that he was joking.
If they had had the slightest premonition that the city would indeed
be devastated, they would have fled for their lives. If we were to hear
on the news that there was a fifty percent chance of our neighbor-
hood's being destroyed would we remain there? Certainly not! We
would flee even if the chances were far less than fifty percent! Today
too many people fear coming to visit Israel, where, Baruch Hashem,
far fewer than fifty percent of the residents have been harmed. Lot's
sons-in-law, though, were convinced beyond a shadow of a doubt

that Sodom would not be destroyed and there was no need to heed his warnings.

How could they not believe him? Lot was a great man, whom Chazal compared in many respects to Avraham Avinu.[2] It is true that Chazal voice disapproval of many of his actions, but all in all he was a great man. Even after his parting from Avraham Avinu, which Chazal criticize heavily,[3] Lot still had the merit of conversing regularly with angels. In addition, his prayers saved Tzoar from destruction.[4] Furthermore, Lot must have spoken sincerely after all that had just happened. The residents of Sodom had descended on his house and attempted to take him prisoner; he was miraculously rescued by the angels. Lot knew that the entire town was evil. In fact the *midrash*[5] relates that his own daughter was killed by the people of Sodom, so he could not have been too surprised that Hashem planned to destroy the city. If he warned his sons-in-law eloquently and convincingly, his words should have had a tremendous impact on his listeners. How could his sons-in-law dismiss it as a joke?

In Noach's Footsteps

Perhaps Lot's sons-in-law were following in Noach's footsteps. The Torah records, "Noach, with his sons, his wife, and his sons' wives with him, went into the Ark because of the waters of the flood."[6] Scripture stresses that Noach went into the Ark only after the rains began. Chazal comment on this, "Even Noach was one of those with little faith. He believed, yet did not believe that the Flood would come, and therefore he did not enter the Ark until the waters forced him to."[7] The fact that Hashem warned him, "I am about to bring the floodwaters upon the earth to destroy all flesh in which there is a breath of life from under the heavens,"[8] did not spur him to seek protection. He entered the Ark only when the rain began to fall and he could no longer remain outside. How can we understand Noach's behavior? Noach was a prophet, an איש צדיק תמים – "a righteous, perfect man"[9] with total faith in Hashem! He must have believed that the Flood would come about – why else did he spend one hundred and twenty years warning his generation? Why did he argue so vehemently with people who did not heed him, who believed that even if a flood occurred, they would be able to protect themselves[10]? Does this sound like a man "of little faith"?

The *baalei mussar* explain that Noach certainly believed strongly in Hashem's ability to bring about the Flood, but he did not think that Hashem would actually implement his Attribute of Justice so harshly. Hashem, after all, is a God of kindness, Who bestows good on all His creations. It was Noach's great belief in Hashem and His love of *chessed* that convinced him that Hashem would never turn the entire world into water and destroy all life, leaving only a few survivors. Perhaps this understanding can serve as a rebuttal to Chazal's criticism of Noach. The *Zohar*[11] says that when Noach emerged from the Ark to find a world in ruins, he cried to Hashem, "Creator of the Universe! You should have had mercy on Your creations," to which Hashem responded, "Now you are telling Me this? Why did you not speak up before the Flood? Had you done so, perhaps your prayers would have succeeded in preventing the Flood." When Hashem warned Moshe Rabenu that he wished to destroy the entire nation following the *chet haegel*, Moshe prayed and the nation was saved. Similarly, Avraham's lengthy negotiations with Hashem on behalf of Sodom succeeded in saving at least one righteous person. The Flood is referred to as "the waters of Noach"[12] because Noach's failure to pray on behalf of his generation means that he was somewhat responsible for it.[13] On the basis of an explanation of the *baalei mussar*, perhaps we can give Noach the benefit of the doubt. He did not pray for his generation because he refused to believe that the Flood would actually take place. He believed that there was no need to pray because Hashem is a God of *chessed*, Who would never do such a terrible thing. By the same token it could be argued that Lot's sons-in-law did not believe him because it was incomprehensible that Hashem would punish Sodom so harshly!

The difficulty with this explanation is that Lot and his family lived after the Flood, so surely they were well aware of the mighty power of Hashem's Attribute of Justice and His willingness to activate it when required. Although Hashem promised that He would never again bring a Flood upon the world, some opinions claim that "a flood of water He will not bring, but perhaps He will bring a flood of fire."[14] Secondly, Hashem promised that He would not destroy the entire world – Sodom was just one evil city. Our question therefore remains: why did Lot's sons-in-law refuse even to consider that Hashem would destroy Sodom and its neighboring cities by fire?

Perhaps this was simply the work of the *yetzer hara*. The *yetzer hara* not only tries to mislead a person into acting improperly, but can convince him (as happened with the people of Sodom) that his improper acts are indeed righteous. Haman, for example, said to himself, למי יחפץ המלך לעשות יקר יותר ממני – "Whom would the king want to honor more than me?"[15] Chazal comment[16] that when the *Megilla* uses the word המלך by itself, without the name Achashverosh, it refers to Hashem, the King of kings. Haman was therefore asking himself, "Whom would the King of kings want to honor more than me?" Am I not a great *tzaddik*? It is true that I declared myself a god[17] and passed myself off as the creator of the world, so to speak, but even so, Hashem thinks very highly of me. Perhaps on *Erev* Purim we could elaborate on this theme, but meanwhile let us try to understand what could possibly have been going through Haman's mind. As evil as he was, he truly believed that he was righteous. Similarly, the people of Sodom, among them Lot's sons-in-law, were sure that their corrupt behavior was completely justified. After all, why should they support parasites who sit idle? Why give bread to the poor? Let them go out and find a job! The people of Sodom believed that they had the proper *hashkafa*. Lot's sons-in-law were *tzaddikim* who strictly adhered to the *minhagim* of the holy congregation of Sodom, so why would Hashem destroy them with a flood of fire? Lot had to be joking – "He seemed like a jester in the eyes of his sons-in-law."

Not Very Convincing

I do not know if I am permitted to say this, but perhaps Lot's sons-in-law were not the only ones to blame. Lot himself was also somewhat responsible for their rejection of his words. The Gemara relates an incident: "The Roman regime once enacted decrees forbidding the Jews to keep the *Shabbos*, or circumcise their sons, or to keep the laws of family purity. Rav Reuven ben Istroboli cut his hair (to hide the fact that he was Jewish) and went and sat with the Romans. He said to them: 'If one has an enemy, does he want him to become poor or to become rich?' They said to him: 'To become poor.' He said to them: 'If so, let them not do work on the *Shabbos* so that they should become poor.'"[18] The Romans were convinced by his argument and the decree against *Shabbos* observance was annulled. Rav Reuven now tried to have the other decrees rescinded. He said to them, 'If one has an enemy, does he want him to become weak or to become strong?' They said to him: 'To become weak.' He said to them: 'If so, let them circumcise their sons on the eighth day, and they will become weak.' They were impressed with this argument as well and revoked the decree against circumcision. He then tried to have the decree against observing *taharas hamishpacha* rescinded. He said to them: 'If one has an enemy, does he want him to increase or decrease?' They said to him: 'To decrease.' He said to them: 'If so, let them not cohabit with *niddos*.' (i.e. Let them observe the laws of family purity, which limit the time a man may cohabit with his wife.) They accepted this argument and annulled that decree as well.

Later, when the Romans realized that Rav Reuven was Jewish, they reinstated the decrees, which remained in force until Rebbi Shimon bar Yochai and Rav Elazar ben Rav Yossi managed to have them annulled. What difference did it make to the Romans that Rav Reuven ben Istroboli was Jewish, if he presented them with convincing arguments? When they realized that in actual fact he observed the *mitzvos* which they had banned, it became clear that he had his own agenda and did not believe a word of what he was saying! If he did not believe what he was saying, why should they?

Lot's sons-in-law did not believe him, because Lot himself was not convinced that the city of Sodom was about to be overturned. The angels may have "struck with blindness, from small to great,"[19] the people of Sodom who converged upon his house, yet Lot was still not convinced. Lot went to warn his family only because the angels instructed him to. If his words did not come from his heart, how could they be expected to penetrate the heart of another person? "He seemed like a jester in the eyes of his sons-in-law."

Why should we assume that Lot did not believe what he was saying? We are not permitted to speak of Lot in such a manner, but from the *pesukim* his behavior clearly indicates this. What should Lot have done when his sons-in-law refused to listen to him? At least he should have taken his wife and daughters and fled. What actually happened? "And just as dawn was breaking, the angels urged Lot on saying, 'Get up, take your wife and your two daughters who are present, lest you be swept away because of the sin of the city.'"[20] Had it not been for the urging of the angels, he would not have moved! How did Lot react to the angels' urging him to flee from the city? ויתמהמה "Still he lingered..."[21] Interestingly the cantillation mark is a *shalsheles* – a prolonged, wavering note signifying that he tarried for a long time. Why did he wish to remain behind? Rashi tells us, "In order to save his money." Even though Sodom was about to be destroyed, he wanted to pack his bags and liquidate his bank account! Given that the bank was closed in the evening, he would have to wait until the morning. What about all his sheep and cattle? He had to wake them and bring them along too. Traveling with sheep and cattle limits a person's mobility, as Yaakov remarked to Esav, "My lord knows that the children are tender, and the nursing flocks and cattle are upon me; and they will drive them hard for one day, then all the flocks will die."[22] In fact during the Middle Ages, Jews usually did not own livestock because they feared that at any moment they could be expelled and it would be very difficult to flee with this extra burden. How could Lot possibly have been expected to flee in such a hurry?

Lukewarm Beliefs

If Lot had truly believed the angels, would he have remained behind to gather his money and his flocks? If he had believed that Sodom was about to be destroyed, he would have grabbed his wife and daughters and fled immediately, even if it meant leaving behind all his material possessions. Perhaps Lot believed that Hashem would bring a fire down upon Sodom, but not today – perhaps tomorrow or the next day. Just as Hashem did not destroy Tzoar, perhaps he would cancel the decree against Sodom as well. If Lot himself was not convinced of Sodom's impending destruction, is it any wonder that he was unable to convince his sons-in-law?

Discussing the laws of cooking on *Shabbos*, the Talmud states, "A כלי שני – second vessel (that was not directly on the fire, rather one into which hot food was transferred) is not capable of cooking"[23] because the vessel itself was not heated by the fire. One who gets "fired up" about something is able to transfer the "heat" to others in a convincing manner. (Perhaps Lot adopted the stringent Ashkenazic view forbidding placing food that is easily cooked even in a כלי שני. Nevertheless, Lot's sons-in-law were clearly not "easily cooked".) When a person himself is not convinced that something is true, he does not have the intensity to convince others.

According to the Chazon Ish the *halacha* of מורידין ולא מעלין "Cast in and not brought up"[24] does not apply today. This *halacha* permits casting an evil person into a pit and rules that one does not have to save such a person if he is already in a pit. The Chazon Ish believed that as long as the evil person was not properly rebuked for his sins this law would not apply, and he maintained that in this generation there isn't really anyone able to rebuke effectively. Why did the Chazon Ish believe that no one in our generation is capable of giving proper reprimand?

We are not worthy of speaking this way about the *gedolim*, but at least when it comes to ourselves, we should first do some introspection before we go and rebuke a secular Jew. How strong is our own belief? Do we truly live what we preach? Perhaps if our *emunah* were stronger, we would learn Torah and not waste a single moment. We would sprint like an athlete racing for a gold medal to grab an opportunity to perform an act of *chessed*. Avraham Avinu had his *bris milah* at the age of ninety-nine. While he was recovering, Hashem "turned up the heat." Even so, Avraham gathered all the strength he could muster and ran to search for guests. Can we say the same about ourselves?

What about our *tefilla*? Do we truly pour out our hearts to Hashem? Our voices need not be as loud as the *shofar* on Rosh Hashana, but do our hearts shout? I cannot speak for others, but I can certainly speak for myself. If my *emunah* were stronger, my *tefillos* and *mitzvos* would be more "heated". The fact that this is not the case indicates that something is missing from my faith. If our *emunah* is not strong enough, how can we even hope to have any influence on others? When we arrive late for *Shacharis*, are we distressed at having missed an opportunity to answer: אמן יהא שמי-ה רבא מברך לעלם ולעלמי עלמיא or do we simply resign ourselves, saying, "Baruch Hashem, we arrived in time for יוצר אור," and console ourselves with the fact that there will be other opportunities to hear a *Kaddish*? We have no realization of how much was lost by not being able to answer *Kaddish* and *Borchu*! If this is who we are, how can we possibly expect to convince others to follow the true path in life?

Strengthening *Emunah*

How can we improve our attitude? By realizing our own greatness and potential! With every step we take we can build worlds or destroy worlds; it is up to us. Every word of Torah we learn, every Rashi and every *Tosafos* creates entire worlds that while not visible, certainly exist. If a person wastes his time when he should be learning, it destroys worlds, God forbid.

A child cries when his toy breaks. As sensitive parents we either try to console him with a candy or we spend a few shekels on a new toy. Imagine for a moment if the sun were to break in half. A few shekels are not going to fix it. I cannot even imagine all the ramifications of such a disaster – I'll leave those calculations to the scientists. We would first have to figure out the paths each half of the sun would take independently. This would also affect the orbit of the earth which until now was more or less elliptical. We would feel a great increase of temperature on one side, and a sharp decrease on the other side. The force of gravity would cease to function. Although Hashem has not made me privy to His secrets, I do not believe we need to fear this happening in the near future. The sun and the moon were placed in the universe to remain "continuously all the days of the earth."[25] The Rambam writes that even the materials found on these luminaries are meant to remain there for eternity. I am not sure how to understand this Rambam, given that in recent years astronauts have managed to remove soil from the moon and bring it to earth. Some scientists claim that the sun is burning itself up, but I am not worried that this phenomenon will have any immediate effect on our lives. The fact remains that if the sun were to split into two it would have immeasurable ramifications.

Every Jew Is A Star!

We must realize that a Jew is not a mere child's toy in which a crack is of no great significance – we are not only as great as the sun, we are even greater! Hashem instructed Avraham, "'Gaze now toward the Heavens, and count the stars if you are able to count them,' and He said to him, 'So shall your offspring be!'"[26] I believe this refers to the greatness of the Jewish people not only in quantity but in quality. From our vantage point such a great distance away, a star appears very small. In reality each star is immense – some of them several times larger than the sun. The sun itself, as we know, is many times the size of the earth. Each and every Jew is like a star – he appears small and insignificant because we do not have the tools to measure his true greatness. A crack in a Jew is like a crack in the sun – the implications are immeasurable.

Each word that issues from our mouths, whether good or bad, has as much significance as the movements of the sun. Conversely, in our *parsha* Avraham Avinu expresses himself as "dust and ash."[27] Similarly, Moshe Rabenu and Aharon Hakohen ask of themselves "... for what are we?"[28] This dichotomy is a cornerstone of our belief. On the one hand, we are required to be humble, to live with the realization that we are totally insignificant in relation to this vast world. On the other hand, we must realize how great our potential is. How could Moshe Rabenu sincerely ask "... for what are we?" Did he not realize that he was the greatest of all prophets and that it was he who saved the Jewish nation from Egypt and brought the Torah down for us? Of course he knew! He also knew, however, that all of this was given to him by Hashem and he did not ascribe any greatness to himself. We must be aware of our greatness, while at the same time realizing that this greatness is a heaven-sent gift. We have nothing to be haughty about, but it is incumbent on us to act in a manner befitting a great person.

Tefillah As A Shield

The current situation here in *Eretz Yisrael* is very difficult.[29] We do not need Lot or the angels to explain this to us. We must realize that it is within our power to improve the situation. Every word of Torah we learn has the power to change things. Our *tefillos* must be an outpouring of our hearts to Hashem. The commentaries explain that the *berachos* of מצמיח קרן ישועה, בונה ירושלים, and המחזיר שכינתו לציון refer to the Final Redemption, may it arrive speedily in our day, while the *beracha* of גואל ישראל – "Redeemer of Israel" – is a prayer to Hashem to save us from the troubles we encounter along the way. When we say this *beracha* we should concentrate on this interpretation. Hashem has saved us from many evil people like Haman and Antiochus, yet Chanukah and Purim were not the only salvations. Throughout history Hashem has spared us from many enemies, and if we are worthy, Hashem will deliver us from our current situation too.

Meriting Divine Protection is within our reach. Our Torah, our *tefilla*, and our acts of *chessed* have the power to save us. For every act of *chessed* we perform, Hashem acts towards us "מדה כנגד מדה" – "measure for measure."[30] This is the only form of protection we have against war (and in peacetime as well!) Government leaders have spent time in Washington pursuing peace (and may Hashem protect us from such peace, especially here in the Jewish Quarter. I always refer to שלום עכשו – Peace Now – as חס ושלום עכשו). Today, in addition, the government is attempting to bring about what they call a Secular Revolution[31] – may Hashem protect us from that as well.

Do Hands Win Battles?

I heard the following *chiddush* in the name of my esteemed teacher HaRav Bezalel Zolty zt"l. Chazal say, "Whoever sees the stone

---

29   This sicha was given at the height of the second Intifada.

31   Towards the end of Ehud Barak's tenure as prime minister he became an advocate for "secular rights".

upon which Moshe sat when Yehoshua waged war against Amalek must give thanks and praise to the Omnipresent."[32] Why did Chazal not enact a similar *beracha* for when one views the actual site on which Yehoshua conducted the battle? Chazal wanted to ensure that we do not credit Yehoshua and his army with the victory. Yehoshua may have chosen soldiers who were "strong and feared sin, that their merit should assist them,"[33] but the victory resulted from Moshe's raising his hands, as the Torah states: "It happened that when Moshe raised his hand, Israel was stronger."[34] Chazal ask, "But do Moshe's hands win a battle or lose a battle? Rather, the verse comes to tell you, so long as Israel gazed upward and subjugated their heart to their Father in Heaven, they would prevail, but if not, they would fall."[35] The victory can be seen on the battlefield; Yehoshua killed the strong Amalekites, "with the sword's blade."[36] The true source of victory, however, was Moshe's raised hands. *Am Yisrael* won the battle because they submitted their hearts to our Father in Heaven. Therefore we recite this *beracha* not upon seeing the battlefield, but upon seeing the place where war was really waged – the stone upon which Moshe sat.

We may not be on the level of Moshe or Yehoshua, but we must try our utmost to completely surrender our hearts to Hashem. We must strengthen our Torah learning, as well as our *tefilla* and *chessed*, our *Shabbos* observance, *shmiras halashon*, and whatever else needs strengthening.

May Hashem bring salvation to the Jewish nation so that once again, as in the war against Amalek, we can say, "Israel was stronger," speedily in our day. Amen.

Notes

1   *Bereishis* 19:14

2   See Rashi on *Bereishis* 13:8.

3   See Rashi on *Bereishis* 13:11.

4   See *Bereishis* 19:20-21.

5 *Pirke D' Rabbi Eliezer* 25

6 *Bereishis* 7:7

7 Rashi ibid.

8 *Bereishis* 6:17

9 Ibid. 9

10 See Rashi ibid. 14 and *Sanhedrin* 108b.

11 Section I 254:2

12 *Yeshayahu* 54:9

13 See *Zohar* section I 67:2.

14 *Zevachim* 116a

15 *Esther* 6:6

16 *Esther Rabba* 3:10

17 See Rashi, Esther 3:2

18 *Meila* 17a

19 *Bereishis* 19:11

20 *Bereishis* 19:15

21 Ibid. 16

22 *Bereishis* 33:13

23 *Shabbos* 40b

24 *Avoda Zara* 26b

25 *Bereishis* 8:22

26 *Bereishis* 15:5

27 *Bereishis* 18:27

28 *Shemos* 16:7

30 *Shabbos* 105b

32 *Berachos* 54a

33 Rashi *Shemos* 17:9

34 *Shemos* 17:11

35 *Rosh Hashana* 29a

36 *Shemos* 17:13, see Rashi.

The Trials Of Avraham

קח נא את בנך את יחידך אשר אהבת את יצחק ולך לך אל
ארץ המוריה והעלהו שם לעולה על אחד ההרים אשר אמר אליך
Hashem instructs Avraham Avinu: "Please take your son,
your only one, whom you love, Yitzchak, go to the land of
Moriah, and bring him up there as an offering upon one of
the mountains which I shall tell you."[1]

Hashem Appeals To Avraham

Why does Hashem begin His instructions with the word נא –
'Please'? Chazal explain, "This is analogous to a king of flesh and
blood who had been confronted with many wars and he had one
mighty warrior who won all the battles. One day, a particularly
fierce war confronted the king and he turned to his warrior and said
to him: "'I beg of you, stand fast for me in this war, so that people
should not say that the earlier wars were of no substance.' Similarly,
the Holy One, Blessed is He, told Avraham, 'I have tested you with
many trials and you have withstood them all. Now, stand fast for
me in this trial, so that people should not say that there was no
substance to the earlier trials.'"[2] Hashem was appealing to Avraham

Avinu to pass this test, for should he fail, God forbid, people would conclude that Avraham Avinu was only able to pass the other nine tests because they were less challenging, yet when it came to difficult tests, Avraham was unable to stand up to the challenge.

Going Against His Nature

In what way was the test of the binding of Yitzchak considered the greatest trial of all? The other tests did not require him to go against the dictates of his conscience. His first test of faith came when Nimrod threw him into the furnace for believing in Hashem. Avraham, however, was steadfast in his beliefs and would rather have died than deny what he held to be absolute truth. The same applied to the other tests. It was very difficult for him to receive guests on the third day following his *bris milah*, especially at his advanced age, yet in his quest to emulate Hashem who is all *chessed*, he endeavored to welcome the guests and provide for them in the best way he could.

Doing What Is Right

Some of the tests went against his nature, yet he realized deep down what was the right thing to do. As we discussed in *Parshas Lech Lecha*, the Torah states[3] in describing the war against Amrafel and his allies: ויבא הפליט ויגד לאברם העברי – "Then there came the fugitive and told Avram, the Ivri."[4] What is the meaning of the description עברי? The *midrash* tells us, "The entire world is מעבר אחד (on one side) and he is on the other side."[5] The description of the entire world as being on one side included Avraham Avinu himself. The war against Amrafel pitted Avraham against the entire world, including himself. Avraham, who by nature, was a man of *chessed* had to act in a manner which was the antithesis of *chessed*, by killing Amrafel and his accomplices.[6] Avraham realized that saving Lot from these evil people would bring about a great *Kiddush Hashem*. If the way to sanctify Hashem's Name meant acting in a manner contrary to his ways of *chessed*, then that is what had to be done.[7]

Later Hashem instructed Avraham to send away his son Yishmael – an extremely difficult task for him, as the Torah makes clear: "The matter greatly distressed Avraham regarding his son."[8] It was

Sarah who had demanded that Yishmael be sent away and Hashem supported her, telling Avraham, "Be not distressed over the youth. Whatever Sarah tells you, heed her voice, since through Yitzchak will offspring be considered yours."[9] Yishmael will not be your spiritual heir, rather Yitzchak will follow in your footsteps. As painful as it was for Avraham to have to send away his son, he knew that it was the right thing to do.

Here he is about to undergo an even greater internal struggle – *Akeidas Yitzchak*. Here too, his attribute of *chessed* does not stand in his way. If it is Hashem's wish that Yitzchak is to be sacrificed, then that is what he will do. How is Avraham Avinu expected to understand the command to sacrifice his beloved son, who Hashem had just told him would be the continuation of the Jewish nation? What about the great *chillul Hashem* this would cause? Avraham had preached to the entire world about living a life of *chessed* and the sin of sacrificing one's children for *avoda zara*. He taught how Hashem has no desire for human sacrifice, for He wants people to live. What would the other nations say now? They would scoff at Avraham for his hypocrisy – first he preaches against killing and then he goes and kills his own son. All of the "souls they made in Haran"[10] – the ones whom Avraham and Sarah brought close to the ways of Hashem – would now leave the fold. The sacrificing of Yitzchak would also be evidence for "the scoffers of the generation who claimed that Yitzchak was Avimelech's son and not Avraham's, for Sarah spent many years with Avraham and was unable to conceive."[11] For what real father would be willing to sacrifice his own flesh and blood? The potential *chillul Hashem* it could cause made this Avraham's greatest test.

We mention *Akeidas Yitzchak* on several occasions, most notably on Rosh Hashana, when we ask Hashem to remember us and to grant us a good year in the merit of the binding of Yitzchak. Why was this event singled out? Have there not been many people throughout history who have given up their lives and the lives of their children to sanctify Hashem's Name?

Paving The Way

Perhaps one way we can explain this is that it was a far great-er test for Avraham Avinu than it would have been for an ordi-nary person. As we discussed above, Avraham's love of *chessed* was so great that the idea of killing anyone, let alone his beloved son, was totally contrary to his nature. An insight of Rav Chaim Volozhiner suggests a different explanation: The *pasuk* states: מתהלך בתמו צדיק אשרי בניו לו – "One who walks in his innocence is a righteous man; fortunate are his sons after him."[12] Why are his sons fortunate? Rav Chaim explains: "The traits that the *tzaddik* toiled and labored to attain become part of the nature of his children after him, and with just a slight effort on their part, they too can reach this level. We see for ourselves how many people have sacrificed their lives and died *al Kiddush Hashem*. This is ingrained in our nature and passed down to us from our father Avraham Avinu, who was will-ing to give up his life in the furnace in Ur Kasdim for his belief. The same may be said of the other nine trials of Avraham; they paved the way for us to be able to withstand similar trials."[13]

If a Jew is *moser nefesh* and makes the sacrifice of leaving his home in America and settling in *Eretz Yisrael*, it is because of that strength instilled in him since Avraham Avinu. A Jew who is willing to sac-rifice himself or his children *al Kiddush Hashem*, has inherited the ability to do so from Avraham Avinu, who gave himself up to be burned in the furnace in Ur Kasdim and was willing to sacrifice his son on Mount Moriah. It was Avraham's passing this test of faith that paved the way for his descendants to be able to withstand these terrible trials.

My esteemed teacher HaRav Chaim Shmuelevitz zt"l used this idea to clarify a passage from the Gemara. The Gemara describes the tragic story of Chana and her seven sons. As her youngest son was being taken away to be killed, Chana said to him, "My son, go and tell Avraham your father, 'You bound a sacrifice on one altar, but I bound sacrifices on seven altars.'"[14] Was Chana implying that her sacrifice was greater than Avraham's? Rav Chaim explains that Chana was praising Avraham Avinu, for it was his heroic act of placing his son upon the altar that imbued her with the superhuman emotional strength to sacrifice her seven sons.

Yitzchak Defers To The *Gadol Hador*

There is another interesting point we can make regarding *Akeidas Yitzchak*. The Torah records Yitzchak's question to his father, "Here are the fire and the wood, but where is the lamb for the offering?" Avraham responds, according to Rashi, that Yitzchak himself is to be offered upon the altar. We learn from our Sages that a vision of prophecy given to one prophet is also seen by other prophets. Yitzchak too was a prophet. He must have been aware that Hashem had never intended Avraham to slaughter him but only to "bring him upon the altar."[15] Realizing that it was not he who was to be brought as an offering, Yitzchak wondered "Where is the lamb?" Avraham responded that Yitzchak misunderstood and it was he who was to be offered. Although Yitzchak perceived things differently, he deferred to Avraham's understanding and was willing to allow himself to be sacrificed. After all, Avraham was the *gadol hador*. We can now say that Avraham's test was to see whether he would follow the word of Hashem, while Yitzchak's test was to determine whether he would follow the word of Avraham. In other words, Avraham's test in the *Akeida* was a Torah commandment while Yitzchak's was Rabbinic. Perhaps this can explain why the section of *Akeidas Yitzchak* is read on the second day of Rosh Hashana which is a Rabbinic requirement. It was a major test for Yitzchak the prophet to be willing to accept Avraham's interpretation of the prophecy, even when it went contrary to his own understanding and especially when it meant giving up his own life.

HaRav Yoseph Ansbacher shlit"a added to this. Chazal tell us, "Sarah's death is juxtaposed with the binding of Yitzchak because when she heard the news of the *Akeida* and learned that her son was readied for slaughter and was nearly slaughtered, her soul flew from her and she died."[16] Based on what we have said, we can understand the sequence of events. Because "Avraham was secondary to Sarah in prophecy,"[17] Sarah did not have to concede her understanding of the prophecy to Avraham's perception the way Yitzchak did. She therefore understood initially, as Yitzchak did, that Avraham was never meant to slaughter Yitzchak. "Her soul flew from her," because she feared that Yitzchak was about to be slaughtered in vain.

Moshe Rabenu: Prophecy Through A Clear Glass

Based on this perspective of prophecy, my esteemed teacher HaRav Shach zt"l suggested another explanation for why this was a particularly difficult test for Avraham Avinu. He cites the Rambam's explanation of the difference between Moshe Rabenu's prophecy and that of other prophets. In *Parshas Behaaloscha*, Hashem says to Miriam and Aharon, "If there shall be prophets among you, in a vision shall I, Hashem, make Myself known to him; in a dream shall I speak with him. Not so is My servant Moshe; in My entire house he is trusted. Mouth to mouth do I speak to him, in a clear vision and not in riddles, and at the image of Hashem does he gaze."[18] Only Moshe Rabenu had a clear vision of what Hashem was telling him, while the others saw a vision which they had to interpret. Chazal tell us, "One prophetic signal may come to several prophets, but two prophets never communicate a prophecy in exactly the same words."[19] The Godly light shines upon all prophets in the same manner; all see the same prophetic vision yet they do not perceive the vision in an identical style. This is because the prophet's reception of the vision is influenced by the intricacies of his own personality. The prophet only relates the prophecy after it has been influenced by his own character. This idea goes so far as to suggest that if two prophets are found prophesying in precisely the same language, we can conclude that they are false prophets who coordinated their "prophecy" beforehand.[20]

In fact, any two people viewing the same thing may interpret and describe it in two different ways. One person walking into our *Beis Midrash* may describe it as a place filled with students and *talmidei chachamim* studying Torah, while another walking in at the same moment will speak about the many books, tables, and *shtenders* he sees. Similarly, one witness to a crime describes the incident as taking place on a warm night, while the next person may describe the evening as being cool. Neither of them is lying, but each is interpreting the scene in his own manner. For this reason, as is the case where two prophets prophesy in the identical words, if two witnesses testify using precisely the same words, we must assume that they are false witnesses who colluded in advance and we are obliged to disqualify their testimony.

The only prophet who relayed the original word of Hashem and not his own interpretation of a vision was Moshe Rabenu, because Moshe Rabenu was so close to Hashem that he completely negated himself for Hashem. Through this total self-negation, Moshe merited receiving his prophecy *"be-aspaklaria hameira"* – through a clear glass, as the Gemara teaches us. "All the prophets looked into a dim glass, but Moshe looked through a clear glass."[21] What does it mean to see through a 'clear glass'? I don't really know how prophecy works, but from the little I can comprehend, it appears that we can explain in this way. When light passes through a clear glass it appears on the other side with no discernible change. This means that if it enters as white on one side, it will emerge as white on the other side. This is in contrast to tinted glass in which white light entering from one side emerges colored by the glass. The prophet's personality 'colors' his interpretation of the vision. Moshe Rabenu, however, totally negated his own personality, so there was no color for the prophecy to pass through, thus the vision he presented was precisely Hashem's words. Thus he was the only prophet who could faithfully bring us the Ten Commandments and the other words of Hashem.

Because Moshe saw Hashem's vision clearly, no one could suspect him of not transmitting Hashem's Torah precisely as Hashem gave it to him. Every word, every vowel, every note in the Torah is written as Hashem dictated to Moshe. When the *pasuk* says "לא תבשל גדי בחלב אמו" – "Do not cook a kid in its mother's milk,"[22] no one can claim that Moshe transmitted the Torah improperly, and that instead of *chalav* – milk, Hashem meant *chelev* – fat. If the Torah says milk, then milk it must be, for Moshe wrote verbatim what Hashem dictated. Moshe's prophecy was not clouded with his own bias. "In My entire house he is the trusted one."[23] What Moshe taught us was precisely what he heard from Hashem.

The Prophecy Of Bilaam

There was another prophet who was also given a clear prophecy, and that was Bilaam. Chazal comment on the *pasuk*, ולא קם נביא עוד בישראל כמשה – "Never again has there arisen in Israel a prophet like Moshe."[24] "Never ... in Israel, but in the other nations one has arisen. Which prophet did they have who was like Moshe? Bilaam, son of Beor."[25] How do we explain this? Could it be that the wicked Bilaam was as great as Moshe Rabenu? Was Moshe Rabenu not the greatest *tzaddik* who ever lived, while Bilaam was one of the most evil people in the history of mankind? That is true, yet in prophecy they were equal. As we mentioned, each prophet prophesies based on his own 'glass'; the transparency of the glass depends on his level of *ahavas Hashem*, *yiras Hashem*, and other *middos*. The glass which Bilaam's prophecies passed through was totally black. Even if he were shown a vision which clearly meant that he must bless *Bnei Yisrael*, there would be no chance of his understanding and interpreting the vision in the correct manner. Therefore in order to draw from him a blessing for *Am Yisrael* and not a curse, the prophecy had to be given to him in clear and unambiguous terms, as it was told to Moshe Rabenu. Each of them was given a clear prophecy, Moshe's through his 'clear glass,' and Bilaam's prophecy was handed to him directly, circumventing his 'glass.' Bilaam had to be told precisely: "The Jewish people must be blessed using these exact words: 'The words of Bilaam son of Beor, the words of the man with the open eye, How goodly are your tents O Jacob, your dwelling places, O Israel,'[26] for there to be even a chance that it would be presented as a blessing.

Avraham: Prophecy Through *Yiras Shamayim*

Avraham Avinu's prophecy was not through a 'clear glass,' the way Moshe Rabenu's was. Avraham prophesied through the lens of *yiras Shamayim*. The level of his *yiras Shamayim* was such that he interpreted the vision as requiring him to sacrifice his own son. Perhaps had his *yiras Shamayim* not been of such a high caliber, he would have interpreted the vision as demanding that he send his son to Yeshiva or that he sacrifice a lamb. Ordinary people do not have

the option of interpreting a vision in the manner that he did. They
are guided by the dictates of the *Shulchan Aruch* and other *poskim* as
to whether Hashem requires them to sacrifice themselves or their
children or not. Only someone on the level of Avraham Avinu could
interpret the vision as requiring him to make the ultimate sacrifice
for Hashem.

It was only after Avraham stood up to this test that Hashem bestowed on him the title ירא אלקים – "for now I know that you are a
God-fearing man."[27] Although Avraham underwent many trials and
tribulations prior to the *Akeida*, it was only when he demonstrated
this willingness to negate himself totally for Hashem that he was
referred to as 'God-fearing.' This is why the merit of עקידת יצחק is so
great and this is why we use it as a powerful defense on *Yom HaDin*.
May this merit soon bring about the sounding of the ram's horn
blown by *Moshiach*, or by the Almighty Himself.

והיה ביום ההוא יתקע בשופר גדול ובאו האובדים

בארץ אשור והנדחים בארץ מצרים והשתחוו לה' בהר הקודש בירושלים.

*"It shall be on that day that the great shofar will be blown, and those
who are lost in the land of Assyria and those cast away in the land of
Egypt will come together and they will prostrate themselves to Hashem
on the holy mountain in Jerusalem."[28]*

Notes

1   *Bereishis* 22:3

2   *Sanhedrin* 89b

3   *Sicha* II

4   *Bereishis* 14:13

5   *Bereishis Rabba* 42:8

6   See Rashi, *Bereishis* 14:1.

7   See also *Sicha* II for *Parshas Lech Lecha.*

8   *Bereishis* 21:11

9   Ibid. 12

10   *Bereishis* 12:5

11   See Rashi, *Bereishis* 25:19.

12   *Mishle* 20:7

13   *Ruach Chayim* on *Maseches Avos* 5:3.

14   *Gittin* 57b

15   *Bereishis* 22:2

16   Rashi, *Bereishis* 23:2

17   Rashi, *Bereishis* 21:12

18   *Bamidbar* 12:6-8

19   *Sanhedrin* 89a

20   See ibid.

21   *Yevamos* 49b

22   *Shemos* 23:19

23   *Bamidbar* 12:7

24   *Devarim* 34:10

25   *Bamidbar Rabba* 14:20

26   *Bamidbar* 24:3,5

27 *Bereishis* 22:12

28 *Yeshayahu* 27:13

Parshas Chaye Sarah

Acquiring Eretz Yisrael

Expulsion Of The Sons Of Ketura

In this week's *parsha* we learn that Avraham Avinu marries again after the death of Sarah. He takes a wife called Ketura, who bears him a number of children who are listed by name in the Torah. We then read, "Avraham gave all that he had to Yitzchak, but to the concubines' children who were Avraham's, Avraham gave gifts; then he sent them away from Yitzchak his son, while he was still alive, eastward to the land of the east.["](1) In *Parshas Vayera* we read of Yishmael's expulsion. Sarah instructed Avraham, "Drive out this slave-woman with her son,["](2) and Hashem supported her: "Whatever Sarah tells you, heed her voice." The decision to expel the children of Ketura, however, was made by Avraham alone without any sort of revelation from Hashem. Perhaps Avraham based his decision on a *kal vachomer*: if Yishmael, for whom he had prayed, "O that Yishmael might live before you"[3] and to which Hashem had responded: "But regarding Yishmael I have heard you,"[4] was expelled, then the Bnei Ketura, on whose behalf Avraham did not pray and for whom Hashem made no promise about their future, should certainly be expelled.

On the other hand, there seems to be more reason for the Bnei Ketura to remain with Avraham Avinu than for Yishmael. The Rambam[5] rules that the Bnei Ketura were commanded to perform *bris milah* and that this mitzvah applies to their descendants as well, whereas the commandment to Yishmael was exclusively for him and it is not binding upon his descendants. Although Rashi offers a dissenting opinion, it appears according to the Rambam that the ensuing generations' keeping this mitzvah was more reason for the Bnei Ketura to remain associated with Avraham Avinu than for Yishmael to do so. Furthermore, we never read of any negative behavior by the Bnei Ketura like that exhibited by Yishmael, who would worship idols and shoot arrows at Yitzchak. "Sarah saw the son of Hagar, the Egyptian, whom she had borne to Avraham, mocking."[6]

Why then did Avraham expel the Bnei Ketura? Although they would have performed the mitzvah of *bris milah* and perhaps they would have produced offspring who would have been assets to mankind, Avraham Avinu believed them to be unworthy of living in *Eretz Yisrael*. Living in the Holy Land demands that one be of special character and rise above the level of Yishmael.

"The Land Which Hashem Seeks Out"

The expulsion of Yishmael was not only for Yitzchak's sake. As Sarah said, "For the son of that slave-woman shall not inherit with my son, with Yitzchak,"[7] but it was for Yishmael's own good as well. If one is not worthy of living in the special Land, it will actually harm him to dwell there, for in *Eretz Yisrael*, judgment is more stringent and more immediate than in *chutz la'aretz*. It is a far more serious offense to anger the King in his own palace, so to speak. *Eretz Yisrael* is the "Land that Hashem, your God, seeks out; the eyes of Hashem, your God, are always upon it."[8] Hashem keeps a constant vigil over what happens in *Eretz Yisrael*, which can be for the benefit of someone who behaves properly, but is to the detriment of one who does not. One who does not behave in a seemly fashion is better off living in "the land of the east." Now we can understand Avraham's sending away the Bnei Ketura, not as a punishment but rather for their sake, for their own protection.

Divine Providence In *Eretz Yisrael*

The Ramban asks a question: if we know that Sodom was not the only city in the world whose inhabitants were wicked, why was Sodom singled out for destruction? He explains that it was because Sodom was located in *Eretz Yisrael* and the Land cannot tolerate such behavior. While even in *chutz la'aretz* such sinful behavior does not go unpunished, nevertheless outside the Land of Israel, judgment is not an urgent matter. The Sodoms in *chutz la'aretz* can last many generations and may still be around today. In *Eretz Yisrael*, however, where Divine Providence is constant, immediate, and more apparent, a place such as Sodom cannot continue to exist.

About the seven original nations who had dwelt in the Land of Israel, we read, "The Land disgorged its inhabitants."[9] The Land was unable to tolerate their behavior, just as a person who is unable to tolerate certain foods vomits them out. If we wish to ensure that the "Land does not disgorge" us,[10] we must begin by behaving properly. The *yichus* of being a descendant of Avraham Avinu and thereby entitled to the Land is only of value when we act like an Avraham, or a Yitzchak or a Yaakov. Failure to do so will result in the Land's spitting us out, "as it disgorged the nation that was before you."[11] There is no immunity against being spat out.

The Ramban asserts that this is what happened to the Kutim. In the days of Yeravam ben Nevat, the people left the dictates of the Torah and turned to idol worship and other iniquitous behavior. As punishment, the Almighty exiled them from their Land and gave *Eretz Yisrael* into the hands of Sancheriv, the king of Ashur. In order to repopulate the now empty cities of Israel, the king of Ashur "imported" foreigners from places such as Bavel and Kutah and settled them in the Shomron. These Kutim, as they came to be known, continued their former practice of idol worship. As punishment Hashem sent lions among them.[12]

Why did Hashem suddenly punish them in this fashion? They were not Jewish and they were simply continuing the lifestyle they had practiced for years in *chutz la'aretz*. The Ramban explains that in *chutz la'aretz* it was not as urgent that Hashem punish them. Had they remained in Kutah they could have lived in this manner and at worst they would have been sent to Gehinom. When the idol worship reached the borders of *Eretz Yisrael*, however, it had to cease immediately. The Kutim, in panic over being attacked by lions, sent a message to the king of Ashur, explaining that they were not familiar with "the law of the God of the Land."[13] What is the meaning of "the God of the Land"? Is Hashem not God of the entire universe? Even the Kutim were able to recognize that Hashem's Providence is different in *Eretz Yisrael* from what it is elsewhere.

The Kutim ultimately converted to Judaism, yet for generations a dispute continued among the *halachic* authorities regarding the sincerity of their conversion. As the Tanach states, "They feared Hashem, but they worshipped their own gods."[14] Both opinions concur that their level of *avoda zara* diminished, as it was forced to, because the Land was unable to tolerate their previous degree of worshipping foreign gods. In *Eretz Yisrael* judgment is immediate.

Galus As *Chessed*

In our Yom Tov prayers, we recite: ומפני חטאינו גלינו מארצנו – "Because of our sins we have been exiled from our Land." Contrary to what many people think, living in Brooklyn is not a great reward! Like all other exiles, though, this one is not only a punishment but a form of protection as well. The Gemara tells us, "Hashem acted charitably with the Jewish nation ... that he exiled them two years earlier than *venoshantem*."[15] This refers to the *pasuk*, "When you beget children and grandchildren and 'ונשנתם – you will have been long' in the Land ... that you will surely perish quickly."[16] The numerical value of ונשנתם is 852. Hashem did us a tremendous favor by exiling us after only eight hundred and fifty years, thus preventing the fulfillment of this prophecy, which would have caused the entire nation to perish. *Am Yisrael* was exiled to Bavel, where they flourished and produced "the Torah scholars of Bavel who make buds and blossoms for the Torah."[17] The Babylonian exile produced people of the caliber of Ezra and Mordechai, as well as many other Torah giants. Had the Jewish people, in their current state, remained in *Eretz Yisrael*, they could not have continued to exist; only in *chutz la'aretz* could they hope to have a future. In this way we can see that the exile was a *chessed* from Hashem, but God forbid that we should ever be in need of such *chessed*! We would prefer to choose the *chessed* of being close to Hashem in *Eretz Yisrael* and Yerushalayim, but we must be worthy of it.

The Gemara states: "Jerusalem of the World to Come is not like Jerusalem of this world." Perhaps "the World to Come" here is referring to the days of *Moshiach*. The Gemara explains: "Anyone who wishes to go up to Jerusalem of this world may go up; of the World to Come, only those invited to it may go up to it."[18] We may be living in *Eretz Yisrael* now, yet who knows if we will still be worthy of it when *Moshiach* arrives.

It is a tremendous privilege to live in *Eretz Yisrael* and an even greater one to live in Yerushalayim. However, this privilege brings with it an obligation to behave in a manner appropriate for someone living in Hashem's palace. We should be happy to accept this obligation on ourselves because it brings us close to Hashem. Three times a day we pray:

ברכנו אבינו כלנו כאחד באור פניך

"Bless us, our Father, all of us as one, with light of Your Countenance."[19]

We ask Hashem not to hide behind harsh decrees, God forbid, but that we see the light of His Countenance. May Hashem shower us with love and *chessed* so that our secular brethren too will see His light and come closer to Hashem and His Torah. The spread of secularization is the result of *hester panim* – Hashem's hiding His countenance. When we merit *ha'aras panim*, all these terrible sins will disappear.

In The Darkness Of Exile

Exile, as we have just mentioned, is also a form of blessing, but a blessing we would rather live without. Exile is symbolized by darkness. ברכנו אבינו כלנו כאחד באור פניך "Bless us, our Father, all of us as one, with light of Your countenance." *Birkas Kohanim*, the priestly blessing, begins with יברכך ה' וישמרך – "May Hashem bless you and safeguard you."[20] In what way do we wish Hashem to bless us? The second *pasuk* defines the blessing: יאר ה' פניו אליך ויחנך – "May Hashem illuminate His Countenance for you and be gracious to you."[21] We desire the blessing of light and not darkness, even if at times that too could be a blessing.

The Torah tells us that *maaser sheni* is brought to Yerushalayim, "So that you will learn to fear Hashem your God all the days."[22] Although in context this *pasuk* refers to the fear and awe of the onlookers watching the Kohanim serving in the *Beis HaMikdash*, I believe that even today Yerushalayim has the power to inspire a person to Torah and *yiras Shamayim*.

We beseech Hashem during *Selichos*: אל תשליכנו מלפניך – "Do not cast us away from Yourself." One possible meaning is that מלפניך refers to *Eretz Yisrael* which is לפני ה'. We learn this from the book of Yonah. When the prophet fled from *Eretz Yisrael*, we are told, "It was from before Hashem that he was fleeing."[23] Yonah could receive prophecy only when he was before Hashem in *Eretz Yisrael*; it was impossible in *chutz la'aretz*. We pray that Hashem not send us out מלפניך – from the Land of Israel, but rather that we should merit that our presence in *Eretz Yisrael* and Yerushalayim help to open our hearts to Torah, *yiras Shamayim*, and to coming closer to Hashem.

Opportune Times And Places

Those of us privileged to live in *Eretz Yisrael*, and especially in Yerushalayim, who do not achieve this closeness to Hashem, will have far more to answer for than someone living in Moscow, where the opportunity to learn Torah is minimal. A person in New York has a greater opportunity than a person in Moscow, but neither can compare to a Jew living in *Eretz Yisrael*. We are privileged to walk among Torah giants, and anyone who does not learn from them or at least try to follow in their footsteps will have much to answer for.

Our sages teach us an important principle: "Greater is the punishment for the non-observance of the white threads than for the non-observance of the blue threads."[24] Regarding *tzitzis*, even when *tcheles* was available, it was always more costly, thus a person may very well have been exempt from this requirement. No such exemption, however, exists when it comes to the white threads, for they are easily acquired and therefore the penalty for one who does not wear them is far greater. Here in *Eretz Yisrael*, Torah is as accessible as the white threads of our *tzitzis*. The charge against us for not achieving an appropriate level of Torah and *yiras Shamayim* will be far greater than against one living in Russia or even the United States for whom access to Torah is comparable to *tcheles* strings.

This principle of availing ourselves of opportunities applies not only to favorable places, but to favorable times as well. Days of greater sanctity such as *Shabbos*, Yom Tov and Yom Kippur, are auspicious times for spiritual growth. Wasting these special times on trivialities and foolishness is a more severe offense than wasting ordinary days.

By the same token, a person in Yeshiva has a greater opportunity to acquire Torah than someone on the outside and thus will also be judged more severely for not taking advantage of it. The Gemara clarifies this verse in the *Navi*: "Tell My nation of their willful transgressions and the House of Yaakov their unwitting transgressions.[25] 'My nation' refers to the Torah scholars, whose unwitting transgressions are considered like willful transgressions. '... and the House of Yaakov' refers to the ordinary people, whose willful transgressions are considered like unwitting transgressions."[26] Compared to the outside world, we are *talmidei chachamim* and therefore the appellation 'My nation' in the *pasuk* refers to us, the *bnei Yeshiva*. Our accidental transgressions are viewed as willful. We could have become great *talmidei chachamim* but we did not avail ourselves of this golden opportunity. The ordinary people outside of the Yeshiva are not judged as severely and their intentional transgressions are viewed as accidental.

Understanding the Gemara in this light, a person may decide that he is better off remaining an *am ha'aretz*. Then any transgression, even intentional, will be viewed as accidental! Obviously this is not what the Torah wants from us. In fact if someone has the opportunity to become a *talmid chacham*, yet elects to remain an *am ha'aretz* that in itself is a very severe transgression. As the Gemara states: "The beginning of man's judgment concerns only his study of Torah."[27] It is incumbent on a *ben Yeshiva* to utilize his opportunities to strive for greatness. He must not be satisfied with becoming just a minor *talmid chacham*, but endeavor to be the best he can. When it comes to physical matters, we can be satisfied with little, but in spiritual matters, we must strive to reach the top, as the *pasuk* states: "Open wide your mouth and I will fill it."[28]

Similarly someone may ask, 'Why bother living in *Eretz Yisrael*? Are we not endangering our lives by settling in a place where we are judged immediately and more harshly? Would we not be better off in *chutz la'aretz* where the demands are much less?' This is distorted reasoning! We should desire the greatness of *Eretz Yisrael* and yearn to achieve the greatness demanded of its inhabitants. We must strive for greatness and not flee out of fear that we will not be able to live up to the required standards.

Eretz Yisrael Is To Sanctify Hashem's Name

Yehoshua gathered the entire nation in Shechem just before his death, in order to make another covenant between them and Hashem. He charged them: "Choose today whom you will serve."[29] He prefaced his request with the historical background familiar to us all from the Pesach Haggadah, "Your forefathers – Terach, the father of Avraham and the father of Nachor – always dwelt beyond the Euphrates River and they served other gods."[30] He was demanding that they decide now if they would rather return to worshipping the gods of Terach or other *avoda zara*, for serving the God of Avraham is far more difficult. He warned them, "You will not be able to serve Hashem, for He is a holy God; He is a jealous God; He will not forgive your rebellious sins or your transgressions."[31] It is so much less threatening to serve Terach's *avoda zara*, so why should they bother serving Hashem? Yehoshua continued: "... but as for me and my house, we will serve Hashem!"[32] For others this might be too difficult an undertaking. The people's response was, "We shall serve Hashem, our God, and we shall heed His voice."[33]

Eretz Yisrael was given to us as a tool with which to serve Hashem, not for worshipping *avoda zara*. The people's response was exactly what Yehoshua wanted to hear – that they undertook to serve Hashem not only before conquering *Eretz Yisrael* but afterwards as well. Satisfied, Yehoshua made a new covenant in Shechem between Hashem and the Jewish people.

The only purpose in entering *Eretz Yisrael* is to become closer to Hashem. Moshe Rabenu said to Hashem, "If Your Presence does not go along, do not bring us forward from here."[34] Hashem may have promised, "Behold! I send an angel before you to protect you on the way, and to bring you to the place that I have made ready."[35] An angel will actually bring them into the Land, but Moshe Rabenu insisted that if Hashem Himself did not accompany them, he would rather the nation remained in the desert.

Similarly, following the setback in the war against Ai, when Achan took from the *cherem*, Yehoshua lamented, "If only we had been content to dwell on the other side of the Jordan."[36] It would have been better to remain on the other side of the Jordan than to suffer this great *chillul Hashem* of being defeated and ruled by other nations. Now, note that it was Yehoshua who together with Calev objected to the spies' report that the Jewish people were better off in the desert. The purpose of *Eretz Yisrael* is to sanctify Hashem's Name; when it ends up producing a *chillul Hashem* it is better to remain in the desert. Hashem eventually instructed Yehoshua to destroy Achan and the cherem and promised that He would help *Am Yisrael* conquer *Eretz Yisrael*. We must be worthy of living in this Land, and worthy of Hashem's Providence, otherwise there is no point in remaining here. We should pray that by our dwelling in this Holy Land, we bring about only a *Kiddush Hashem*.

Acquiring *Eretz Yisrael* In Modern Times

The only way to acquire the Land is through observance of Torah and *mitzvos*. Any promise from political parties to safeguard our security is worthless, whether they are left-wing or right-wing. The lottery of the goat which was sent to *Azazel* on Yom Kippur was sometimes drawn by the Kohen Gadol's left hand and sometimes by his right hand. Only Torah and *yiras Shamayim* can protect us. We must give our support only to parties which fight for Torah and *Shabbos* observance. Any bridge between us and the secular Jews will not last if it involves sanctioning desecration of *Shabbos*!

Chazal tell us, "The world continues to exist only in the merit of the breath of schoolchildren."[37] Today's secular children are referred to as *tinokos shenishbu*[38]. What a deplorable situation! Children should be "*tinokos shel beis raban*" – "children of houses of learning"! We must see to it that all children receive a proper Torah education, based on Torah and on *yiras Shamayim*. We cannot support parties who do not make this their top priority.

Today[39] we have one barak attempting to draft the Yeshiva students (then Prime Minister Ehud Barak), and another barak (Chief Justice Aharon Barak) trying to bring in the Reform and Conservative. Indeed we *Yidden* support a *barak* – the *barak*, the lightning, of the Torah which was given with "*kolos ubrakim*" – "thunder and lightning."[40] The Ne'eman Commission is also trying to bring in the Conservative and Reform. The Ne'eman that we know is "*Kel Melech Ne'eman*," "God, trustworthy King," or Moshe Rabenu regarding whom Hashem said "*bechol beisi ne'eman hu*" – "In My entire house he is the trusted one."[41] We do not need any Reform or Conservative assistance in keeping *mitzvos*.

The prophet says, "As for what you say, 'We will be like the nations, like the families of the lands, to worship wood and stone,' as I live – the word of the Lord Hashem Elokim, I will rule over you with a strong hand and with an outstretched arm and with outpoured wrath."[42] In Germany, where the Jewish citizens were in favor of assimilation and wished to be like the other nations, we witnessed Hashem's "outpoured wrath" in its fury. Although Rav Nachman expresses the wish, "O that the Merciful One would bring all this wrath upon us and redeem us,"[43] we would prefer not to have this outpouring of anger, but would rather Hashem rule over us with *chessed* and great love.

I am embarrassed even to mention it but there was actually a motion in the *Knesset* suggesting that there should be a new law declaring the *Kosel* a non-holy site. (Perhaps it never reached the plenum, but it was certainly suggested.) There was even a party which at-

---

38   Literally "children taken captive" because they never had the opportunity to receive a proper Torah education.

39   This *Sicha* was delivered in 5759. (1998)

tempted to undermine *bris milah*. Maybe the *Knesset* should also vote on whether the Seventh Day should remain holy or whether the Jewish people should remain a holy nation! That is precisely where they are heading and we must keep far away from this. We must always זכור את יום השבת לקדשו – "Remember the Sabbath Day to sanctify it."[44]

We see that not distinguishing between קודש לחול – "holy and secular," and between יום השביעי לששת ימי המעשה – "the Seventh Day and the six days of labor" leads to not distinguishing בין ישראל לעמים – "between Israel and the nations." Certain political parties today care more about the fate of the Arabs than their fellow Jews, and I am not referring only to Arab parties. They have lost not only the distinction between "Israel and the nations," but even between אור לחשך – "light and darkness" – they do not see what is going on before their eyes – they are blind! They are handing *Eretz Yisrael* over to murderers.

As mentioned, we pray every day ברכנו אבינו כלנו כאחד באור פניך, we want to merit הארת פנים, the illumination of Hashem's Countenance, so that we may strengthen the Name of Hashem and Torah and *yiras Shamayim* in *Eretz Yisrael* and among *Am Yisrael*. We must ensure that there are Yeshivos and *Shabbos* and *bris milah*, and if the *Kosel* is no longer a holy site, it should only be because it now forms the border of a still holier place, the *Har HaBayis*.

Today we are in a disgraceful situation, unknown in all previous exiles. Titus and Antiochus may have captured *Har HaBayis* but no one ever announced formally that it belonged to them. Today there is an agreement that the *Har HaBayis* belongs to King Hussein of Jordan – he is the שומר משמרת הקודש – "guardian in charge of the sanctity."[45] I haven't heard whether he is a Kohen or a Levi but nevertheless he has been appointed שומר משמרת הקודש! We pray that the holiness of the *Kodesh HaKodashim* spread to the *Kosel*, to Yerushalayim in its entirety and to the entire Land of Israel. "... and your eyes will behold it, and you will say upon the territory of Israel, 'May Hashem be glorified.'"[46] This can only come about through observance of *Shabbos* and other *mitzvos*: "Whoever delights in the *Shabbos* is granted a boundless heritage."[47]

ופרצת ימה וקדמה צפונה ונגבה – "And you shall burst forth west-ward, eastward, northward, and southward."[48] May we merit Hashem's salvation באור פני ה'.

באור פני מלך חיים – "In the light of the King's Countenance is life."[49]

Notes

1   *Bereishis* 25:5-6

2   *Bereishis* 21:10

3   *Bereishis* 17:18

4   Ibid. 20

5   *Hilchos Melachim, Perek* 10, *halacha* 8

6   *Bereishis* 21:9

7   *Bereishis* 21:10

8   *Devarim* 11:12

9   *Vayikra* 18:25

10   Ibid. 28

11   Ibid.

12   See also *Sicha* II *Parshas Lech Lecha.*

13   *Melachim* II 17:27

14   Ibid. 33

15   *Gittin* 88a

16   *Devarim* 4:25-26

17   *Shabbos* 145b

18   *Baba Basra* 75b

19   The final *beracha* of the *Shacharis Shmone Esrei.* (*Mincha* as well in *Nusach Sefard*)

20   *Bamidbar* 6:24

21   Ibid. 25

22   *Devarim* 14:23

23   *Yonah* 1:10

24   *Menachos* 43b

25   *Yeshayahu* 58:1

26   *Baba Metzia* 33b

27   *Kiddushin* 40b

28   *Tehillim* 81:11

29   *Yehoshua* 24:15

30   Ibid. 2

31   Ibid. 19

32   Ibid. 15

33   Ibid. 24

34   *Shemos* 33:15

35   *Shemos* 23:20

36 *Yehoshua* 7:7

37 *Shabbos* 119b

40 *Shemos* 19:16

41 *Bamidbar* 12:7

42 *Yechezkel* 20:32-33

43 *Sanhedrin* 105a

44 *Shemos* 20:8

45 *Bamidbar* 3:28

46 *Malachi* 1:5

47 *Shabbos* 118a

48 *Bereishis* 28:14

49 *Mishle* 16:15

Constructing Scales Of Values

ולרבקה אח ושמו לבן וירץ לבן אל האיש החוצה אל העין

"*Rivka had a brother whose name was Lavan; Lavan ran to the man outside, to the spring.*"[1]

Ulterior Motives

What a *tzaddik*! Lavan is another Avraham Avinu! Lavan simply hears that a man in need of food and lodging is standing by the spring and he runs to invite him into his tent.[2] We can almost feel the holiness emanating from Lavan as he diligently performs the mitzvah of *hachnosas orchim*. The next few *psukim*, however, reveal Lavan's true motive. "For upon seeing the nose-ring and the bracelets on his sister's hands, and upon his hearing his sister Rivka's words saying, 'Thus has the man spoken to me,' he approached the man, who was still standing with the camels by the spring."[3] Rashi asks, "Why did he run and for what did he run? On seeing the nose ring he said, 'This one is rich,' and he set his eyes on the money." We can be certain that if Lavan had not spotted Rivka's nose-ring and bracelets, he would not have run so enthusiastically towards Eliezer. His reaction would more likely have been, "A man in search of lodging? Why should that concern me? Let him sleep out in the field by the well! What's that ... he has jewelry in his possession? That's a different story! Such a person is welcome in my home any time of day or night!" Chazal tell us that Lavan initially attempted to kill Eliezer in order to appropriate his possessions.[4] When that failed, Lavan concluded that his only chance to get a chunk of the wealth was to honor Eliezer as his guest.

Not only did Lavan not exactly excel in the mitzvah of *hachnosas orchim*; his honesty and integrity too, left much to be desired. When Lavan and Besuel learned of Eliezer's mission, their response was, "Here, Rivka is before you; take her and go,"[5] as if to say, "Your story sounds quite convincing and we are willing to hand Rivka over to you immediately." The following day, however, there was a change of heart. Besuel was no longer alive,[6] and Lavan asked Eliezer, "Let the maiden remain with us a year or ten (months), then she will go."[7] I know that yesterday I promised Rivka to you immediately, but why rush into things? Why not wait until next year?

Many years later, when Yaakov was living in Lavan's house, it was evident that Lavan had not changed one bit. Yaakov Avinu and Lavan had an agreement that Yaakov would work for seven years "for Rachel your younger daughter."[8] Despite there being no ambiguity regarding what was expected of each side, Lavan substituted Leah for Rachel. This was a great *chessed* on Hashem's part because this meant that the Jewish nation would now be built on the foundation set by both of these righteous women – "like Rachel and like Leah, both of whom built up the House of Israel."[9] Who knows where we would be without Leah? Moshe Rabenu, Aharon HaKohen, and David HaMelech all descended from Leah. Of course Lavan, for his part, had no intention of doing anything good for Yaakov or for the Jewish nation. Lavan's only intention was to deceive Yaakov into working for him for fourteen years rather than the seven years that had been agreed on.

It is quite possible that Lavan had an additional, sinister ulterior motive – to forever blemish the holy tribes of Israel.[10] The Gemara tells us that when a man lives with one woman yet his mind is on another – even if he is married to both of them, the child created from such a union will be of bad character. Perhaps this was Lavan's wish; if he gave Leah to Yaakov without his knowledge, their off-spring would be blemished, because only the following morning did he realize: "Behold it was Leah."[11] Even if this was not his intention, Lavan's act was a clear and simple case of deceit. The deceit did not end there. Yaakov accused Lavan of "changing my wage a hundred times"[12] – Lavan reneged on their working agreement one hundred times! When the time came to divide up the flock, he replaced the speckled ones with the spotted ones, the ringed ones with the checkered ones.[13] Yaakov finally left for *Eretz Yisrael* and "Lavan sought to eradicate everything."[14] Had Hashem not given Lavan a stern warning not to dare bring any harm on Yaakov, he would surely have put his evil thoughts into practice.

Remaining True To Form

Lavan's character, in short, was far from praiseworthy – he did not speak the truth, he cheated, he stole, and he even planned the murder of Eliezer as well as of Yaakov and his family. In addition, we know that he was an idol worshipper.[15] Perhaps this last point can actually be viewed in a positive light. Whether or not we condone his *avoda zara*, he apparently had tremendous respect for what he viewed as his deity. When Lavan thought that Yaakov had stolen his idols, he pursued him, shouting, "Why did you steal my gods?"[16] *Avoda zara* is a very serious *aveira*, that one should die rather than commit, yet there is something positive about a person with ideals who accords honor to his gods, for it shows that he has spiritual as well as physical interests.

As we read on, however, we discover what Lavan truly thought about his gods. When Lavan invited Eliezer into his home, he asked him, "Why should you stand outside when I have cleared the house?"[17] Rashi tells us that he cleared the house of all *avoda zara* to be able to declare, 'I have no idols – everything in my house is *glatt kosher*!' What happened? These idols were so dear to him, he had the utmost respect for them, he had gone to great lengths to try to retrieve them. How could he just remove them from his house? How could his actions be so contradictory?

In fact Lavan was consistent! First on his scale of values was not belief in the meaningless entities he referred to as his gods. At the top of the list was money and wealth. He was faithful to his gods and perhaps would even speak the truth, as long as it did not cost him anything. Yet the moment money was involved, the picture changed radically. For Lavan there were three pillars upon which the world stands: money, wealth, and possessions. All other values fell way behind. For money, Lavan would lie, deceive, kill, and evict his gods from the house.

Torah Values

Baruch Hashem, we do not act like Lavan. Even so, each person has his own personal scale of values and priorities. There are people who place heavy emphasis on truth and honesty, while others place greater value on acts of *chessed*. Each person has positive traits which he emphasizes over others. Clearly, when viewing this scale, we must realize that first and foremost one should place the highest value on what the Torah deems most important. For example, the Torah established for us that "*Shabbos* is equal in importance to all other *mitzvos*,"[18] therefore one cannot suddenly declare that he is meticulous not to wear *shaatnez*, to the extent that he is even willing to desecrate the *Shabbos* for it. This is clearly in violation of the set of priorities that the Torah has established for us. Not only is *Shabbos* considered equivalent to all other *mitzvos*, but the penalty for its violation is death by stoning. We have no right to decide to be excessively strict in observing other *mitzvos* if it is at the expense of *Shabbos* observance.

In spite of the importance which the Torah accords to *Shabbos*, there were certain practices pertaining to the *Beis HaMikdash* which would otherwise have been prohibited on *Shabbos*. The *Korban Tomid*, for example, was offered every day of the year including *Shabbosos*. Other offerings too were brought on *Shabbos*. The *Beis HaMikdash* service was of paramount importance, yet certain *mitzvos* take precedence over even that. If a Kohen is on his way to the *Beis HaMikdash* to serve, or for that matter any Jew is on his way to offer the *Korban Pesach*, and en route he happens on a *meis mitzvah*,[19] he is obligated to bury the dead even if it renders him *tamei* and thus prohibits him from serving or offering his *Korban Pesach*.[20] One could argue that the *Korban Pesach* can always be brought at the next opportunity, on *Pesach Sheni*, but what would be the case if just before the 14th of *Iyar* he came across another *meis mitzvah*? The *halacha* is that once again, burying the dead takes precedence and in that case he would be unable to offer his *Korban Pesach* at all that year.

As important as it is to bury a *meis mitzvah* – to the extent that it takes precedence over service in the *Beis HaMikdash*, there is something that has priority over even that – *pikuach nefesh* – saving a life. Given a choice between saving a life and burying a *meis mitzvah*, saving the life comes first. In addition, we must realize that this scale of priorities is not the only yardstick by which to measure the value of the mitzvah or the order of priorities. Despite the fact that burying a *meis mitzvah* takes precedence over serving in the *Beis HaMikdash*, and service in the *Beis HaMikdash* is carried out even if in violation of the *Shabbos*, this does not imply that a *meis mitzvah* may be buried on *Shabbos*.

Chazal also tell us, "The mitzvah of *tzitzis* is equal in importance to all other *mitzvos*,"[21] yet the mitzvah of *tzitzis* does not take precedence over other *mitzvos*. We fulfill the mitzvah of *tzitzis* at the expense of certain negative commandments, as we do any positive mitzvah, but it does not come before other positive commandments.

Ranking precedence in fulfillment of *mitzvos* and defining which *mitzvos* are equivalent to all other *mitzvos* are clearly two different concepts and two different ways of measuring relative importance and severity. We learn, for example, "Settling *Eretz Yisrael* is equal in importance to all the other *mitzvos*,"[22] yet one may not violate a single prohibition, even a Rabbinic one, in order to fulfill the mitzvah of *yishuv Eretz Yisrael*. We know that "when one purchases a house in *Eretz Yisrael*, the deed may be written even on the *Shabbos*,"[23] yet the Gemara qualifies this as referring to a document written by a non-Jew. The only Rabbinic prohibition permitted for the sake of

---

19   A Jewish corpse for whose burial no one takes responsibility.

settling the Land is for a non-Jew to perform the *melacha*. We even find a dispute between the *Shulchan Aruch* and the *Rama* regarding the specifics of this leniency.[24] The *Shulchan Aruch*'s opinion is that for the sake of *yishuv Eretz Yisrael*," one may ask a non-Jew to perform an act which would be in violation of a Torah prohibition if done by a Jew. The *Rama*'s view, on the other hand, is that the non-Jew may only perform an act which would be a Rabbinic violation for a Jew. According to the *Rama*, even though *yishuv Eretz Yisrael* is equivalent to all the other *mitzvos*, one may not even ask a gentile to violate a Torah prohibition in order for us to fulfill this mitzvah.

Saving a life, as important as it may be, is less important than the three cardinal sins for which, rather than violate them, a person must give his life. There are other circumstances, such as during times of persecution, when a person should give up his life rather than transgress any of the *mitzvos*. During the Crusader period, a *machlokes* arose whether Jews who killed themselves and their children *al Kiddush Hashem* rather than allowing them to fall into the hands of the Crusaders were acting properly. Many authorities permitted it, but there were those who viewed it as outright murder and suicide.[25] In the Tisha B'Av *Kinos* recited by the Ashkenazim, these acts are related as praiseworthy. It seems that the Jews of the time followed the opinion that it would be better to slaughter their own children than to have them raised in monasteries and taught to worship *avoda zara*. This view may have been the accepted one, but before we issue any rulings based on it, we must realize that there was a dissenting opinion as well. It is very difficult to determine which takes precedence – the spilling of blood or *avoda zara*. Violation of either of these sins is very severe.

Emunah

The test of the *Akeida* teaches us that belief in Hashem comes before anything else. Avraham's unbending belief in Hashem led him to make all the preparations to slaughter his son, despite his major dilemma about Hashem's promise – "Since through Yitzchak will offspring be considered yours."[26] Hashem commanded him to slaughter his son, and that was all that mattered! What about the potential *chillul Hashem*? What will the other nations say? Here is Avraham Avinu who spent his entire life preaching *chessed*, teaching time and again how wrong child sacrifice is. Suddenly he goes and mercilessly slaughters his son. Imagine the ramifications of such an act – Avraham's many years of hard work would all be for naught. Avraham made no such calculations. What was uppermost in his mind was that Hashem had commanded him to slaughter his son. (Or so it appeared to Avraham, and this is in fact the way Hashem wished that it appear to him. In reality Hashem had no desire whatsoever for Avraham to offer his son; He only told him *ha'alehu* – "Place him upon the Altar." Avraham was never commanded actually to slaughter Yitzchak). For Avraham Avinu there was nothing to question; he was guided solely by his faith in Hashem, even if it meant risking the future of the Jewish nation.

These are *halachos* which every Jew must follow. May we never be tested with an *Akeida*. But should there be, God forbid, a test involving potential *Kiddush Hashem*, the *Shulchan Aruch* gives guidelines on what to do.[27] It stipulates when a person must give his life rather than transgress an *aveira*, and when it is preferable to transgress rather than die. These guidelines apply to all Jews; no one may construct a scale of values for himself.

A Unique *Chelek* In The Torah

In spite of the fact that the whole nation was present at Har Sinai, and we all declared in unison, נעשה ונשמע – "We will do and we will obey,"[28] all of *Am Yisrael* did not receive the Torah equally. I am not only referring to the fact that certain *halachos* apply exclusively to a Kohen, others to a Levi, while some laws pertain only to the king. There is another way to understand the idea that each of us has his own unique share in the Torah. We recite daily *"Vesen chelkenu be-Sorasecha"* – "Give us our share in Your Torah." What do we mean by this *tefilla*? On a simple level, we can explain that we are praying that our share be "with those who dwell in the *Beis Midrash* and not with idlers."[29] Every time he left the *Beis Midrash*, Rav Nechunya ben HaKaneh would thank Hashem for granting us this.

There is, however, a different way to interpret this *tefilla*. Every Jew has his own unique share in the Torah – a portion he can call his own. Although the Torah is "the heritage of the congregation of Yaakov,"[30] each heir has his own share of the inheritance. In the laws of inheritance we find a dispute whether *ein breira* or *yesh breira*. Do we view the entire inheritance as belonging to all the heirs until it is divided? Or do we say that after the division each person's portion retroactively belonged only to him from the moment the father died? Clearly this dispute does not apply to our inheritance of the Torah; each and every Jew has inherited the Torah in its entirety and we are all under the obligation to observe all 613 *mitzvos*. We have no right to pick and choose which *mitzvos* we wish to observe and which we do not.

Even with this understanding, we can say that each person has his unique share of the Torah. We can compare this to the Land of Israel, which is the inheritance of the entire Jewish nation, yet each tribe has its own unique portion (with the exception of Yerushalayim which was not divided among the tribes.[31]) For example the Torah says, "Zevulun shall settle by seashores."[32] By the same token, although the entire Torah was given to all of us, we each have a section of the Torah which was designated for us as individuals. When we beseech Hashem daily, "Give us our share of Your Torah," we are asking for Divine Assistance in locating the portion of the Torah that is set aside for us. According to some opinions, in earlier generations the prophet would reveal this to each individual. Today we may not have prophets, but we have *talmidei chachamim* who can guide us in determining on which portion of the Torah we should place more emphasis. Many people are able to arrive at this conclusion on their own. One person may be drawn to *Kodshim*, others towards monetary laws. We must be very careful, however, when deciding what to emphasize, for the *yetzer hara* works hard at convincing us to choose the easier path: Why struggle? Take the easy way out! When choosing a direction, we need to ask ourselves whether it is truly suitable for us, or whether we are actually driven by laziness. The Chofetz Chaim believed that it was incumbent on all Kohanim to learn how to serve in the *Beis HaMikdash*, may it be built speedily in our day, yet too often a person may choose to delve into *Kodshim* over *Nezikin* because the latter would require him to learn and understand the Rif and the Rosh, commentaries which do not exist on *Kodshim*. I believe that HaGaon HaRav Yechezkel Sarna zt"l used to say to those who spent too much time studying *Kodshim*, "You are lazy, lazy! Therefore you say 'Let us go and bring offerings to Hashem.'"[33] Sometimes, however a person really has a natural inclination to study *Kodshim*. It is incumbent upon us to be honest with ourselves about the real reason we are drawn to one area of Torah study over another.

Every Jew is required to study the entire Torah. Indeed it has been said in the name of the Vilna Gaon that each person will be called to judgment for the material that he did not learn – from Chumash to *maase merkava*. Nevertheless, we find in Shas that there were some Amoraim who would excel in *halacha* while others were expert in *aggada*. Does this imply that those more involved in *aggada* did not learn *halacha*? Certainly not! Rav Abahu, for example gave many *aggadic* discourses, yet he was very well-versed in *halacha* and is often quoted in *halachic* matters. Rav Yehoshua ben Levi was said to have been a great expert in *aggada*,[34] yet we are well aware of his expertise in *halacha*. In fact *Tosafos*[35] tell us that whenever a dispute is found between Rav Yochanan and Rav Yehoshua ben Levi, we rule in accordance with the view of Rav Yehoshua ben Levi – even though Rav Yochanan was one of the greatest Amoraim.

About Rav and Shmuel, the Gemara teaches, "The *halacha* follows Rav in ritual law, and in civil cases the ruling adopted is that of Shmuel."[36] In a number of instances, Shmuel is referred to as Aryoch.[37] Aryoch was king of אלאסר[38] which can be pronounced אל אסר *"al asar"* – "Do not forbid." This comes to hint that Shmuel may be the giant when it comes to areas of monetary litigation, but regarding *issur* – deciding whether something is prohibited or permitted, Rav is the king. Therefore in reference to Shmuel we say *"al asar"* – 'Do

---

33 This quote is from *Parshas Shmos* (5:17). When the Jews asked Pharaoh for permission to leave Mitzrayim to bring an offering to Hashem, Pharaoh accused them of being lazy and trying to get out of working.

not follow his view when it comes to prohibitions.' Does this mean that Shmuel was not well-versed in areas of *issur*? Surely not, for his opinion is quoted throughout Shas in these areas. By the same token, we find Rav quoted quite often on monetary issues. Each was familiar with the entire Torah and observed it. Rav's greatness, however, was most striking in matters of *issur* while Shmuel particularly excelled in monetary laws. When we say that the giants of Torah were each drawn to particular sections of the Torah we do not imply, God forbid, that they neglected other sections. Rather, they particularly excelled in their specific areas.

The Gemara relates that someone asked Rav Yosef the son of the great *amora*, Rabba: "In which mitzvah was your father especially careful?"[39] to which he answered that it was the mitzvah of *tzitzis*. Does this mean that he was lax in his observance of *Pesach*, *Shabbos*, *kashrus*, and *bris milah*? Certainly not! It was simply that he felt a close spiritual connection to the mitzvah of *tzitzis*. The Gemara relates that once while he was climbing a ladder, one of the strings of his *tzitzis* tore and he would not come down the ladder until he was able to replace it. I am not sure how he managed to do that on top of a ladder – perhaps he kept additional strings in his pocket for such an occasion, or he may have sent someone on the ground to bring them to him. What is clear is that he placed such value on this mitzvah that he remained on the ladder until he was able to repair his *tzitzis*. Another Jew may be inclined to place greater emphasis on another mitzvah. None of us has ever violated the prohibition of "The breastplate will not be loosened from upon the *ephod*,"[40] yet I do not believe that any of us would consider this our special portion of the Torah.

The Three Pillars Of The World

The prophet states: תתן אמת ליעקב חסד לאברהם – "Grant truth to Yaakov, kindness to Avraham."[41] Yaakov is known as a man of truth, while Avraham is referred to as a man of *chessed*. This appellation in no way implies that Avraham was not a man of truth or that Yaakov did not perform acts of *chessed*. The holy forefathers each excelled in his own area of service of Hashem. Each forefather's unique portion of the Torah corresponds to one of the pillars upon which the world stands. The Mishna states:

על שלשה דברים העולם עומד על התורה ועל העבודה ועל גמילות חסדים

"On three things the world stands, on Torah, on the service, and on acts of kindness."[42]

Although Chazal teach us: "Avraham Avinu fulfilled the entire Torah,"[43] his special strength was *chessed*. Avraham Avinu is the paradigm of what *chessed* should be. He planted an *eshel*[44] in Be'er Sheva and performed many acts of kindness for his guests, materially as well as spiritually. In fact, Chazal tell us "The attribute of *chessed* said: 'So long as Avraham was in this world, I did not have to perform my job, for Avraham took my place.'"[45]

Avraham Avinu was the personification of *chessed* in this world. Yitzchak was the pillar of *avoda*, service; he was the sheep that was bound upon the Altar. Yaakov personified the attribute of *emes* – truth. Yaakov was the *ish tam* – "the wholesome man," perfect, the tent-dweller who spent all day immersed in the Torah passed down to him by his father Yitzchak, in the Torah of Shem, and in the Torah of Ever[46] – he was the pillar of Torah. We have no doubt that each of the forefathers observed the entire Torah, yet each had a specific role in the building of the Jewish nation and in building the Torah within *Klal Yisrael*. They are the three pillars on which the world stands.

Custom-Made Scales

We mentioned that part of our scale of values has been constructed for us by the Torah, and we must find the other part for ourselves. Are we particularly drawn to areas of *issurim*, monetary laws, *Kodshim*, or any other portion? In the absence of a prophet, each person must construct this scale for himself. In recent times, our scale of

---

44 The Gemara cites a dispute between Rav and Shmuel nature of the *eshel*. One opinion states that it is an orchard from which fruits were brought for guests, while the other states that it is an inn for lodging in which food is also provided. (See *Sotah* 10a, cited by Rashi, and *Bereishis* 21:33.)

values has seen a total transformation. One example of this involves our relationship with non-Jews. The Rav (HaGaon HaRav Shlomo Zalman Auerbach) zt"l ruled that although the *halacha* states that one may not violate the *Shabbos* in order to save the life of a non-Jew,[47] in our day we are obligated to save the life of a non-Jew even if it involves desecration of the *Shabbos*. The Rav claimed that with the development of communications, it would become known immediately to the entire world that Jews in *Eretz Yisrael* refused to provide proper medical care to non-Jews on *Shabbos*. As a result non-Jewish doctors in Argentina, say, may then refuse to treat ailing Jews who could be in life-threatening situations.[48]

In my humble opinion, there is an additional reason to permit violating the *Shabbos* in order to save the life of a non-Jew today. In previous generations a gentile would never complain if a Jew were to let a non-Jew die rather than treat him on *Shabbos*, for he understood the supreme value the Jewish people place on *Shabbos* observance. *Shabbos* was not to be transgressed under any circumstances. Reverence for God was always at the top of the scale of values. The Gemara in fact tells us that the Jews were able to explain to their gentile neighbors: "Only for our own who keep the *Shabbos* may we violate it, but we must not desecrate the *Shabbos* for you, who do not keep it."[49] We are permitted to desecrate the *Shabbos* only in order to save one of our own, because this will result in one more person in the world observing future *Shabbosos*. We see from this Gemara that even a non-Jew understood this point. It is well-known that enemies would often attack on *Shabbos*, thinking that the Jews would not retaliate. Torah-observing Jews, however, understood that *pikuach nefesh* takes precedence over *Shabbos* observance.

During the era of Aristobulus, the Tzdukkim[50] who were the Jewish leaders in Yerushalayim, declared that Jews are forbidden to wage war on *Shabbos* and as a result the Romans succeeded in laying siege to Yerushalayim and conquering it. Of course, they were gravely mistaken, because the *halacha* requires us to violate the *Shabbos* rather than allow ourselves to be killed. Not only are we permitted to protect ourselves, but we are obligated to do so. War for the purpose of conquering *Eretz Yisrael* may also be carried out on

Shabbos. Chazal tell us: "Build a bulwark against the city that makes war with you until it is conquered,"[31] – even on *Shabbos*."[32] We see that the Romans were so convinced that *Shabbos* observance headed our scale of values that they used this to their advantage.

The fact that a Jew would not violate *Shabbos* in order to save the life of a non-Jew was never subject to question. Unfortunately today, due to our many sins, our scale of values has changed completely. Honor of heaven has sunk to the bottom of the ladder. If there are any values left in the outside world, it is only in the realm of *bein adam lachavero* – what they call 'humanitarianism.' Somehow or other, acting properly towards our fellow human beings still remains a value. Even if people do not sincerely believe this, the idea is espoused in public. A non-Jew today would not understand: "Only for our own, who keep the *Shabbos*, may we violate it, but we cannot desecrate the *Shabbos* for you who do not keep it." That would not be humanitarian. Honor of heaven carries no weight whatsoever.

Sadly, a large percentage of the Jewish population does not observe the *Shabbos* today. How could we explain to a non-Jew that we are willing to violate *Shabbos* in order to save the life of a Jew who is obligated to observe *Shabbos* yet does not do so, while we cannot violate the *Shabbos* to save the life of a non-Jew who is under no obligation whatsoever to keep the *Shabbos*? From this perspective, it appears clear to me that the Gemara's ruling that one may not violate *Shabbos* in order to save the life of a non-Jew does not apply today. This does not mean that in general it is no longer incumbent upon us to follow the dictates of the Gemara, God forbid. Observing this particular ruling is beyond our ability today because our scale of values has gotten muddled.

"In Times Of Gathering-In Distribute ..."

The Talmud teaches: "In a time of those who gather in, distribute, in a time of those who distribute, gather in."[33] This means that if Torah learning is emphasized and widespread, then we are obligated to place our emphasis on other areas, but if insufficient emphasis placed on learning Torah, then it is up to us to create that emphasis.

HaGaon HaRav Yisrael Salanter zt"l in his *mussar* sermons used to emphasize the *mitzvos* of *bein adam lachavero*, because in his day these *mitzvos* were not taken as seriously as they should have been. He pointed out that the *mussar* movement was founded as a result of a specific terrible incident, when a person embarrassed another in public. Today, if we have the power to do so, we should establish a *mussar* movement with emphasis on *mitzvos bein adam laMakom*. Even the secular Jew of our time acknowledges to some extent the importance of *mitzvos bein adam lachavero*; it is the *bein adam laMakom* that is severely neglected.

Obviously this does not mean that from tomorrow we can begin to ignore our obligations to our fellow man and start fighting with each other, cursing, or speaking *loshon hara*, God forbid. Certainly we must continue to be strict in the realm of *bein adam lachavero*, but the area of *bein adam laMakom* requires strengthening.

Talmud Torah needs attention as well. As the Mishna teaches us, "The study of Torah is equivalent to them all."[54] This does not imply that we need not worry about the other *mitzvos* in the Mishna such as *hachnosos orchim* and *bikkur cholim*. This does not even imply that Torah study takes precedence over visiting the sick and inviting guests. In fact, *bikkur cholim* takes precedence if the mitzvah cannot be carried out by others in the same manner. *Pikuach nefesh* certainly comes before Talmud Torah. All things considered, however, we must be aware of the great reward awaiting us for Talmud Torah – every word we learn is equivalent to all the *mitzvos*.

Other areas that need strengthening are: *Shabbos* – we must understand with all our hearts that *Shabbos* is equivalent to all the *mitzvos*; the laws of *taharas hamishpacha* with all their detailed *halachos* such as not touching, not gazing at forbidden sights and so on, and the mitzvah of *kashrus*.

The mitzvah of *yishuv Eretz Yisrael*, as important a mitzvah as it is, we must realize that settling the Land is conditional on using it as a tool to observe *mitzvos* and not in order to build secular settlements where Torah is openly violated. This idea is spelled out explicitly: "And He gave them the lands of nations, and they inherited the toil of regimes, so that they might safeguard His statues and observe

His teachings."[55] The prophet decries one who settles the Land for purposes other than observing *mitzvos*: "But you contaminated My Land, and made My heritage into an abomination."[56] Twice daily we declare that without Torah, the Land will not remain in our hands: "It will be that if you hearken to My commandments,"[57] then you will remain in the Land. If, God forbid, the opposite is the case, then "You will be swiftly banished from the goodly Land that Hashem gives you."[58] Nothing will be gained by observing the mitzvah of *yishuv Eretz Yisrael* without Torah and *mitzvos*. This *pasuk* is not limited to the days of Moshe Rabenu and Yirmiyahu; it applies to our times as well: "This Torah will not be exchanged."[59] Whatever is written in the Torah applies to all generations.

Strengthening *mitzvos bein adam laMakom* clearly does not give us license to disregard *mitzvos bein adam lachavero*. Chazal express this in very sharp terms: "Better a man should throw himself into a fiery furnace than publicly put his neighbor to shame."[60] Many authorities take this passage literally.[61] Even though the *halacha* does not follow the literal interpretation[62], Chazal's strong language demonstrates how terrible an offense it is to embarrass someone in public. The same applies to all other *mitzvos* of *bein adam lachavero*.

Building Ladders

Chazal relate that the residents of *Eretz Yisrael* were especially careful not to embarrass their fellow man in public.[63] Is this prohibition one of the *mitzvos* dependent on the Land? Perhaps in *Eretz Yisrael* in particular they witnessed the tragic results this *aveira* could bring. The Gemara[64] tells us that the shaming of Bar Kamtza brought about the destruction of the *Beis HaMikdash*. Clearly, Bar Kamtza was not a great *tzaddik*. He informed on the Jewish people to the authorities, which led to the destruction of the *Beis Ha-Mikdash*, as well as thousands upon thousands of deaths and two thousand years of suffering. In addition the Jewish nation lost sovereignty over the Land of Israel. He may not have been one of the

---

59   One of the Thirteen Principles of Faith listed in אני מאמין at the end of daily Shacharis.

righteous people of his generation, but that did not justify publicly putting him to shame. At that time Hashem wanted retribution for the honor of Bar Kamtza, so it was through this man that the *Beis HaMikdash* was destroyed and the Jewish nation was sent into exile. Chazal sum up the incident: "Come and see how great is the power of shame, for the Holy One, Blessed is He, assisted Bar Kamtza in his plot to avenge the shame to which he had been subjected, and He destroyed His Temple and He burned His Sanctuary."[65] In *Eretz Yisrael*, they personally witnessed the terrible results of such behavior, and therefore the inhabitants were extra careful not to trample on each other's honor.

Regarding the Land of Israel, Calev said, "We shall surely ascend and conquer it, for we can surely do it."[66] Chazal explain that he meant "We shall surely ascend – even to the heavens"[67] – they will listen to Moshe. "He brought us out of Egypt, divided the Red Sea for us and fed us with manna. If he were to tell us to prepare ladders and ascend to heaven, should we not obey him?"[68] I don't know how to construct a ladder to heaven, but there is a concept of a ladder planted on this earth and reaching the heavens on which we can ascend.[69] We climb the ladder by observing *mitzvos*, toiling in Torah, and doing *teshuva*. With this ladder one can truly reach the heavens, and with this ladder we can inherit the Land of Israel as well, speedily in our day. Amen.

Notes

1   *Bereishis* 24:29

2   See *Bereishis* 18:2.

3   Ibid. 30

4   See *Yalkut Shimoni, Bereishis* 109.

5   *Bereishis* 24:51

---

69   This is an allusion to *Parshas Vayetze* in which Yaakov dreams of a "ladder set on earth and its top reached heavenward." (*Bereishis* 28:12)

6 See Rashi, *Bereishis* 24:55.

7 *Bereishis* 24:55

8 *Bereishis* 29:18 – see Rashi there.

9 *Rus* 4:11

10 See Rashi *Bereishis* 29:21

11 *Bereishis* 29:25

12 *Bereishis* 31:41

13 See Rashi, *Bereishis* 31:41.

14 Rashi, *Devarim* 26:5

15 See Rashi, *Bereishis* 31:19.

16 *Bereishis* 31:30

17 *Bereishis* 24:31

18 Yerushalmi, *Berachos* 1:5

20 See *Megilla* 3b.

21 *Nedarim* 25a

22 *Tosefta, Avoda Zara* 5:2

23 *Baba Kama* 80b

24 See *Orach Chaim* 306:11.

25 See *Bedek HaBayis* in *Beis Yoseph* to *Yoreh Deah* 157:1.

26 *Bereishis* 21:12 See Rashi, *Bereishis* 22:12.

27   See *Yoreh Deah* 157.

28   *Shemos* 24:7

29   *Berachos* 28b

30   *Devarim* 33:4

31   See *Yoma* 12a.

32   *Bereishis* 49:13

34   See *Baba Kama* 55a.

35   See *Avoda Zara* 35a "...*chada*."

36   *Bechoros* 49b

37   See *Shabbos* 53a, *Chullin* 76b.

38   See *Bereishis* 14:1.

39   *Shabbos* 118b

40   *Shemos* 28:28

41   *Micha* 7:20

42   *Avos* 1:2

43   *Yoma* 28b

45   *Sefer HaBahir* page 86, note 191.

46   See Rashi, *Bereishis* 25:27.

47   See Orach Chaim 330:2.

48   See *Shmiras Shabbos KeHilchosa* chapter 40, note 2.

49 *Avoda Zara* 26a.

50 Sadducees

51 *Devarim* 20:20

52 *Shabbos* 19a

53 *Berachos* 63a

54 *Peah, Perek* 1, Mishna 1

55 *Tehillim* 105:44-45

56 *Yirmiyahu* 2:7

57 *Devarim* 11:13

58 Ibid. 17

60 *Sotah* 10b

61 See *Tosafos* there, "... *noach*" and *Shaarei Teshuva* by Rabenu Yona, Shaar 3, Note 139.

62 As appears from the Rambam, who omits this *halacha* entirely, as well as the *Meiri* in *Sotah*.

63 See *Baba Metzia* 58b.

64 *Gittin* 55b

65 *Gittin* 57a

66 *Bamidbar* 13:30

67 Rashi there.

68 *Sotah* 35a

Parshas Toldos

"Esav Ish Seir"

The Seir Of Rosh Chodesh

Rivka Imeinu instructs Yaakov to impersonate Esav in order to receive his father's blessings. Yaakov protests: "My brother Esav is an אִישׁ שֵׂעִיר!"[1] שֵׂעִיר comes from the word שֵׂעָר, meaning 'hair.' Yaakov is telling Rivka that he cannot pretend to be Esav because Esav is a hairy man, as he was described at birth – כֻּלוֹ כְּאַדֶּרֶת שֵׂעָר – "entirely like a hairy mantle."[2]

The word שֵׂעִיר also means 'goat.' *Parshas Toldos* always falls around Rosh Chodesh Kislev, so perhaps there is an allusion here to the goat *chatas*-offering of Rosh Chodesh. Chazal tell us that when Hashem created the two great luminaries, the sun and the moon, the moon complained, "Is it possible for two kings to wear the same crown? Hashem said to the moon: 'Go and make yourself smaller.'"[3] The Gemara continues, "The moon said before Him, 'Master of the Universe, is it fitting that because I said a correct thing before You, I must diminish myself?'" The Gemara then relates Hashem's attempts to appease the moon: "Go and rule by day and by night," to which the moon replies, "What is the greatness in that, for of what use is a candle in the daytime?" Hashem then gives the moon an army of stars to rule alongside it.

If the moon really sinned, why does it need to be appeased? If we can use such an expression when speaking about Hashem, it would appear that Hashem acted לפנים משורת הדין, – "not by the letter of the law."[4]

The Gemara describes a few more attempts at appeasement which the moon rejects, until finally Hashem commands the Jewish people to bring as an offering on Rosh Chodesh a שעיר עזים אחד לחטאת לה' – "a goat for a sin-offering to Hashem."[5] This is the only *mussaf*-offering described by the Torah as a "sin-offering to Hashem." Chazal tell us that Hashem said: "This goat shall be atonement for my diminishing the size of the moon."[6]

This seems even more incomprehensible. What does it mean to atone for Hashem's sin? Is Hashem not the epitome of perfection? Is not the entire world His? How can He require atonement? Although we cannot understand it fully, perhaps there are some lessons we can derive from this. We can learn how far we must go to avoid hurting others, even if we are wronged. Hashem was certainly justified in punishing the moon, yet He felt that He had punished the moon too harshly, so to speak, and thus required some degree of atonement.

In the light of this explanation, we can review Yaakov Avinu's protest against posing as the איש שעיר and thus receiving the *berochos* intended for Esav. Although Esav was a murderer, a cheat, and a liar and certainly deserved whatever he had coming to him, Yaakov felt that if he personally hurt him in any way he would be required to bring a שעיר, similar to the one offered on Rosh Chodesh, as an atonement.

Intentions For The Sake Of Heaven

Similarly, the Book of Shmuel describes how Penina caused Chana to become angry: "Her *tzara* (her husband's other wife) provoked her again and again in order to irritate her ... Whenever Penina would go up to the House of Hashem, she would provoke her."[7] Chazal tell us "Penina's intention was for the sake of Heaven,"[8] to goad her into praying for a child. Penina's method succeeded, for ultimately Chana broke down and prayed. She was granted a son, Shmuel, who merited establishing the kingdoms of Shaul and David, and who in some respects was considered the equivalent of Moshe and Aharon.[9]

The proof that Penina's provocations were לשם שמים can be seen from the fact that she provoked her only in the House of Hashem, which was an auspicious place for prayers to be accepted. The rest of the year she acted towards her as a good friend.

Despite Penina's noble intentions, Chazal tell us that she was punished. The *pasuk* states, "While the barren woman bears seven, the one with many children becomes bereft."[10] Rashi questions how it is possible that she gave birth to seven children when only a few *psukim* later we are told that she had three sons and two daughters. Rashi explains "For Hashem had remembered Chana and she had given birth to three sons and two daughters. For every child Chana gave birth to, Penina buried two. When Chana was expecting her fifth child, after Chana had given birth to four children and Penina had buried eight, Penina pleaded for mercy. Chana prayed on the children's behalf and they lived. For this reason Penina's remaining two children are referred to as Chana's."

If Penina's actions were truly לשם שמים, why was she punished so severely? Should she not have been rewarded? In my humble opinion, we can explain Penina's punishment as follows. Penina realized that it was wrong to hurt Chana, as we see from the fact that the rest of the year she refrained from doing so. On her annual pilgrimage to Shilo, however, when she had a "היתר" to hurt Chana לשם שמים in order to spur her to pray for a child, she felt the slightest tinge of gratification. Jealousy between two wives of the same man is only natural and thus there was a tiny bit of שלא לשמה intertwined with her לשמה. For this she was punished. There is no doubt that in the Next World she is being rewarded for her actions and for her good intentions. In this world however, she was punished for the element of שלא לשמה in the pain she caused Chana.

"A Loud And Bitter Cry"

In contrast, Yaakov Avinu was disturbed by the thought of having to hurt Esav, even if Esav deserved it. Furthermore, Yaakov was an *ish tam*,[11] a wholesome, perfect man, as well as a man of truth.[12] The prospect of having to deceive his father also troubled him greatly. He was worried that Yitzchak might discover his act of deception:

"Perhaps my father will feel me and I shall be as a mocker in his eyes."[13] – The Gr"a comments that the word אולי, – "perhaps," is a form of wishful thinking – הלואי – 'if only it were true.' He hoped that his father would get wind of what was taking place and therefore he would not have to deceive him.[14]

On a profound level this was not really an act of deception. Could a *tzaddik* such as Yitzchak truly wish to bless a wicked man like Esav? Esav was the one who hid his true character from his father; Yitzchak's desire to bless him was based on his deception. At this point it was Yaakov's job to reveal the truth, and his mother was willing to take full responsibility for his doing so: "Your curse be on me, my son."[15] After all, Hashem had told Rivka, "The elder shall serve the younger." Our Sages remark that even though this subterfuge was justified, Yaakov was bent over in tears as he approached his father. Yet despite all the justification and Yaakov's hesitation, he was still punished to some extent for having hurt Esav. As Chazal comment, "When Esav heard his father's words, he cried an exceedingly great and bitter cry.[16] Many generations later, Yaakov's descendant Mordechai 'cried a loud and bitter cry'[17] when he heard what Esav's descendant Haman planned for him and his people."[18] While Yaakov was simply following the will of Hashem and did try not to hurt Esav, he was punished for not being still more sensitive to Esav's plight.

Closing The Box Too Tightly

Later we read of Yaakov's reunion with Esav. The Torah tells us that when Yaakov reached Yabok, "He took his two wives, his two handmaids, and his eleven sons and crossed the ford of Yabok."[19] Rashi comments on the fact that only eleven of Yaakov's children crossed over. "And where was Dina? Yaakov put her into a chest and closed it over her, so that Esav should not set his eyes upon her. Yaakov was punished because he withheld her from his brother, when she might have returned him to virtuous conduct, so she fell into the hands of Shechem." The Alter of Slobodka questions why Yaakov was punished for not wishing to take his wicked brother Esav as a son-in-law. Even if the *shidduch* would have caused Esav to do *tes-*

huva, can we expect a father looking for a match for his daughter to consider a murderer, with the goal of bringing him to repent? Does it even enter our minds that such a man would be an appropriate *shidduch* for the daughter of Yaakov Avinu, the prophet, our holy forefather and pillar of Torah? The Gemara is full of sources proving that a man must seek out a *talmid chacham* for a son-in-law. Furthermore, Esav had three wives already and had no need for another!

The Alter comments that Yaakov acted correctly in concealing Dina from Esav, yet it should have pained him to have to do so. He explains in his inimitable way that Yaakov "closed the box too tightly." Because "Hashem deals strictly with those around Him even to a hairsbreadth,"[20] someone on the level of Yaakov Avinu was held accountable.

We can learn from this incident how far we must go not to inflict harm on others. There are many stories about the lengths our great leaders would go to in order to avoid offending others.

The Brisker Rav once convened a meeting of Rabbis to discuss the local *shechita*. Halfway into the meeting one of the local *shochtim* entered the venerable assembly. For fear of hurting his feelings, the Rav refrained from asking him to leave the room, yet clearly they could not continue the discussion in his presence. The Brisker Rav adroitly changed the topic of conversation and it was only after the man left that the original discussion resumed.

Yaakov, as we said, did not wish to harm the איש שעיר. He knew that harming his brother would require atonement like the שעיר offered on Rosh Chodesh. In fact the moon was partly to blame for any harm that befell Esav. Had the moon not invented difficulties at the prospect of two kings ruling with the same crown, there would have been nothing wrong with "two nations in your womb,"[21] as Hashem tells Rivka about the impending birth of twins. Why should they not both become great nations? Why must one nation be stronger than the other?[22] The moon set a precedent with her complaint, making it impossible for two kings to rule simultaneously. One would always have to be stronger than the other. Rivka was therefore told ורב יעבד צעיר "The elder shall serve the younger."[23]

Prophecy Is Determined By Our Actions

If Hashem promised Rivka ורב יעבד צעיר, where was Esav's free choice? I do not believe that this prophecy negated Esav's free choice. It was not Esav's obligation to fulfill the prophecy. Grammatically speaking, the prophecy could have been interpreted in two ways: The expression ורב יעבד צעיר can be understood to mean that the elder will serve the younger or that the elder is the one whom the younger serves. Similarly, the *pasuk*[24] כאכל קש לשון אש can be read to mean 'Straw consumes fire,' but in reality it means 'Straw is consumed by the fire.'[25] Had Esav acted properly, the prophecy would have been interpreted to mean that the elder is the one whom the younger serves.

By the same token, Avraham Avinu was promised "In Yitzchak will offspring be considered yours."[26] Chazal remark: "In part of Yitzchak but not all of Yitzchak."[27] This could be a reference to either Esav or Yaakov. Because Esav chose the path he did, Yaakov was chosen as the "part of Yitzchak" to continue his father's legacy. Rivka, who was well aware of the real Esav, knew how the prophecy was to be interpreted. Esav's actions were not bound by the prophecy; rather his behavior determined the interpretation of the prophecy.

We find a similar case when the prophet Yonah entered the city of Ninveh and announced עוד ארבעים יום ונינוה נהפכת "Forty days more and Ninveh shall be overturned."[28] The *midrash* tells us that the word נהפכת could refer either to an upheaval in Ninveh itself which would suffer the fate of Sodom, or to a transformation through the people's repentance. Indeed the people of Ninveh repented and נהפכת took on the meaning of a transformation within the people. The conduct of the people determined the interpretation of the prophecy.

Similarly, in the *Bris bein haBesarim*, Hashem promised Avraham that his descendants would be exiled for four hundred years, but he did not stipulate from when the four hundred years would be counted. Would it be immediately or from the birth of Yitzchak; from their descent to Egypt or from the moment the hard labor began? The sooner the count began, the sooner the exile would end. Ramban remarks that the people in Mitzrayim were not worthy of the count's beginning immediately, but because they cried out to

Hashem, He retroactively caused the count to begin from the birth of Yitzchak and not later. Prophecies can have multiple interpretations and it is our actions that can determine which interpretation is used. The same applies to the many prophecies involving the End of Days.

"An Ox Knows His Owner"

איש שעיר - perhaps by describing Esav in this manner, the Torah is also alluding to the two goats (שעירים) used in the Yom Kippur service. In what way was Esav similar to those goats? The goats must be identical in height, appearance, value etc. and they must be purchased together.[29] Only a lottery could determine which goat would be "for Hashem" and which one "for *Azazel*." The goat ultimately chosen for *Azazel* was a goat with all the credentials necessary to be "for Hashem."

Why did the Torah insist on a lottery? Why could the Kohen Gadol himself not determine which goat was for Hashem and which for *Azazel*? Perhaps we can gain some insight into this by analyzing an interesting incident in the Tanach. During the reign of Achav and Izevel there was rampant idol worship within the Jewish nation. The prophet Eliyahu decided that the only way to tear the nation away from the spiritual corruption of their leaders was to demonstrate Hashem's greatness publicly and prove the utter powerlessness of the idols and false prophets. Eliyahu asked Achav to gather the entire nation, including all the prophets of the idol Baal, at Har HaCarmel. He then instructed the people to choose two bulls, each to be placed on a wood pile without any fire. The prophets of Baal would then call out in the name of their gods and Eliyahu would call in the Name of Hashem: "The God Who responds with fire is the true God!"[30] The people approved of the proposal. Eliyahu then turned to the prophets of the Baal and said, "Choose for yourselves one bull and prepare it first."[31] We then read, "They took the bull that he (Eliyahu) gave them and prepared it."[32] If Eliyahu had instructed them to choose a bull, why did he end up giving it to them? Chazal relate that they chose a bull, but the bull refused to budge. The bull protested to Eliyahu that he and the other bull had grown up together, so why should he be the one chosen for the Baal? Eliyahu explained to the animal that two bulls were needed to prove that Hashem is God, one bull for Hashem, and one *lehavdil* for *avoda zara*. Thus the bull designated for the Baal would also play an essential role in sanctifying Hashem's Name. The bull answered, "In that case, I allow the other bull to be for the Baal. I want to be offered upon the Altar for Hashem!" Four hundred prophets of the Baal could not succeed in budging the bull and Eliyahu finally had to use force. Although the people chose the bull, it was Eliyahu who ultimately had to give it to them.[33] Chazal teach us that the bull was in the right and that the *pasuk*, "An ox knows his owner"[34] refers to this animal which desired to serve Hashem.

On Yom Kippur each goat has the same necessary credentials and each desires to be chosen for Hashem and not for *Azazel*, yet only Hashem can determine which is which. Despite Esav's evil behavior, Yaakov did not wish to make this איש שעיר the שעיר לעזאזל – only Hashem can make that determination. Rivka, by instructing Yaakov to impersonate Esav, was informing him that because Esav had chosen the life that he did, the heavens had already ordained that he would be the שעיר לעזאזל.

Lessons From The Moon

Only Hashem can correct the moon's blemish. As we request each month in *Kiddush Levana*, "Hashem, fill the flaw of the moon," but we for our part, must learn from its being made smaller. Perhaps the moon's complaint about two kings not sharing the same crown rings true for professionals and tradesmen, for we know that "every craftsman hates others of his craft."[35] Torah scholars, however, must welcome others: "Torah scholars increase peace in the world."[36] Clearly members of other professions should not be jealous of their colleagues either, but a *talmid chacham* must take even greater care. וכל בניך למודי ה' – "And all your children will be students of Hashem."[37] The success of another scholar cannot detract from my share in the Torah, for every Jew has his own share in the Torah. Another person's brilliant insights cannot diminish my honor or my share in the Next World. In fact the opposite is true; the greater the number of *talmidei chachamim*, the greater the blessing brought to the world. The entire world therefore benefits from the presence of yet another *talmid chacham*.

The Gemara records a dream of Rav Eliezer ben Pedas, in which Hashem promised to reward him in the Next World with thirteen rivers of balsam oil as clear as the Tigris and the Euphrates.[38] Not only can I not understand what a person would do with so much oil in the Next World, but I don't even know what I would do with a river full of oil in this world. Yet Rav Eliezer asked Him, "Is that all?" Hashem replied, "If I give you more, what will I then give all your colleagues?" Rav Eliezer responded, "Am I making this request of a person who is limited in what he can give? Everything belongs to You, and You have the wherewithal to give abundantly to my fellows and to me." There is no end to the abundance Hashem provides us with, and therefore no one can receive anything at the expense of another. Why should we be jealous of the success of others, whether physical or spiritual? There is no limit to the number of *talmidei chachamim* the world can hold.

Hashem Himself taught us "A person cannot encroach upon what is set aside for his fellow."[39] The manna fell in measured amounts of "an *omer* per person."[40]

No one went without because another received his share. Hashem determines our livelihood; more or less *hishtadlus* – human effort – on our part is of no consequence. If so, why does the Torah tell us, "They gathered, whoever took more and whoever took less?"[41] How could some take more and some take less, if they each took "an *omer* per person?" Perhaps some interpreted Moshe's instructions according to the stricter and larger measurements of the Chazon Ish while others understood it to mean the smaller measurements of Rav Chaim Naeh, which is the accepted practice in Yerushalayim! In any event, the end result was that no matter how much each person gathered, everyone ended up with the same amount. "They measured in an *omer* and whoever took more had nothing extra and whoever took less was not lacking."[42] Unfortunately we have no record of whose opinion Moshe Rabenu followed, but what we do know is that each person came home with precisely the same amount. Was there any reason for the moon to complain? Did the honor accorded the sun detract from the moon's honor?

Strive To Be The *Seir LaHashem*!

From the bull in the story of Eliyahu, and from the goats offered on Yom Kippur, we can learn that we must all strive for greatness. The goat sent to *Azazel* was also an essential component of the Yom Kippur service, but it is not our responsibility to fill that role; we must strive to become the *seir laHashem*. Eliyahu needed the bull offered by the Baal to demonstrate that "Hashem is God,"[43] yet if someone has the opportunity to serve Hashem, why should he be satisfied with a lesser role which can be filled by someone else?

Many types of people with all their various skills are required in this world, yet why should we fulfill another role when we can become Torah leaders? Why should we be shoemakers if we can become *Roshei Yeshivos*? Chazal tell us, "It is not possible for the world to function without spice merchants and without tanners. Happy is he whose occupation is that of a spice merchant, and woe is to him whose occupation is that of a tanner."[44] There is more demand for tanners than for spice merchants; the spices are only required once a week for *havdalah*, and if a person does not possess them, he has still fulfilled the mitzvah of *havdalah*. The tanner, on the other hand, is needed to provide shoes and even parchment for *tefillin* and *Sifrei Torah*. What Chazal meant was that if one has the choice, he should choose a profession which surrounds one with a good fragrance, rather than one that causes a bad smell! This means a bad smell not only in the physical sense but in the spiritual sense as well. Our task is to be involved in Torah. The world may need shoemakers, but others can fill that role.

The *halacha* states: "All can bring up to *Eretz Yisrael*."[45] If a Jew expresses a desire to live in Syria, it is our duty to inform him of the mitzvah to live in *Eretz Yisrael*. On the other hand, the *halacha* is that one may purchase a house in Syria, which is adjacent to *Eretz Yisrael*, from a non-Jew even on *Shabbos* – through a non-Jew.[46] From the perspective of *Hilchos Shabbos*, purchasing a home in Syria is the same as purchasing a home in *Eretz Yisrael*. The fact that it is a greater mitzvah to live in *Eretz Yisrael* in no way contradicts the fact that a non-Jew may perform acts that are prohibited on *Shabbos* in order to assist us in purchasing a home in Syria. For *Am Yisrael* as a whole, it is preferable for Syria to be in Jewish hands. The individual, however, must strive to live in *Eretz Yisrael*. Let other people see to it that Syria is in Jewish hands.

Strive To Live In Yerushalayim

By the same token we learn, "All can bring up to Yerushalayim, but none can take out."[47] A man may coerce his wife to live in Yerushalayim and a woman may force her husband to do so, even though the rest of the Land would remain desolate if the entire nation were to settle in Yerushalayim. As a people, we must see to it that the entire Land from Dan to Be'er Sheva, from Peras to the Nile, is settled by Jewish people. On an individual level, however, every Jew must strive to live in Yerushalayim. Hashem will see to it that the rest of the Land is also settled. The fact that the world needs other professions should not prevent anyone from striving to become a Torah leader.

Chazal tell us that the half shekel donated by each individual for the *mishkan* amounted to far more than was needed for the public offerings of the year. (I once attempted to calculate how many shekalim were spent in the *Beis HaMikdash* for all the sacrifices throughout the year, and I concluded that the amount spent was very little compared to the donations of six hundred thousand people.) All the donations were piled together in a basket and coins would be removed as needed. The Mishna points out an interesting fact. The house of Rabban Gamliel would somehow try to ensure that it was precisely their half-shekel that was used.[48] Does it really make a difference? Do all the people not have an equal share? They do all have an equal share, yet wouldn't it be nice if my half-shekel was used to purchase the *Korban Tomid*?

There are many necessary components for the world to survive. I must ensure that my share is in Torah and nothing else. As we mentioned above, the world needs tanners as well as spice merchants, yet blessed is he who is a spice merchant. We must do our best to become Torah leaders, to influence the world with Torah and *yiras Shamayim*. *B'ezras Hashem*, may we reach the stage of וכל בניך למודי ה' – "All your children will be students of Hashem."

Notes

1   *Bereishis* 27:11

2   *Bereishis* 25:25

3   *Chullin* 60b

4   *Brochos* 7a

5   *Bamidbar* 28:15

6   *Chullin* 60b

7   *Shmuel* I 1:6-7

8   *Baba Basra* 16a

9   See *Brochos* 31b

10   *Shmuel* I 2:5

11   *Bereishis* 25:27

12   "Grant truth to Yaakov." – *Micha* 7:20

13   *Bereishis* 27:12

14   See *Parshas Miketz*, Sicha I

15   Ibid. 13

16   *Bereishis* 27:34

17   *Esther* 4:1

18 See *Bereishis Rabba* 67:4.

19 *Bereishis* 32:23

20 *Yevamos* 121b

21 *Bereishis* 25:23

22 Ibid.

23 Ibid.

24 *Yeshayahu* 5:24

25 *Yeshayahu* 5:24

26 *Bereishis* 21:12

27 *Sanhedrin* 59b

28 *Yonah* 3:4

29 See *Yoma* 62b

30 *Melachim* I, 18:24

31 Ibid. 25

32 Ibid. 26

33 See *Midrash Tanchuma Parshas Masei, Siman* 6.

34 *Yeshayahu* 1:3

35 *Rashi, Bereishis* 3:5

36 *Brochos* 64a

37 *Yeshayahu* 54:13

38   See *Taanis* 25a.

39   *Yoma* 38b

40   *Shemos* 16:16

41   Ibid. 17

42   Ibid. 18

43   *Melachim* I 18:39

44   *Pesachim* 65a

45   *Kesubos Perek* 13, *Mishna* 11

46   The *Shulchan Aruch* and the Rama differ as to the extent of
     what the non-Jew may do, but in any case it is permitted to
     purchase the house even on *Shabbos*.

47   Ibid.

48   *Shekalim Perek* 3, *Mishna* 3

Digging Wells

וכל הבארות אשר חפרו עבדי אביו
בימי אברהם אביו סתמום פלשתים וימלאום עפר

*"All the wells that his father's servants had dug in the days of
Abraham his father, the Plishtim stopped up, and filled them
with earth."[1]*

Stopping Up The Wells

One can never have too many wells. Why did the Plishtim stop
up the wells? Were they not beneficial to them and to their land? If
they had stolen the wells, despicable though the act might have been,
we could at least have understood their motivation as the desire for
a greater water supply. History records several incidents of stolen
wells; Avimelech's servants stole Avraham's wells[2] and the Plishtim
fought with Yitzchak claiming, "The water is ours."[3] What did they
hope to achieve here by sealing the wells that Avraham had already
dug?

The Plishtim clearly had an ulterior motive which was to eradicate
any remembrance of Avraham from the land. If, many years later,
someone were to happen upon one of the wells, he might remark

that it was Avraham Avinu who had dug it. He would be reminded that a righteous man had once walked this land and everywhere he went, he had taught *chessed* and spread belief and fear of Hashem. The Plishtim thought that the best way to erase Avraham's memory was to remove anything that would remind people of him. Thus, even though they could have benefited from the wells, they stopped them up.

Of Mockers And Scoffers

Our Sages teach us that the verse in *Tehillim*, "Praiseworthy is the man who walked not in the counsel of the wicked, and stood not in the path of the sinful, and sat not in the session of *leitzim* (scoffers)[4] refers to Avraham Avinu, who did not walk in the counsel of the *dor hahaflaga* and did not stand in the path of Sodom and did not sit among the Plishtim, who were well-known *leitzonim*. The Gemara[5] then cites a *pasuk* which demonstrates the Plishtim's *leitzonus*: "It happened when their heart became merry that they said: 'Summon Samson and let him entertain us.'"[6] At first glance the Gemara appears to be telling us that hundreds of years hence, the Plishtim's love of amusement would brand them *leitzonim*. Do Chazal mean that anyone who enjoys a bit of entertainment from time to time is categorized as a *leitz*? It is clear that this entertainment that they sought was a sign of something much deeper, something distasteful that was ingrained in their personality. Avraham was able to discern this early on and thus elected not to sit in their company.

What *leitzonus* are we referring to? As far as I know, archaeologists have yet to discover ancient Philistine joke books. To understand Chazal we must first define the term *leitz*. A *leitz* is not one who tells a joke once in a while, but someone who mocks things of value. Rav Chanina ben Tradyon tells us, "If two sit together and there are no words of Torah between them, that is a *moshav leitzim*."[7] This does not mean that they are telling jokes or clowning around rather than learning. They may even be discussing the weather or the situation in the territories. If such talk comes at the expense of learning, it is classified as a *moshav leitzim*, for it proves that they have no appreciation of the value of Torah, of time, or even of their own lives and souls. The Plishtim were classified as *leitzonim* because they wished to erase from the world the name of Avraham Avinu as well as all that he accomplished. Only people devoid of spiritual values would attempt to eradicate the memory of the man who paved the way for serving Hashem – they are *leitzonim*. (Chazal tell us that in the *pasuk*: "Strike the *leitz* and the simpleton grows clever,"[8] the *leitz* refers to Amalek[9] of whom it is said, ולא ירא אלקים – "He did not fear God."[10])

Following In His Father's Footsteps

What did Yitzchak do when he discovered that the Plishtim had sealed the wells? "Yitzchak dug anew the wells of water which they had dug in the days of Avraham his father, and the Philistines had stopped up after Avraham's death, and he called them by the same name that his father had called them."[11] On a simple level, Yitzchak called the wells by the names his father had given them for sentimental reasons. On a deeper level, however, the Torah is telling us that Yitzchak was following in his father's footsteps. The Plishtim had tried to uproot and eliminate all of Avraham's spiritual influence; Yitzchak repaved the path of serving Hashem.

Yitzchak did not serve Hashem precisely in the same way his father did. Avraham served Hashem out of love, while Yitzchak developed the concept of serving Hashem out of יראה – awe. His עבודה alone was described as פחד יצחק.[12] Their goal, however, was the same – to promulgate the existence of the God of the entire universe and His Providence over all His creatures. The forefathers served Him, and each in his own way sought to spread this message to all the surrounding nations. We find that Hashem told Moshe, "I am the God of your father, the God of Avraham, the God of Yitzchak, and the God of Yaakov,"[13] while in another instance, He told Moshe that He is "the God of Avraham, Yitzchak, and Yaakov."[14] The first *pasuk* emphasizes that He is the God of each of them individually, while the second emphasizes that He is the God of them all collectively. Each of the forefathers had His own special relationship with Hashem, yet the common denominator was that they all served the same God.

Pluralistic Judaism

Today we hear much talk about pluralism – recognition of many streams and forms of Judaism. What does this mean? Is Judaism not already pluralistic? Do we not have the different approaches of Beis Shammai and Beis Hillel, the Rambam and the Raavad, Rashi and *Tosafos*? This type of pluralism is very good and it is healthy for the dissemination of Torah. Differing views are to be encouraged, but only when they stem from pure sources and have as their goal to fulfill the directives of the Torah as given to Moshe at Sinai. The common denominator must be like the wells of Yitzchak – that they all want to serve the same God. The Rambam may rule that one who performs a מלאכה שאינה צריכה לגופה[15] on *Shabbos* has violated a Torah prohibition,[16] while the Raavad may disagree, yet each of them is seeking proper fulfillment of the Torah's commandment, זכור את יום השבת לקדשו – "Remember the Sabbath day to sanctify it."[17] They are not taking issue with the relevance of these *psukim*. Regarding the disputes between Beis Shammai and Beis Hillel, our Sages teach us that a heavenly voice announced: "Both are the words of the living God"[18] – each of their opinions is pure and holy. We fulfill our obligation of Torah study by learning the opinions of Beis Shammai and Beis Hillel, the Rambam and the Raavad, Rashi as well as *Tosafos*. This type of pluralism is to be encouraged.

There are many styles of learning Torah: the Brisker method, the Hungarian approach, that of the Sefardim and Moroccans, etc. If each of these approaches has as its goal to arrive at the true *pshat* and understanding of the Gemara as well as the final *halachic* ruling, then they are equally valid. In fact, I do not believe that any single approach can be used to solve all difficulties. I heard from HaRav Yisrael Dzimitrovski shlit"a that *Tosafos* prefer the logic to be crystal clear, even if it has to be forced into the Gemara's language. To the Rambam, on the other hand, it was of paramount importance that his rulings fit into the language of the text, even if at times the logic was not so clear. The *Shulchan Aruch* and the Rama had varying ap-

---

15   Every *melacha* is associated with an action and an intention. When the action is performed for an unconnected intention, it is called a מלאכה שאינה צריכה לגופה.

proaches to *halachic* rulings. The Amoraim themselves had several methods of solving difficulties. At times they concluded that the Mishna is missing information (חסורי מחסרא והכי קתני), while at other times they concluded that one Mishna is in accordance with the opinion of one Tanna, while another Mishna follows the view of another. Yet another way of resolving contradictions is the Brisker approach of *tzvei dinim*.[19] Is there only one way? Absolutely not! The Torah is pluralistic! The one criterion however is that the source and the goal of the method are pure. If this requirement is fulfilled, the mitzvah of Talmud Torah has been fulfilled.

(The one approach that the *gedolim* have always objected to is פלפול הבל – the attempt to connect two concepts that are not at all similar. *Pilpul* is a desirable approach only if its goal is to arrive at the true meaning of the Torah. If so, it is preferred to a more superficial approach. And learning on a superficial level is greatly preferred over not learning at all, for with time the person will desire a deeper understanding. Outside of *pilpul hevel*, all approaches to learning are valid and encouraged.)

Pluralism is not to be encouraged however, if it means adopting the practices of the other nations, rather than seeking to fulfill Hashem's will. Such 'opinions' are not Judaism. Reform Judaism does not seek to delve into the writings of the Torah, to fulfill the word of God, but rather to emulate the other nations and to rid its followers of the 'burden' of keeping Torah and *mitzvos*. This is not spreading Judaism, but rather uprooting it. From the very beginning, Reform denied that the Torah was ordained from heaven. Today their 'rabbis' publicly deny the existence of a Creator, *Hashem yerachem* (They of course cannot use such an expression, because they do not believe in God and He certainly will not save them!) We can only beseech Hashem to save us from such blasphemy. Even Christianity and Islam claim to have had a prophet who transmitted the word from Heaven, while the Reform and Conservative deny even this.

19　The two passages that appear contradictory are not referring to the same topic.

The Israeli Supreme Court, which refers to itself as the High Court of Justice, made a grave mistake by ruling that Reform and Conservative must have representation on Religious Councils. This is preposterous – it is neither Judaism nor is it a religion! What the court should have done was to permit them to establish their own council and allow them to construct their own *mikvaos* and cemeteries that conform to their standards. They should be permitted to do as they please. Call them a social group or whatever you wish, just let them not be recognized as a 'stream of Judaism.' I believe this was the approach of HaGaon HaRav Moshe Feinstein zt"l.

Sticking With Winners

While it may seem to be a modern problem, Reform is nothing new. The movement in fact emulates the Hellenism of years ago. The Hellenists did not have an intellectual or idealistic approach, but they always chose the winning side, as explained by Rav Yitzchak Aizik HaLevi z"l author of *Doros HaRishonim*. When the Greeks were in power, they wished to become Greeks; when the Chashmonaim became victorious, it was no longer 'fashionable' to be Greek so they abandoned Greek culture and sided with the Chashmonaim. However, they limited their affiliation with the Chashmonaim, claiming to be disciples of Tzaddok and Baitus who adhered only to the Written Torah. They would not accept the Oral Law, but 'religiously' observed the dictates of the Written Torah. In reality they did not fully adhere to the Written Law either. They claimed not to believe in life in the Next World, for it is not written explicitly in the Torah. However, in many places the Torah speaks of Divine Providence and about reward and punishment. What other reward could the Torah have been referring to? We live in a world of צדיק ורע לו רשע וטוב לו – where "misfortune befalls the righteous and the wicked prosper."[20] Clearly they did not totally believe in the Written Law either.

At the end of the period of the second *Beis HaMikdash*, when *Am Yisrael* were once again at a low point, the Hellenists suddenly became Romans. What happened to their belief in the Written Torah? The Hellenists-Tzdukkim-Roman converts in fact took a very consistent approach – they always sided with the victor. What would they have done if an election were a tie? That is uncertain, but when it was clear who was in power, that was whom they followed.

The Reform movement uses the same technique. When the movement began in Germany, its leaders removed from their *siddur* any reference to Zion and Jerusalem. Many of them observed the Sabbath on Sunday because that was the practice in Germany, and it was important to be good Germans. When the Germans spat them out, they moved on to America and then it was time to become American. Following World War II when, Baruch Hashem, the Jewish presence in *Eretz Yisrael* became strengthened, they were suddenly reminded of the existence of Zion and Jerusalem and it was time to become Zionists. It is known that during World War II, many Reform Jews went so far as to interfere with attempts to rescue the Jews of occupied Europe. "How will we be able to integrate with other nations if there are too many Jews here, especially those from Eastern Europe, whom they despised. The non-Jews will not like this at all!"

Then Reform established a foothold in Israel and their women began to arrive at the *Kosel* wearing *talleisim*. Funnily enough, it does not seem to concern them at all that their men do not wear them. The women however adhere to this mitzvah *lemehadrin min hamehadrin*! Presumably if, God forbid, the Palestinians were to gain the upper hand, they would cease coming to the *Kosel* and once again remove any reference to Zion and Jerusalem from their siddur. If I am not mistaken, they did not appear this year (5761) at the *Kosel* for the High Holidays and Sukkos, for the Arabs were throwing stones, and prayer at the *Kosel* was no longer one of the foundations of their faith. Once the violence stopped, their *halachic* authorities permitted them to come once again to the *Kosel*. Is this a 'stream of Judaism'? It is a stream of anti-Judaism, a stream of Jews it is, but Jews devoid of Judaism! The term 'Judaism' implies accepting and adhering to the Torah as given to us by Moshe Rabenu, searching for a deeper understanding of the Torah, with the Brisker, or the Hungarian, or the Moroccan approach, but always adhering to tradition.

Repaving Old Paths

Yitzchak not only re-dug the wells that his father had dug; he also dug new ones, but with his father's goal of spreading the word of Hashem, of spreading *chessed*, and *yiras Shamayim* throughout the world. Yitzchak devised new ways to reach out to Hashem, as did Yaakov in his time. Their ultimate goal however was to establish a relationship with that same God of Avraham.

We must follow the path paved by our holy forefathers, by Moshe Rabenu, and all the *gedolim* after him, all the way down to Rav Eliashiv shlit"a and the other *gedolim* of our generation. The forging of new paths is encouraged, but only with the proper motivation. We can introduce new approaches, but only within the confines of the Torah. We are allowed to question a ruling of the Beis Yosef or the Rama. After clarifying the *sugya* and the Rishonim, we may feel that a different *halachic* ruling makes more sense to us – but only after delving deeply into the *sugya* and working it through. Our goal must be to reach a true understanding of the same Gemara and the same Torah, not to introduce ideas aimed at uprooting the Torah, God forbid.

Chazal issued rulings aimed at strengthening observance of the Torah and not as some people mistakenly believe. For example, the *pruzbul* was not meant to annul the observance of the monetary aspects of *shemitta*. The Mishna in *Shviis*[21] teaches us that Hillel introduced the idea because he noticed that people refrained from lending money, in direct violation of the commandment: "Beware lest there be a lawless thought in your heart, saying, 'The seventh year is approaching, the *shemitta* year,' and you will look malevolently upon your destitute brother and refuse to give him."[22] The *pruzbul* thus serves to strengthen Torah observance. Many Rishonim[23] rule that the *pruzbul* is not effective when *shemitta* is Torah-ordained. Other Rishonim differ, claiming that even when shemitta is *mid'Oraysa* it is permitted to use a *pruzbul*. The institution was set up not to uproot a mitzvah of the Torah, but to prevent violating the Torah.

A similar concept exists in the *heter iska*. This is not Chazal's way of permitting violation of the prohibition of *ribis*, God forbid. Let us try to understand how this concept works. When lending or borrowing money, the Torah forbids us to accept or give any payment above the value of the loan. A loan is defined as something the lender gives to the borrower, with the borrower taking full responsibility for returning the value of the loan, not necessarily the exact same bills or coins. Claiming the money was burned, lost, or stolen, therefore, does not absolve the borrower from his responsibility to repay the loan. Returning more than the amount borrowed is a violation of the prohibition of *ribis*.

A *pikodon*, on the other hand, is an object given to another for safekeeping. The person charged with guarding the object is responsible for the safe return of the specific object. If the object is lost or stolen or unable to be returned due to other extenuating circumstances, depending on the terms of the agreement, the person caring for the object may be absolved of any responsibility. Another distinction between a loan and a *pikodon* is that while it is forbidden to profit from a loan, it is permitted to profit from a *pikodon*.

The *heter iska* is a system in which a portion of the money borrowed is viewed as a loan, with all the associated responsibility, while the remaining portion has the status of a *pikodon*. If the borrower were to claim that he was held up at gunpoint and all his money was taken, and if it can be proven that this is indeed true and that no negligence was involved, the borrower would only have to repay the loan portion. The profits and losses are associated with the *pikodon* portion. The system obviously would have to include safeguards against dishonest claims. I do not wish to discuss under what circumstances a person is permitted to rely on the *heter iska*, but suffice it to say that Chazal, in their efforts to encourage people to lend money, did not permit anything the Torah prohibited.

Chazal never intended to remove any *mitzvos* from the Torah – not *Shabbos*, not *shemitta*, nor anything else. Chazal's goal was to find ways to strengthen Torah observance. To use those same wells dug by Avraham, Yitzchak, and Yaakov. Anyone who believes otherwise is following in the footsteps of the Hellenists, the Karaites, and the Reformers.

In those days Hashem helped us to overpower the Greeks and the Hellenists. Today we are not fighting the Greeks, but we do have

Plishtim, or Palestinians as they call themselves, to contend with. With the Almighty's help, we can overpower these Plishtim as well. We also need Hashem's help in combating the modern day Hellenists. They will not succeed. We will fight in the Name of Hashem and He will help us to emerge victorious, drawing from the same spiritual wells dug by Avraham, Yitzchak, and Yaakov. I am not sure if the wells dug by the forefathers physically exist today, but they certainly exist spiritually. We must each try to keep these wells open by writing our own *chiddushim*. Every Jew has his own unique share in the Torah of Hashem and we pray for this three times a day: ותן חלקנו בתורתך – "Give us our share of Your Torah."

May we merit that Hashem return His Divine Presence to Zion and, as *Parshas Toldos* always comes out around Rosh Chodesh Kislev, let us pray that soon we will be able to offer the *olah* and *chatas* of Rosh Chodesh. In the Rosh Chodesh prayers we say, "May we prepare he-goats ברצון (with favor); in the service of the Holy Temple may we all rejoice." There are two difficulties with this phrase. Firstly, the goat that was offered is a *chatas* – an obligatory one – while the term רצון is used in conjunction with a voluntary sacrifice. In addition, why do we emphasize "... may we all rejoice"? Would not "may we rejoice" have sufficed?

The Rosh Chodesh offering atoned for the sin of entering the *Beis HaMikdash* or partaking of *Kodshim* while in a state of *tumah*.[24] Hashem promises us that in the future, "I will remove the spirit of impurity from the Land."[25] If impurity no longer exists, there will be no need to atone for coming in contact with consecrated objects while in a state of impurity. At that time we truly will "prepare he-goats with favor," on a purely voluntary basis.

About the injunction that we all rejoice in the service of the *Beis HaMikdash*, Chazal teach us that when a sinner brings an offering, the Kohen and Levi must be in a state of joy, while the sinner must cry and confess his sin. "The sacrifices God desires are a broken spirit."[26] In the future, however, when sin is eradicated from the world, everyone – the Kohanim and Leviim, as well as those offering the *korbanos*, will rejoice. "In the service of the Holy Temple may we all rejoice," speedily in our day, Amen.

Notes

1   *Bereishis* 26:15

2   See *Bereishis* 21:25.

3   *Bereishis* 26:20

4   *Tehillim* 1:1

5   See *Avoda Zara* 19a.

6   *Shoftim* 6:25

7   *Avos* 3:2

8   *Mishle* 19:25

9   See *Shmos Rabba* 27:6.

10 *Devarim* 25:18

11 Ibid. 18

12 *Bereishis* 31:42

13 *Shmos* 3:6

14 Ibid. 16

16 *Hilchos Shabbos* 1:7

17 *Devarim* 5:12

18 *Eruvin* 13b

20 *Berochos* 7a

21 10:3

22   *Devarim* 15:9

23   Among them, the Rambam in *Hilchos Shemitta veYovel* 9:16.

24   See *Shevuos Perek* 1, *Mishna* 5

25   *Zecharia* 13:2

26   *Tehillim* 51:19

Parshas Vayetze

Internal And Eternal Beauty

What Is Beauty?

The Torah informs us, "Leah's eyes were tender, while Rachel was beautiful of form and beautiful of appearance. Yaakov loved Rachel."[1] A cursory glance at the *pesukim* seems to suggest that Yaakov's love for Rachel was based purely on her physical beauty. We would expect more than this even from an ordinary person. How much more so from someone of the stature of Yaakov Avinu. The words of the Torah clearly cannot be interpreted according to their simple meaning.

The Torah commands us:

ולא תתורו אחרי לבבכם ואחרי עיניכם

"Do not explore after your heart and after your eyes."[2]

Does this mean that one must ignore what his prospective wife looks like? Certainly not! On the contrary, the Gemara states, "It is forbidden for a man to betroth a woman until he sees her."[3] The Gemara does not mean, as people mistakenly think, that a person must feel an attraction towards the prospective spouse. The Gemara is simply warning us to make sure that there is nothing about her which he finds repulsive. The attraction, *be'ezras Hashem*, will form and continue to grow over the years they spend living together.

What does the Torah mean by ‏ולא תתורו אחרי לבבכם ואחרי עיניכם‎? Although Chazal mandate that a person see his prospective wife before marrying her, his eyes must not be the sole determining factor; he must use his intellect as well. One must ascertain whether the woman possesses inner beauty – *yiras Shamayim*, character, good family, etc. and he must not be so taken by her physical beauty that he ignores everything else.

Do Not Stray After Your Eyes

The spies whom Moshe Rabenu sent to scout out *Eretz Yisrael* returned with the frightening report that the Land was fortified and full of giants. They let their eyes rather than their *sechel* determine whether the Jewish nation should enter the Land of Israel. Had they thought for a moment, they would have realized that Hashem, Who took them out of Egypt, would have no difficulty conquering this land of giants.

Rashi tells us that in his search for a wife for Yitzchak, Eliezer noticed Rivka by the well, and saw the water rising up towards her. Although this was sufficient evidence of Rivka's righteousness and perhaps a sign from Heaven that he had found the right match, Eliezer refused to rely solely on what his eyes saw and insisted on testing Rivka's level of *chessed*. Even though she had succeeded in becoming an *ovedes Hashem*, despite having been brought up in a house of idol worship, Eliezer feared that this was not enough. If she were to marry Yitzchak and become one of the matriarchs of the Jewish nation, her level of *chessed* was of paramount importance.

Although *yiras Shamayim* is a prerequisite for good *middos*, it is far more difficult for a person to improve his character than his *yiras Shamayim*. HaRav Yisrael Salanter teaches us that it is easier to master the entire Talmud than to change even one character trait. Perhaps had the opposite been true, had Eliezer ascertained that Rivka was a woman of *chessed*, yet remained unsure of whether she had the proper *yiras Shamayim*, he would still have brought her back as a wife for Yitzchak, believing that at worst, just as Avraham and Yitzchak managed to convert many others, they would have succeeded in converting Rivka. Had the woman been lacking in proper character traits, however, it would be very difficult to change and thus she would have been an unsuitable wife for Yitzchak.

Ammon And Moav Vs. Amalek

Support for the above supposition can be found in the Torah's commandments. On the one hand we learn, "An Ammonite or Moabite shall not enter the congregation of Hashem; even their tenth generation shall not enter the congregation of Hashem, to eternity,"[4] yet we are not commanded to destroy them. About Amalek, on the other hand, we are commanded, "You shall wipe out the memory of Amalek from under the heaven,"[5] yet, as with all other Edomites, a third generation convert may marry into *Am Yisrael*. Whose sin was considered more severe – that of Ammon and Moav, who were punished by being forever barred from marrying into *Am Yisrael* or Amalek, the only nation whose name we are commanded to obliterate?

Their sins were different in nature. In connection with Amalek we are told, "They did not fear Hashem."[6] *Yiras Shamayim* is the foundation of everything; the world cannot tolerate a lack of it and such people must be removed from the world. Yet as serious an offense as this is, a descendant of Amalek who converts has demonstrated a departure from the ways of his ancestors. The Amalekite convert who fears Hashem is no different from other Edomites, who need not be destroyed and may marry into the Jewish nation after three generations. When it came to fear of God, Ammon and Moav were no worse than the other idol worshipping nations and therefore they did not need to be obliterated. What they lacked was good character – they had no *hakaras hatov*, gratitude to the nation whose ancestor Avraham had saved their ancestor Lot, and they also lacked the willingness and desire to perform acts of *chessed*. These character deficiencies are so deeply ingrained and so hard to change that even the passage of ten generations would not be enough to render them worthy of joining Hashem's Nation.

Eliezer was not satisfied with the mere fact that the water rose towards Rivka. The decision to bring her back as a wife for Yitzchak could not depend solely on what he saw; he had to ascertain that she was of sterling character.

In The Merit Of Rachel

Similarly, it would be wrong of us to assume that Yaakov Avinu was concerned only with Rachel's physical beauty and that he let his eyes be the sole determining factor in choosing her as his wife. Surely he investigated her *yiras Shamayim* and her *middos* and discovered that in her merit, Hashem was to proclaim the eventual return of the Jewish nation to Zion. The *Midrash* relates to us a moving incident that occurred when Hashem wished to destroy the *Beis HaMikdash* and exile the Jewish people: one by one each of the forefathers tried to intercede and pray on behalf of the nation, but Hashem refused to accept their prayers and insisted that the Jewish people be exiled for the sins they had committed. "At that moment, our matriarch Rachel appeared before the Holy One Blessed is He and said, 'Master of the Universe, it is known to You that Your servant Yaakov loved me dearly and worked for my father for seven years in order to marry me. At the completion of those seven years, when the time came for him to marry me, my father plotted to substitute my sister for me. When I found out about his plan, it was very difficult for me and I informed my husband and gave him a sign so that he should be able to distinguish me from my sister and my father would not be able to substitute her for me. Afterwards I reconsidered and had compassion for my sister, fearing that she would be put to shame ... I overcame my desires and gave my sister the sign which I had given to my husband, in order to have him think that Leah was actually me. What am I but flesh and blood, the dust of the earth, and I was not jealous and I did not put her to shame, yet You are the Eternal King, the Compassionate One. If I can overcome my jealousy for my fellow human being, why should You be envious of some *avoda zara* that is of no substance?'"[7] It appears that Hashem had no answer to this question and promised Rachel, "Your children will return to their borders."[8]

Hidden Greatness

Leah was also a great *tzadekes*, yet her righteousness was not as visible – Yaakov Avinu was not even aware of it. It is clear that even her father Lavan had no idea of just who she was, for we recite in the Pesach Haggadah: לבן בקש לעקר את הכל – "Lavan wished to uproot everything." Had he realized what he had, he would never have given away this daughter who was destined to become mother of six of the tribes, not to mention the two born to her by her maidservant. Imagine how the Jewish people would look without Leah, the foremother of Moshe Rabenu, Aharon HaKohen, and Dovid HaMelech!

Lavan could give her away only because her true essence was so deeply hidden that even a prophet of Yaakov's stature was unable to recognize it. None of her righteousness was visible on the outside. Chazal tell us that Rachel was buried "on the road to Efrat"[9] because her righteousness was revealed to all, while Leah was buried in a cave, in *Maaras HaMachpela*, to symbolize her hidden *tzidkus*.

Yaakov investigated who Rachel was, yet part of the reason he chose Rachel as the mainstay of his home was that he did not realize just how great a *tzadekes* Leah was. By substituting Leah for Rachel, Lavan, as evil as his intentions were, was actually fulfilling the Divine Plan that called for Leah to play the key role in building the Jewish nation. Of course, Rachel's selflessness was responsible as well.

Perhaps Yaakov did not investigate who Leah was, because in choosing Rachel he had already carried out his father's instruction to go to Charan "and take a wife from there,"[10] one wife and not two. Yaakov in fact took only one wife; the other one was given to him by deception. It was these two women together "both of whom built up the house of Israel."[11]

Eternal Gifts

The Torah tells us: ועיני לאה רכות[12] Chazal comment: "What is the meaning of the word רכות? If you will say that it means רכות literally, ('tender,' from having shed many tears) this cannot be! Is it conceivable that Scripture does not speak explicit-

ly of the shortcomings of an animal that is *tamei*, as it is written
ומן בהמה אשר איננה טהורה – "of the animal that is not pure"[13] rather
than a בהמה טמאה – an impure animal, but it speaks of the shortcomings of the righteous?[14] The Gemara continues: "Rather Rav
Elazar said: 'רכות means מתנותיה ארוכות' – 'her gifts were long' –
'everlasting.'" (רכות in the *pasuk* comes from the word ארוכות.) Leah
gave birth to Levi, from whom the Kohanim and Leviim descend
and to Yehuda, whose kingdom is eternal. Although Israel's first
king, Shaul, descended from Rachel, his monarchy was not everlasting – it did not remain in the hands of his descendants.

Perhaps what we have discussed can answer a difficulty in Megillas Esther. Mordechai is introduced as:

איש יהודי היה בשושן הבירה

ושמו מרדכי בן יאיר בן שמעי בן קיש איש ימיני

*"There was a איש יהודי in Shushan the capital, whose name was Mor-
dechai the son of Yair, the son of Shimi, the son of Kish, איש ימיני."*[15]

The term איש יהודי seems to imply that Mordechai was a member
of the tribe of יהודה, yet the *pasuk* concludes by describing him as an
איש ימיני, implying that he descended from בנימין. One of the commentaries offered by Chazal is that although Mordechai was techni-
cally a member of the tribe of Binyomin, he owed his life partially to
Dovid HaMelech, who descended from יהודה, for not having killed
his ancestor Shimi ben Gera.[16]

Assuming this is true, why was Megillas Esther chosen as the
place to reveal it? Is the story of Dovid and Shimi ben Gera not
related in the book of Shmuel? In fact Esther is the most appropriate place to mention this, because the Megilla promises us that the
festival of Purim will remain with the Jewish people for eternity:
"and these days of Purim should never cease among the Jews."[17] The
Purim story therefore must at least hint to the tribe of Yehuda, a
descendant of Leah, for if the miracle had come about only through
Rachel's descendant, Binyomin, it would not have been everlasting.
It was because of Leah's influence that קימו וקבלו היהודים – "the

Jews confirmed and undertook,"[18] referring to their reacceptance of the eternal Torah.

Walk Humbly With Your God

Chazal[19] elucidate: "Six hundred and thirteen *mitzvos* were related to Moshe ... the prophet *Micha* came and established the basis for fulfillment of the Torah's commandments upon three ethical requirements, as it is written: 'He has told you, O man, what is good! What does Hashem require of you but to do justice, to love kindness, and to walk humbly with your God.'[20]" Hashem has many attributes, some of which are more visible to us than others. Leah's humility associated her with Hashem's hidden attributes in the upper worlds, whereas Rachel's character emulated Hashem's attributes that are more visible in the lower worlds.[21] We have no right to evaluate the attributes of the mothers, but this apparently is how Chazal see it. Leah's humility concealed her righteousness to the extent that it could not be appreciated even by Yaakov Avinu.

The above Gemara teaches us that the words "... and walk humbly with your God" refer to the *mitzvos* of *hachnossas kallah* and *levayas hameis*, caring for a bride and accompanying the deceased. The Gemara asks: "Do these matters not suggest a *kal vachomer*? If the Torah instructed us to walk humbly, that is discreetly, in matters that are not generally performed discreetly, such as funerals and weddings, then in matters that by their very nature should be performed discreetly, such as giving charity, how much more so must one take care to do them discreetly?"[22] Rashi explains that the Gemara chose weddings and funerals as occasions at which we should act with הצנע לכת because the word לכת, going, appears in the Tanach in the context of weddings and funerals, as the *pasuk* states: טוב ללכת אל בית אבל מלכת אל בית משתה – "It is better to go to the house of mourning than to go to a house of feasting."[23] At funerals and weddings we demonstrate our kindness to our fellow man in public. The Gemara is telling us that even these public demonstrations of kindness should be performed in as understated a way as possible. Belief in Hashem must be displayed publicly, while acts of kindness should be performed in as private a manner as possible.

Perhaps we can see a symbolic representation of this idea in the mitzvah of *tefillin*. We wear *tefillin* on our arm as well as on our head. The *tefillin shel rosh* must be revealed whereas the *tefillin shel yad* must be concealed. The *tefillin* worn on the head represent a person's thoughts. A Jew must never hide the fact that he believes in Hashem and in the Thirteen Principles of Faith. The *tefillin* worn on the arm, on the other hand, represent a person's actions, which should be done modestly.

Going Against One's Nature

Although humility and acting inconspicuously are the ideal, we must at times employ the principle of עת לעשות לה' הפרו תורתך – "It is a time to act for Hashem; they voided Your Torah."[24] Matisyohu and his sons, who were Kohanim and thus descendants of Leah, had to invoke this principle and go against their inherited trait of הצנע לכת in order to win an eternal victory for the Torah and *Am Yisrael*. Matisyohu presumably spent his time in the *Beis Midrash* of Kfar Modiin and traveled to Yerushalayim when it was his turn to serve in the *Beis HaMikdash*. Until the time came to "act for Hashem" and sanctify His name by waging war against the Greeks, his family was not well-known. We can assume that they were not trained soldiers, yet it was in the merit of their actions that the Torah was reestablished for all time within the Jewish nation.

Over the years many have pondered why this very special family, which merited sanctifying Hashem's Name and was responsible for bringing salvation to the nation, to the Torah and to the *Beis HaMikdash,* was eventually lost to the Jewish people. The five brothers were killed by the Greeks, while other descendants became *Tzdukim* and were killed by Herod. Perhaps it was their becoming *Tzdukim* that led to their downfall. These same *Tzdukim*, who were responsible for the civil war between Hyrcanus and Aristobulos, brought about the Roman exile. In fact in his commentary on the *pasuk*, "Alas I knew not how to guard myself from sin! My own devices harnessed me, like chariots subject to a foreign nation's mercies,"[25] Rashi comments that we brought the Roman exile upon ourselves.[26] I would like to suggest a different approach.

First And Second Luchos

Two sets of *Luchos HaBris* – Tablets of the Law – were brought down from Har Sinai. The first set had greater sanctity, as the Torah states: "The tablets were God's handiwork, and the script was the script of God, חרות (literally 'engraved') on the tablets."[27] The Gemara tells us "Do not read it as *charus* – 'engraved,' but rather as *cheirus* – 'freedom.'"[28] The first *luchos* freed us from the clutches of the angel of death. Chazal add another interpretation of the word חרות: "This teaches us that that had the first set of tablets not been shattered, the Torah would never have been forgotten by Israel."[29] Engraving implies permanence. We would have been able to learn the entire Shas once and remember all of it. This does not mean we would have no reason to stay in Yeshiva, for even after having mastered Shas we would be required to study the works of the Rambam, Rashba, and other giants.

The second *luchos*, although they had a high level of sanctity, were clearly not as holy as the first ones. These tablets may have been מכתב אלקים – "the script of God," but they were not מעשה אלקים – "God's handiwork" like the first tablets were, since they were carved by Moshe Rabenu. We would have expected the man-made *luchos* to be more fragile, yet it was the first ones, made by Hashem Himself, that did not last. The Maharal explains that anything which is too holy cannot last in this world.

The *Midrash* provides us with another reason why the second tablets lasted and the first ones did not. The *Midrash* tells us: "The first tablets were given with great publicity and therefore were susceptible to the *ayin hara*, the evil eye, and were broken. Referring to the second tablets, Hashem said, "There is nothing more beautiful than modesty, as it says, 'What does Hashem require of you but to do justice, to love kindness, and to walk humbly with your God.'"[30] The first *luchos* were given at the great assembly at Har Sinai known as יום הקהל.[31] The Torah has great praise for that memorable day: "You have been shown in order to know that Hashem, He is the God! There is none beside Him, from heaven He caused you to hear His voice in order to teach you, and on earth He showed you His great fire, and you heard His words from the midst of the fire ... Has a people ever heard the voice of God speaking from the midst of the fire as you have heard and survived?"[32] Regarding the second tablets, Moshe was commanded: ואיש לא יעלה עמך וגם איש אל ירא בכל ההר – "No man may ascend with you nor may anyone be seen on the entire mountain."[33] The whole thing must be inconspicuous in order to ensure that it remain eternal. There will be no Divine Revelation, no fire, and no great assembly. The second tablets were given privately and were thus made to last.

I am not sure what *ayin hara* the *Midrash* is referring to – certainly not from the other nations, for we know they were offered the Torah and were not interested. Perhaps the Satan gave them an *ayin hara*. What we do see is that the more something is publicized, the less chance it has of lasting for eternity.

Perhaps this can help us understand the tragic end of the Chashmonaim. Matters were desperate – it was עת לעשות לה' – "a time to act for Hashem,"[34] forcing this otherwise modest family to emerge into the public eye, like the first *luchos*. True, they sanctified Hashem's Name, and many died *al Kiddush Hashem*, but the publicity was their downfall. Only something performed בהצנע לכת – "by walking humbly," in the manner of Leah, whose gifts were eternal, can last forever. Rachel's righteousness was visible to all, thus her gifts did not last. We ourselves cannot make such statements, but we are basing our words on the *Midrash*.

The first *luchos*, although physically broken, were not totally destroyed. I am not referring only to the fragments stored in the Ark, but to the fact that each year we commemorate that momentous day. The Gemara tells us about Shavuos, "All agree with respect to Shavuos that we require it to be 'for you' too. What is the reason? It is the day on which the Torah was given."[35] Our entire existence as a nation stems from Shavuos, the day the Torah was given. Those broken tablets did in fact leave a lasting impression.

The same may be said of the Chashmonaim, who may have been destroyed, but left us with a lasting impression. Every year, during the Chanukah festival commemorating their victory, we proclaim Hashem's power: "You delivered the strong into the hands of the weak, the many into the hands of the few ... they cleansed Your

Temple, purified the site of Your Holiness and kindled lights in the courtyard of Your Sanctuary." *Megillas Taanis* and all the festive days recorded there were declared null and void, with the exception of Chanukah. The Gemara explains, "Chanukah is different because the miracle of Chanukah has already been publicized."[36] The same publicity which was so detrimental to the Chashmonaim ensured that their legacy and achievements have remained with us.

We can learn from here that הצנע לכת – walking humbly, does not necessarily mean that a person has to flee from publicity, but rather that whatever a person does should be with humility. The Chashmonaim who emerged into the public eye for the purpose of לעשות לה' merited purifying the *Beis HaMikdash* and re-establishing the Torah for eternity, as we recite in על הניסים:

ולעמך ישראל עשית תשועה גדולה ופרקן כהיום הזה

"And for Your people Israel. You worked a great victory and salvation as this very day."

The salvation brought about through the Chashmonaim did indeed leave a lasting impression, and in addition, as the Rambam writes, the kingdom returned to Israel's hands for over two hundred years.

Notes

1   *Bereishis* 29:17-18

2   *Bamidbar* 15:39

3   *Kiddushin* 41a

4   *Devarim* 23:4

5   *Devarim* 25:19

6   Ibid. 18

7   *Midrash Rabba Eicha Psichta* 24

8   *Yirmiyahu* 31:7

9   *Bereishis* 35:19

10 *Bereishis* 28:2

11 Ruth 4:11

12 *Bereishis* 29:17

13 *Bereishis* 7:8

14 *Baba Basra* 123a

15 Esther 2:5

16 See *Megilla* 12b.

17 Esther 9:28

18 Ibid. 27

19 *Makkos* 24a

20 *Micha* 6:8

21 See *Zohar, Parshas Vayetze* 154a.

22 *Makkos* ibid.

23 *Koheles* 7:2

24 *Tehillim* 119:126

25 *Shir HaShirim* 6:12

26 See *Sicha* II for *Parshas Vayetze*.

27 *Shemos* 32:16

28 *Eruvin* 54a

29 Ibid.

30 *Tanchuma Parshas Ki Sisah, Siman* 31.

31 *Devarim* 18:16

32 *Devarim* 4:35-36

33 *Shemos* 34:3

34 *Tehillim* 119:126

35 *Pesachim* 68b

36 *Rosh Hashana* 18b

"I Would Not Have Slept!"

Leil Tisha B'Av

Yaakov Avinu leaves his parents' home and spends fourteen years at the Academy of Shem and Ever on his journey towards Haran. On the way to Lavan he stops to rest overnight:

ויפגע במקום וילן שם כי בא השמש ... וישכב במקום ההוא

"He encountered the place and spent the night there because the sun had set... and he lay down in that place."

At first glance, the words במקום ההוא – "in that place" seem superfluous. Did the Torah not just record וילן שם? Is there any place other than במקום ההוא that he would have lain down? Rashi quotes the *midrash*: "This expresses exclusion; in that place he lay down, but during the fourteen years that he served in the house of Ever, he did not lie down at night, because he was occupied with Torah." It is difficult to believe that Chazal meant that Yaakov did not sleep at all. In Gemara Sukka we learn: "He who takes an oath not to sleep for three days is to be punished with *malkus* and he may sleep immediately." Not sleeping at all, even for just three days, is impossible! What Chazal meant was that he would doze off at times, but he never actually lay down to sleep. It was only when he arrived "at that place" that he deliberately went to sleep.

Why did Yaakov go to sleep? We would have expected a Yeshiva scholar of his caliber to be engrossed in his learning. It is hardly possible that when he left the Yeshiva, he left his love for learning behind. Furthermore, Chazal tell us that Yaakov went there to *daven*: "When he reached Charan, he said to himself: 'Shall I have passed through the place where my fathers prayed and not pray too?'"[3] This was not merely a stop on the road. Yaakov purposely returned to Har HaMoriah in order to *daven*. If Yaakov realized what the place was, why does he say: אכן יש ה' במקום הזה ואנכי לא ידעתי –"Hashem is present in this place and I did not know"?[4] How could he not have known? His sole motive in returning there was that he knew what it was!

We can gain some insight into this incident through a *midrash* that is also cited in the *halacha*. The night that Yaakov slept "in that place" was the night of Tisha B'Av. Although fourteen Tisha B'Avs had passed during the fourteen years Yaakov was in the Yeshiva, Yaakov did not feel the destruction. It was only when he arrived במקום ההוא – at the site of the *Beis HaMikdash* and he actually saw the destruction that he felt Tisha B'Av. The *Kinos* recited on Tisha B'Av mention the fact that Yaakov saw the destruction. Upon perceiving the *Beis HaMikdash* lying in ruins, Yaakov remarked: אין זה כי אם בית אלקים וזה שער השמים the simple translation of which is "This is none other than the abode of God and this is the gate of the heavens!"[5] According to this *midrash*, we can interpret the words אין זה to mean "it was not there." Yaakov Avinu suddenly realized that the *Beis Hamikdash* – the abode of God – was no longer standing. He stopped learning immediately, since *halacha* mandates that learning Torah is forbidden on Tisha B'Av. Now that he was observing his first Tisha B'Av and could not learn, he lay down to sleep.

When he arrived at the place and beheld the destruction, "Yaakov instituted the *Maariv* prayer."[6] Yaakov established the prayer that is recited at night, because night represents the darkness of the exile. Avraham and Yitzchak established *Shacharis* and *Mincha*, which are recited during the hours of daylight, corresponding to the time when the *Beis HaMikdash* was standing. *Shacharis* and *Mincha* are obligatory, but "the evening prayer is elective."[7] Perhaps this is because the exile too was "elective"; it did not have to take place. If we had not deserved it, it would not have happened. On Tisha B'Av, the *halacha* states, one should sleep with some discomfort, which explains why Yaakov placed a rock under his head when he lay down

"Had I Known I Would Not Have Slept!"

Perhaps we can offer another understanding of Yaakov's declaration: "This is none other than the abode of God and this is the gate of the heavens." Chazal teach us that while the *Beis HaMikdash* stands, "Their interiors are consecrated but their rooftops are unconsecrated."[8] There was no sanctity in the roofs of the Sanctuary. Following the destruction, the sanctity was boundless and continued upward to the heavens. Yaakov knew that this was the place where his fathers had prayed, but on witnessing the destruction in all its darkness, he thought that the Divine Presence had left. When he awoke, he realized that the *Shechina* was indeed present, even during times of destruction, and so he exclaimed: אכן יש ה' במקום הזה ואנכי לא ידעתי – "Hashem is present in this place and I did not know!" Had he been aware of the fact that Har HaMoriah retained its holiness even after the destruction, he would have known that it was an inappropriate place to sleep. Yaakov realized that this night had offered him a golden opportunity to grow to new heights, and he had wasted it.

Yirmiyahu the prophet declared: אתה ה' לעולם תשב כסאך לדור ודור – "You, Hashem, are enthroned forever, Your throne is eternal."[9] What does this *pasuk* teach us that we do not already know? We can understand it in the context of the previous *pasuk*: על הר ציון ששמם שועלים הלכו בו "For foxes prowl on Mount Zion which lies desolate."[10] Yirmiyahu is teaching us that even at times when foxes tread on Har Zion, during times of destruction, when it lies desolate, "You, Hashem, are enthroned forever, Your throne is eternal." This is what Yaakov Avinu learned: the Divine Presence had not departed, therefore it was inappropriate to sleep "in that place."

Rav Aryeh Levin, who was the *Mashgiach* in Yeshivas Etz Chaim, quoted this reaction of Yaakov's: "Had I known, I would not have slept." This, he told his students, is how a Yeshiva *bochur* should feel. He must realize the importance of the Yeshiva and the opportunities it presents. The years should not be wasted in sleep! Obviously sleep is a necessary bodily function and none of us can be expected to be like Yaakov Avinu, who did not sleep during his fourteen years in Yeshiva. However, it should be confined to its appropriate time and place, not during the *shiur* or during time which should be set aside for learning.

"Had I known I would not have slept." Even during his sleep Yaakov Avinu achieved tremendous heights. He dreamt of a ladder:

והנה סלם מצב ארצה וראשו מגיע השמימה
והנה מלאכי אלקים עולים ויורדים בו

"A ladder was set earthward and its top reached heavenward; and behold! angels of God were ascending and descending it."[11]

He dreamt of Hashem's promise to grant him *Eretz Yisrael* and to protect him, as well as Hashem's other promises mentioned in the Torah. Despite this, he regretted that he had wasted the opportunity of a night at the site of the *Beis HaMikdash* by sleeping.

This is how a Yeshiva student should feel. He should realize the holiness of the place and value the years in which he has the opportunity to sit in Yeshiva and study Torah. It would be sad if when the time came to leave the Yeshiva, the student were full of regrets for not having realized what a tremendous place it is, and instead he wasted his time sleeping! Of course, a student must eat when it is time to eat and sleep when it is time to sleep, but he must also learn when it is time to learn! The years in Yeshiva must not go to waste.

A Torah Patched Together From Tattered Pieces

The Gemara[12] tells us: "If someone sleeps in the *Beis Midrash*, his Torah becomes קרעים קרעים – 'tattered,' as it says, 'and a slumberer will wear tattered clothing.'"[13] Although this statement of Chazal has profound meaning, it can be understood on a simple level as well. Let us imagine, for example that a student asks the Rav a *she'eilah*: "Is cooking permissible on *Shabbos*?" The Rav obviously answers that it is forbidden. Another student then asks the Rav if cooking is permissible on Yom Tov and of course the Rav answers that it is allowed. What would happen if a student dozed off after the first question and woke up just before the second answer? He would mistakenly believe that cooking is permissible on *Shabbos*! His Torah becomes קרעים קרעים – patched together from tattered pieces.

Information And Logic

Although we should attempt to accumulate as much knowledge as possible in the Yeshiva, to learn as many pages of Gemara, *Tosafos*, and Rav Chaim as we can, we must realize that spending the time in Yeshiva merely amassing volume of knowledge constitutes wasting time in the preference of quantity over quality. The purpose of Yeshiva is also to teach us how to think using the Torah's logic.

Knowledge can be gained outside the Yeshiva as well. All one needs do is sit in a Beis *Midrash* and open up some books. However, learning to think in a logical manner and to uncover the depths of the Torah is very difficult to learn elsewhere. Obviously the Torah giants of the world can do so outside the Yeshiva as well, but an ordinary person can only accomplish this within the walls of the Yeshiva. We must take advantage of the time we have here, to understand why Rashi rules as he does, why *Tosafos* did not accept this, and why the Rambam differed from both of them. Did the Rambam simply have a different version of the text or was there another reason for his divergent view? Although the knowledge we gain without discovering the logic may be true, life is not conducted solely based on the cases mentioned in the Gemara, thus it is important to understand and to be able to compare one case to another.

The Gemara cites a *halacha* in the name of Rav Evyatar. Rav Yoseph asked: "Who tells us that Rav Evyatar is reliable?" Abaye says: "It is understandable that you can discredit the standing of a scholar for a mistake in something dependent on logic, but an oral teaching? He may never have heard this oral tradition."[14] No person can master the Torah in its entirety. There is no end to the amount of information one can still learn. We must strive to master everything, all the while remembering: לא עליך המלאכה לגמר – "You are not required to complete the task."[15] However, the ability to use logic is an art which a person must master, and it is not found in any book. If a person uses logic incorrectly, he cannot achieve greatness in Torah, while in the area of information, he may be unaware of a particular point and yet still be considered great. Paradoxically, the Gemara teaches us: רב יוסף סיני, רבה עוקר הרים – "Rav Yosef was a well-read scholar (literally, like Har Sinai). He was familiar with the many precepts of the Torah. Rabba, on the other hand, was a keen dialectician (literally, he could uproot mountains with his logic.) An inquiry was sent: Which of these should take precedence? The reply came back: 'A well-read scholar is to take precedence.'"[16] This implies that amassing knowledge is preferable to developing one's thinking ability. The reason for this is that without basic knowledge, logic cannot produce correct results. Once there is a basis of knowledge, one can compare one thing to another using his own logic and draw his own conclusions on particular *halachic* issues.

"Rolling Obstacles" – Applying A Principle

How does one infer *halacha*? Let us view an example. Nowadays, most stores have tiled floors and do not generally contain a *bor*, or 'pit.' At one time sugar and salt were kept in large sacks. When a customer came in to the store, she would tell the owner how much salt she wanted and he would take the appropriate amount from the large sack and transfer it into whatever container she had. One time several women came in to a store at the same time. They all requested sugar. The shopkeeper gave them what they asked for and they each brought it home and used it as an ingredient in the food that they cooked. A short while later it was discovered that there had been a mix-up and they had been sold salt instead of sugar. One woman's cake was ruined, another's tea, and another's fish. Is the storekeeper obligated to reimburse them for their losses? The Rav (Rav Shlomo Zalman Auerbach) zt"l ruled that he is. This ruling was based on the concept of *bor hamisgalgel* "a pitfall that is moved about."[17] The Rav explained that a

---

17   See *Baba Kamma* 6a. A person placed a large stone in a public area which caused no damage while stationary. The stone was then kicked by people walking and caused damage in its new location (Rashi).

bor hamisgalgel need not be in the form of a pit, but can be, as in this case, in the guise of a bag of sugar or salt. This is what true learning is. We must know how to compare one thing to another.

Yeshiva students commonly ask why they need to learn Baba Kamma if they neither own an ox nor have pits in their yards! It is indeed possible that they have a *halachically* defined *bor* in their house. I believe that each us has some type of obstacle in our homes, for example, a child may fall off a chair or table and break his leg. The child does not realize the ramifications of what has occurred, but when he grows up he should actually be able to sue his father for damages! Although I am not a *dayan*, this would seem to be the *halacha*. This is just one of many examples of how the study of Gemara is relevant to our daily lives.

Some people might not understand how to use the laws as practical guidelines. They view the Gemara as esoteric concepts that have no connection to their lives. A person might be in the middle of learning, "If one leaves a jug in a public domain and someone else comes along and stumbles over it and breaks it ..."[18] yet on his way out of the *Beis Midrash*, he throws a banana peel into a public domain. The banana peel now has the status of a בור ברשות הרבים, "a pit in a public domain."[19]

The Gemara states: "He who wishes to be pious must fulfill the laws of *nezikin*."[20] One way to attain piety is to fulfill the precepts relating to laws of damages, one of which is not to throw a banana peel into the street. Where in the entire Shas is it mentioned that one should not throw a banana peel in the street? Does the Talmud even mention bananas? Rabenu Nosson Rosh HaYeshiva states that the word 'banana' is hinted at in Shas in the words *bnos shuach*.[21] *Bnos shuach* is a type of fruit described by the Gemara as "white figs." Even if he is correct, it does not say anywhere in Shas that a person should not throw the peels of *bnos shuach* into the street! The only way to derive a *halachic* conclusion regarding the banana peel is to apply the principles of *Maseches Baba Kamma*. Torah is not irrelevant abstract pieces of information. It is our life!

We learn that if a person steals something and is caught, he must pay double the value of the item he stole. The Torah specifies that this applies "from an ox to a donkey to a lamb."[22] Presumably this includes other things as well, even if they are worth significantly less. Chazal teach us that the entire Torah comprises one unit. Every *maseches* has information relevant to other subjects. Not only can we learn laws of damages in *Baba Kamma* and laws of *Shabbos* in *Maseches Shabbos*, but laws of damages are found in *Maseches Shabbos* and laws of *Shabbos* can be found in *Maseches Baba Kamma*.

Authorities such as *Eglei Tal* and the Rogatchover demonstrate how the entire Torah is one large picture. When the *Eglei Tal* discusses issues related to the prohibited *melachos* of *Shabbos*, he brings proofs from *Kodshim, Taharos, Nezikin*, and the rest of Shas. The Rogatchover also makes reference to sources from all over Shas. One would have to work extremely hard to gain expertise in all these areas. As we mentioned before, one must not only have knowledge in all areas of Torah, but one must also understand its inner logic as well as the Rishonim and Acharonim and know how to apply all of it.

The Ibn Ezra writes, "The empty-headed will wonder what Moshe did on Har Sinai for forty days and forty nights."[23] They wonder why it took Moshe forty days and forty nights to master the Torah. Why does Ibn Ezra refer to them as "empty-headed"? Perhaps if they believed that they could master the entire Written and Oral Torah including Rashi, Rambam, Ketzos, Nesivos, etc. in less than forty days and nights, they must be the Torah giants of the world! The Ibn Ezra explains that they are empty-headed because they do not realize that "If Moshe stood there with Hashem for this number of years (forty) and double double of this number (an additional 160 years totaling 200), he would not be able to understand even one thousandth of the ways of Hashem, and what lies behind His *mitzvos*." This means that even if someone were as great as Moshe Rabenu and had two hundred thousand years to learn, he would still not be able to achieve a complete understanding of the Torah through natural means. I would therefore suggest that everyone spend as much time as he can in Yeshiva.

The Thirteen Rules By Which The Torah Is Expounded

Chazal describe the Torah as a gift from Hashem. If so, what did Moshe spend his time studying during these forty days? It seems to me that he studied the outlines and patterns of the *mitzvos*. Moshe learned, for example, what a Sukkah should look like and what *tefillin* should look like. He studied the מדות שהתורה נדרשת בהן – "the rules by which the Torah is elucidated," the methods of logic and in-depth study. For example, Moshe learned what can be derived from a קל וחומר[24] and from a גזרה שוה[25].

Without some basic knowledge, using the tool of קל וחומר alone can produce warped ideas of what the Torah is trying to say. By means of a קל וחומר one can theoretically conclude that one is required to eat matzah on Sukkos! The קל וחומר would be that if even on Pesach when one is not required to live in the Sukkah, one is required to eat matzah, then *kal vachomer* on Sukkos when one is required to live in the Sukkah, he should certainly be required to eat matzah as well. Applying the principle of *gezera shava* without basic knowledge can also lead to error. An example of this is *"chamisha asar chamisha asar"* comparing Pesach to Sukkos because they each fall on the fifteenth of the month, can lead to the same erroneous conclusion. It is not enough to read the thirteen principles as they are written in the *siddur*; we must know how to apply them in order to learn what can be derived using which principle.

Chazal relate the story of a Tzdukki (Sadducee) who invented the following *kal vachomer*: if one is permitted to live with one's own wife but not with her daughter, then when it comes to someone else's wife with whom one is forbidden to live, certainly he should be forbidden to live with her daughter. Of course this is absurd because it means one is forbidden to marry the daughter of a married woman! We must know how to determine which *kal vachomer* is correct and which is not. This is how Moshe Rabenu spent those forty days – learning how to study the Torah in depth.

---

24 Logic dictates that if a lenient case has a stringency, the same stringency applies to the stricter case.

25 Tradition teaches that two similar words in different contexts are meant to clarify one another.

This too is what Yaakov did during those fourteen years he was in the Yeshiva of Shem and Ever. I don't know whether he only studied the seven *mitzvos* required of all descendants of Noach or the Torah in its entirety. He was mainly busy acquiring methods of analysis – first in the house of Yitzchak, then in the Yeshiva of Ever.

Removing Rocks

After spending fourteen years in the Yeshiva, Yaakov began his journey towards Charan. He was not a young man at this point – he was seventy-seven years old. Despite this, he succeeded in removing the large rock placed on the mouth of the well to prevent robbers from stealing the water.[26] It usually took all the shepherds together to remove the rock: "When all the flocks were assembled there, they would roll the stone from the mouth of the well and water the sheep."[27]

Yaakov removed the rock with ease. "like a person who removes a plug from the mouth of a flask, to let you know that his strength was great."[28]

My esteemed teacher HaRav Chaim Shmuelevitz zt"l asked where Yaakov Avinu got such strength. Certainly not from studying in the Yeshiva for fourteen years! In *Tefillas Geshem*, the prayer for rain recited on Shmini Atzeres, Ashkenazim recite: יחד לב וגל אבן מפי באר מים "He dedicated his heart and rolled a stone off the mouth of a well of water." Yaakov's strength was not physical, but came from the dedication of his heart and his faith in Hashem.

One who studies the Torah as he should, and attains this יחוד הלב can accomplish anything. The most difficult task will become like removing a plug from the mouth of a flask. Even the spiritual rock – the *yetzer hara* is referred to as a rock – can be removed with the proper amount of *yichud halev*. It all depends how much we involve ourselves in Torah study. When one does not delve into the Torah and serve Hashem properly, the rock is insurmountable.

On Chanukah in *Al HaNissim* we thank Hashem because:

מסרת גבורים ביד חלשים ורבים ביד

מעטים וטמאים ביד טהורים ורשעים ביד צדיקים וזדים ביד עסקי תורתך.

"You delivered the strong into the hands of the weak, the many into the hands of the few, the impure into the hands of the pure, the wicked into the hands of the righteous, and the wanton into the hands of the diligent students of Your Torah."

The final praise in this sentence – "the wanton into the hands of the diligent students of Your Torah" – sheds light on all the "pairings." The weak defeated the strong because the weak were עוסקי תורתך. When one is involved in Torah, the Greeks are not insurmountable – even the elephants of the Greeks are like that plug on the flask.

Reinstating The Kingdom Of Heaven

The war against the Greeks was a holy one. The Chashmonaim fought not only for the sake of Kiddush Hashem, but in order to save the study of Torah and keeping of *mitzvos* which the Greeks had forbidden. They were victorious because they had יחוד הלב.

According to the Rambam, as a result of the war, Israel was victorious in that the kingdom lasted for more than two hundred years. However this was not the main purpose of the Hasmonean uprising. Had Antiochus permitted the Jewish people to observe the Torah, they would have been willing to accept him as their king. Since this was not the case, they rebelled, not to return the kingdom to Jewish hands, but to reinstate the Kingdom of Heaven. Their rebellion was for the sake of giving our sons a *bris milah* and observing *Shabbos*, Rosh Chodesh, and other *mitzvos*.

Involving themselves in the study of Torah and holy pursuits was *Am Yisrael*'s יחוד הלב against the Greeks – making them like a mere plug on a flask.

It is well-known that the Chazon Ish was able to perform miracles, particularly in the area of medicine, but in other areas as well. I once asked the Rav (HaRav Shlomo Zalman Auerbach) zt"l whether I am required to believe these stories, to which he answered 'Yes.' At the time, similar stories were circulating regarding another individual who supposedly was also a miracle worker and when I asked the Rav whether I should believe those stories, he replied in the

negative. (Later I happened to be present when the Chazon Ish performed one of the miracles described, and when the other person
attempted to do so unsuccessfully.) The difference between them
was that while the other man was observant and had studied some
Torah, the Chazon Ish's entire being was the Torah. He delved into
it and had insights into all sections of the Shulchan Aruch. Anyone
familiar with his *seforim* can see that the entire Torah was open to
him. Such a person can perform miracles.

Yaakov Avinu achieved his *sheleimus* (perfection) by being a *yoshev
ohalim* – by "sitting in the tents (of Torah),"[29] by spending fourteen
years in the Yeshiva of Shem and Ever without sleeping. This was
the only reason Yaakov had the ability to roll that rock off the mouth
of the well.

Taking Upon One's Self The Yoke Of Torah

In Sefer Daniel, the *pasuk* states: "It will throw truth to the ground,
and it will achieve and prosper,"[30] referring to kingdoms he saw in a
vision. The Yerushalmi comments that the *pasuk* teaches us that the
kingdom of evil succeeded because truth was thrown to the ground.
Truth refers to the Torah. When *Klal Yisrael* is involved in Torah,
the other nations cannot exert control over us.

הקול קול יעקב והידים ידי עשו – "The voice is Yaakov's voice, but the
hands are Esav's hands."[31] When the voice of Yaakov is strong in the
ways of Torah, the hands of Esav cannot rule over us, but when the
voice of Yaakov is not strong, when Yaakov is not involved in the
Torah, the hands of Esav can overpower us.

"If someone takes upon himself the yoke of Torah, the yoke of
government is removed from him."[32] It does not matter whether
it is the government of Rome or Greece, or America. If today we
are obligated to listen to everything America dictates, it is because
something is lacking in our acceptance of *ol haTorah*, the yoke of
Torah. Had we observed the *mitzvos* better, created more Yeshivos
and *Kollelim*, put more effort into our Torah study during our time
in Yeshiva, the *ol malchus* would not be able to overpower us. We
must hope and pray that by accepting the yoke of Torah and *mitzvos*
properly, we will be able to rid ourselves of the burden of the other

nations, and speedily in our day may we reach the stage of "Then You Hashem will reign alone over all Your works on Mount Zion, resting place of Your glory."[33]

Notes

1   *Bereishis* 28:11

2   *Sukka* 53a

3   *Chullin* 91b

4   *Bereishis* 28:16

5   *Bereishis* 28:17

6   *Berachos* 26b

7   Ibid. 27b

8   *Pesachim* 86a

9   *Eicha* 5:19

10 Ibid. 18

11 *Bereishis* 28:12

12 *Sanhedrin* 71a

13 *Mishle* 23:21

14 *Gittin* 6b

15 *Pirke Avos* 2:21

16 *Horayos* 14a

18 Mishna *Baba Kamma Perek* 3, Mishna 1

19 *Shabbos* 99a

20 *Baba Kamma* 30a

21 See *Berachos* 40b.

22 *Shemos* 22:3

23 Ibn Ezra's commentary to *Shemos* 31:18.

26 See *Bereishis* 29:2.

27 *Bereishis* 29:3

28 Rashi, *Bereishis* 29:10

29 *Bereishis* 25:27

30 Daniel 8:12

31 *Bereishis* 27:22

32 *Pirke Avos* 3:6

33 *Shmone Esrei* of Rosh Hashana and Yom Kippur

Ein Od Milvado

"Like Removing A Plug From The Mouth Of A Flask"

וירא והנה באר בשדה והנה שם שלשה עדרי צאן רבצים
עליה כי מן הבאר ההיא ישקו העדרים והאבן גדולה על פי הבאר

*"He looked and behold a well in the field. And behold! Three
flocks of sheep lying beside it, for from that well they would
water the flocks and the stone on the mouth of the well was
large.[1]"*

After inquiring after the welfare of his Uncle Lavan, Yaakov says
to the shepherds, "The day is still long; it is not yet time to bring the
livestock in. Water the flock and go on grazing."[2] The sheep will eat
more grass and become fatter, and you will then have more meat.
The shepherds answered, "We cannot until all the flocks have been
gathered and they will roll the stone from upon the mouth of the
well and we will water the flock."[3] We are not strong enough to remove the massive stone on our own, we need the help of the other
shepherds for whom we are waiting. Presumably the large stone
was placed on the mouth of the well to control distribution of water
among the local residents – to prevent one person from taking more

than his share,' as well as to prevent outsiders from taking. Remember, there had already been an incident in which a stranger arrived in town with ten camels, and a little girl from one of the local families drew enough water for all his camels! The only way to prevent such a thing from recurring was to cover the well with a large stone.

This time there was no need to wait for the other shepherds, for "While he was still speaking with them, Rachel had come with her father's flock, for she was a shepherdess, and it was when Yaakov saw Rachel, daughter of Lavan, his mother's brother, and the flock of Lavan, his mother's brother, Yaakov came forward and rolled the stone from upon the mouth of the well and watered the sheep of Lavan, his mother's brother."[4] Yaakov was able to remove the rock on his own. How did a seventy-seven year old man[5] manage to move a rock which normally required the combined effort of a number of shepherds? Rashi tells us that removing the rock from the mouth of the well required no physical prowess whatsoever on Yaakov's part: "Like a person who removes a plug from the mouth of a flask," as if it had no weight, "to let you know that his strength was great."[6]

Where did Yaakov acquire such strength? As far as we know, he had spent the last fourteen years in the *Beis Midrash* of Ever,[7] where presumably he learned Torah exclusively and devoted no time to any strength-training program. Furthermore, even if Yaakov possessed such incredible superhuman strength, what did he want from the shepherds? Why did he instruct them to "water the flock and go on grazing"? Did he not realize that they could not remove the stone? It would be difficult to believe that such a great Sage and prophet of Hashem would overestimate the strength of the shepherds.

Dedication Of Heart

My esteemed teacher HaGaon HaRav Chaim Shmuelevitz zt"l explained that it was not physical might that enabled Yaakov to accomplish this feat, but spiritual strength. He cites the words of the *piyut* that Ashkenazim recite in the prayer for rain on Shemini Atzeres: "He dedicated his heart and rolled a stone off the mouth of a well of water." Yaakov did not flex his muscles but rather "flexed" his heart – he dedicated his heart to his Father in Heaven.[8]

What does it mean to dedicate one's heart? Does it mean to believe that Hashem is One? Do we not all believe this? Do we not declare twice daily *"Shema Yisrael Hashem Elokenu Hashem Echod"* – "Hear O Israel, Hashem is our God, Hashem is the One and Only"?[9] No matter how hard we tried, I doubt that any of us could have removed the rock from the mouth of the well. While we may declare that Hashem is One, we do not feel it the way Yaakov did. Do we truly believe with all our heart that there is no other force in this world but Hashem? When we see a large rock, we assume that it is very heavy. When we ponder the military strength of our enemies or the nation's economic, military and security woes, we immediately ascribe causes to them. Yaakov Avinu understood that the Almighty is One and *"ein od milvado"* – "there is none beside Him." His entire being felt it. The large stone did not weigh any more to him than the cork of a flask. Any apparent weight the stone may have had was not the stone itself but rather Hashem, the only Force in the world. When a person truly feels *"ein od milvado,"* – "there is none beside Him," all other forces in the world cease to exist. When a person dedicates his heart, and his thoughts are focused purely on the only Master of the Universe, all other powers become null and void.[10] Heavy objects present no problem, because there is no force in the world that can affect Him – not even the force of gravity!

At the outset of World War II, when the Nazis, *yimach shmam*, occupied Poland, HaRav Yitzchak Zev Soloveitchik, the *Brisker Rav,* was forced to flee Warsaw along roads filled with German murderers. Throughout his flight, he put all his efforts into concentrating on the thought *"ein od milvado"* – "There is none beside Him." He was miraculously able to escape to Vilna which at the time was outside German jurisdiction.[11] Even though the Germans had bombs, machine guns, and other weapons of destruction, they have no control over us when we understand that they are all nothing, and we can be saved from them. Although there were many other *tzaddikim* in that generation who certainly believed "ein od milvado," apparently they did not reach the profound perception of the *Brisker Rav.* This world can have control only over someone who ascribes power to it.

When a person truly negates the entire world in his heart, the world cannot dominate him.

When Yaakov instructed the shepherds to "water the flock and go on grazing," he was telling them to strengthen their faith and dedication to Hashem. As descendants of Noach, they too were forbidden to worship *avoda zara*. If they had sincerely believed *"ein od milvado,"* they would have been able to overcome any obstacle, remove the stone, water the flock and continue grazing. However the shepherds were idol worshippers and had no interest in believing in One God. Their refusal to believe made it impossible for them to roll the stone off the well.

"Nature" Vs. Miracles

The power of dedicating one's heart to Hashem can be seen from the following fascinating story in the Talmud. The daughter of R' Chanina ben Dosa once mistook a vessel containing vinegar for one containing oil, and she accidentally filled her *Shabbos* lights with vinegar. Asked her father, "What difference is there? After all 'The One Who commanded oil to burn, can command vinegar to burn as well.'"[12] And so it was – the candles burned until *Motzoei Shabbos*! What did R' Chanina do to merit such a miracle? Rav Eliyahu Dessler zt"l explains that nature is simply an illusion that exists as a way of testing man. Does he truly believe that only the will of Hashem causes the world to function? Someone who has already passed such a test and understands, as Yaakov did, that "there is none beside Him" and that it makes no difference whether oil or vinegar ignites, no longer needs to be dealt with according to the laws of nature. Such a person has already come to the realization that nature does not really exist, therefore Hashem can create miracles for him even when there is no pressing need.[13]

The *Beis Yosef* posed a well-known question about Chanukah. If there was sufficient oil to burn for one day and the lights burned for eight, the miracle was actually only for the last seven days. Why did *Chazal* institute an eight-day festival?[14] Over the years many solutions have been offered, among them those of Rav Kook and Rav Frank who suggested that if the requirement had been to kindle the lights for only seven days, we would have ended up making for ourselves replicas of the seven-branched *menorah* in the *Beis HaMikdash*, which is prohibited by the Torah.[15] The explanation most relevant to our discussion is attributed to R' Simcha Zissel Ziv zt"l, the Alter of Slobodka. According to his explanation, a seven-day Chanukah would have given the impression that a distinction exists between "miracle oil" and "natural oil." There was sufficient natural oil for one day and Hashem added miracle oil which burned for seven more days; miracle oil requires Divine Intervention, while natural oil does not. To dispel this notion, Chazal established an eight-day festival to highlight the fact that there is no difference between natural oil and miracle oil. Just as miracle oil is not bound by any laws of physics, but burns because the King of kings commanded it to, so too with natural oil. In other words, the One Who declared that oil burn for eight days, is the same One Who declares that oil burn for the 'usual' amount of time.[16]

What is the distinction between nature and miracle? Nature is the way Hashem generally runs the world. What we are accustomed to seeing in our daily lives, we call 'nature' while we refer to what appear to us as exceptional one-time occurrences as 'miracle'. The truth is that both are decrees of the King; to Him there is no distinction between miracle and nature. He created nature and He creates miracles.

When we turn a cup upside down, the water spills to the ground. Why? Everyone knows about gravity! Who created gravity? When Hashem declared, "Let the waters be gathered beneath the heavens into one area,"[17] He established the law that water travels downwards and not upwards. Until then water was spread out across the entire earth.[18] The water did not begin to flow downwards immediately. Hashem commanded the water to "... ascend mountains, descend to valleys, to the special place founded for them"[19] – and the waters rose up into the mountain and valleys in order to fulfill Hashem's commandment of "Let the waters be gathered beneath the heavens into one area." It was only then that what we term 'Nature' came into being, establishing the rule that water descends and does not ascend. If Hashem so desires, the waters can stand upright like a wall as happened with Yam Suf and the Jordan. It is all decided by the word of Hashem.

"You Have Trained Them As Rulers Over You!"

However when we attribute too much power to people or things, it spells trouble. The prophet Yirmiyahu warned *Am Yisrael* not to be too surprised when Hashem sent the king of Bovel to rule over them: "What will you say when He punishes you? You yourself have trained them as rulers over you."[20] When did the Jewish nation ever place themselves under Babylonian rule? The chief causes of the sub-jugation were the sins committed during the period of the first *Beis Hamikdash*,[21] yet Bovel would not have been able to rule over the Jewish people, if the people themselves had not allowed it to happen, by according the Babylonians too much importance.

This is what happened: as a sign to king Chizkiyohu, who was on his deathbed, that Hashem would add fifteen years to his life, Yeshayahu HaNavi caused the sun to move backward.[22] As evening was about to descend, it suddenly became morning! As we may expect, this made a tremendous impression throughout the world. In honor of the great miracle, "Merodach-baladan son of Baladan, the king of Babylonia, sent letters and a gift to Chizkiyohu. Chizkiyohu rejoiced with them and showed the messengers his whole treasure house – the silver, the gold, the spices, the fine oil, his entire warehouse and everything that was found in his treasuries; there was nothing that Chizkiyohu did not show them in his palace and in all his realm."[23]

Why was Chizkiyohu so joyous? Surely a righteous man of his stature was not looking for honor or publicity? Chizkiyohu HaMelech was rejoicing over the great *Kiddush Hashem* that was taking place! Merodach-baladan, son of Baladan had sent the messengers "to inquire about the miracle that happened in the land."[24] Chizkiyohu was excited that Hashem's miracle was perceived even in Bovel. It was clear to all that the God of Chizkiyohu had turned the sun "back". The letters and gifts Chizkiyohu received overwhelmed him with joy at the realization that even the king of Bovel recognized the power and sovereignty of Hashem.

Yirmiyahu however was able to discern (or perhaps Hashem told him) that Chizkiyohu was attaching undue significance to the honor meted out to *Am Yisrael* by the *Bavlim.* Chizkiyohu went so far as to make an elaborate feast in their honor, at which his own wife waited on them.[25] We can understand that emissaries of a foreign king should be treated to a royal feast – but should the queen herself have to serve them? No foreign dignitary deserves such honor! Chazal tell us that he went so far as to open up the *Aron HaKodesh* to display the *Luchos HaBris* to them.[26] This was going too far – the Babylonian emissaries were being treated with much more honor than they deserved.

"They Came To Me From A Faraway Land"

Hashem then sent the prophet Yeshayahu to Chizkiyohu with a question: "What did these men say, and from where did they come to you?"[27] The logical response from Chizkiyohu should have been, "You are a prophet of Hashem, and you are asking me?"[28] Rather he became very proud and answered, "They came to me from a faraway land, from Bovel."[29] Even if we were to suppose that Chizkiyohu was under the impression that the prophet did not know where the people came from, he did not need to emphasize that they came from a distant land. He should have said simply, "They came to me from Bovel." Did Yeshayahu ask for a geography lesson? We can assume that Yeshayahu knew where Bovel was! Chizkiyohu added the description "from a faraway land" because he was excited that word of Hashem's miracle had reached distant Bovel – even the great and powerful Bovel recognized the Hand of Hashem. It was in this that Chizkiyohu ascribed too much importance to Bovel.

The prophet then foretold to Chizkiyohu: "Behold, the days are coming when everything in your house, and whatever your forefathers have accumulated, will be carried off to Bovel; nothing will remain. And they will also take some of your children who will issue from you, whom you will beget, and they shall become officers in the palace of the king of Bovel."[30] What a frightening decree! Because Chizkiyohu had been excessively impressed by the Babylonians, all the treasures he had shown off to them were given to them. The prophet explained that Chizkiyohu's admiration and perhaps the Jewish nation's too, would lead, one hundred years later, to Bovel's domination over the Jews, which culminated in the destruction of the First Temple, and the Babylonian exile which followed. Had they not been so impressed, Bovel would not have had the power to rule over them.

We find a similar development in the case of the second *Beis Ha-Mikdash* and Rome. The *pasuk* states, "I knew not how to guard myself from sin! My own devices harnessed me, like chariots subject to a foreign nation's mercies."[31] Rashi explains: "My own devices harnessed me, to have the noblemen of the other nations ride upon me … I myself appointed them over me." The Jewish people themselves appointed the Romans as rulers over them. It began when Yehuda HaMaccabee forged an alliance with Rome against Greece.[32] This granted the Romans far more honor and importance than they deserved. Yehuda even called on them to arbitrate in a dispute over the leadership between the Chashmonai brothers Hyrcanus and Aristobulus.[33] The outcome was that the Romans seized power, took control of Yerushalayim and eventually destroyed the *Beis HaMikdash*. "I myself appointed them over me" – by granting them excessive significance, we have only ourselves to blame for the Romans ruling over us!

The Ramban points out that responsibility for Roman rule actually began many years earlier when Yaakov instructed his messengers, "Thus shall you say to my lord Esav, so said your servant Yaakov."[34] Was Yaakov the servant and Esav the master? Chazal criticize Yaakov for this and attribute to him the following *pasuk* "Like one who seizes a dog's ears, so is one who grows wrathful over a dispute that is not his."[35] Why should you grab a dog's ears? Let the dog take his stroll; why must you get involved with him? Esav was on his way to Seir – to the fields of Edom. Why did Yaakov have to send messengers to invite him? This led to his meeting with Esav, which began with the struggle against Esav's angel. We ourselves have no right to criticize Yaakov in this way, but Chazal, and following them the Ramban, find something negative in Yaakov's actions. He attached unnecessary and excessive importance to Esav, which led to Esav's eventual dominance over the Jewish nation and ultimately to the destruction of the second *Beis HaMikdash*.[36]

Neutralizing The Power Of *Avoda Zara*

The Torah relates: "Rachel had taken the *terafim*, put them into the camel's pack-saddle and sat on them."[37] Why did she place them in the pack-saddle? On a simple level, we can explain that she wished to hide them from her father, who desired to use them for his idol worship.[38] Our Sages, however, suggest an additional explanation. Chazal tell us that these idols were imbued with a particular power (based on sorcery and *tumah*) which enabled them to reveal their location to Lavan. This power, however, could only function when the idols were treated with respect. If they were denigrated, they become powerless. Rachel sat on these idols not only to hide them from her father, but to belittle them and thereby leave them bereft of their powers. Had she not done so and hidden them elsewhere, perhaps they would have shouted out to Lavan and revealed their location.[39]

This idea has *halachic* ramifications as well. We are forbidden to derive any benefit from *avoda zara*.[40] The moment the non-Jew rejects it and no longer relates to it as a god, it has lost the status of *avoda zara* and there is no longer any prohibition against deriving any benefit from it.[41]

Borrowing Silver And Gold

We learn something similar from an incident that took place during *Yetzias Mitzrayim*. The *pasuk* states, "And He took them out (of Egypt) with silver and gold, and there was no failed one among His tribes."[42] What is the connection between the two parts of the *pasuk*? On a simple level, we can explain that although the Jewish nation emerged from Egypt with a heavy load of gold and silver, which would normally make the journey very difficult, Hashem aided them and not a single one failed to make the journey. What help did Hashem send them? Chazal tell us, "There was not a Jewish person who did not possess ninety Libyan donkeys, laden with the

silver and gold of Egypt.["43] The load was borne by the donkeys and
the Jewish people were able to proceed with their hands free.

Perhaps we can understand the *pasuk* differently. Hashem commanded them, "Let each man request from his (Egyptian) neighbor
and each woman from her (Egyptian) neighbor silver vessels and
golden vessels."[44] They borrowed silver and gold from their neighbors. Why did they need to borrow? Why would these same Egyptians who until then had harbored such hatred for the Jewish nation
and oppressed them with bricks and mortar graciously agree to lend
them their valuable items all of a sudden? "Hashem gave the people
favor in the eyes of the Egyptians and they granted their request."[45]
Just as at the beginning of the bondage, "He turned their hearts to
hate His nation,"[46] here He turned their hearts to love His nation,
so they were willing to lend them their gold and silver vessels. If so,
we may ask, once Hashem is already performing a miracle, why not
carry that miracle one step further and have the Egyptian people
love the Jews so much that they would be willing to give away their
precious belongings to them as a gift? Why must they first lend the
vessels to them, and only later, after their owners drowned in the sea,
did the Jews acquire them through the laws of *hefker*?

Perhaps we can explain it in this way: The Egyptian vessels presumably had engravings of *avoda zara* on them and it was therefore
forbidden for the Jewish people to derive benefit from them.[47] Had
the Jewish people received these items as gifts, the vessels would
have had the status of *avoda zara* belonging to a Jew, which could
never be nullified. There would be no recourse but to place them in
genizah.[48] Hashem commanded them to borrow the precious vessels
so that they would remain under Egyptian ownership. Following
the slaying of the firstborn, when Hashem declared, "Against all the
gods of Egypt I shall mete out punishment,"[49] – "wooden idols rotted
and metal ones dissolved and melted to the ground."[50] The Egyptians realized that their idols were worthless, so they were therefore
no longer classified as *avoda zara*.

This, I believe, is the meaning of the *pasuk*. "He took them out
with silver and gold, and there was no failed one among His tribes."
Because Hashem commanded the Jewish people to borrow gold and

silver vessels rather than accepting them as gifts, "there was no failed one among His tribes." No Jew violated the prohibition against deriving benefit from *avoda zara*.

Nullifying *Chametz*

Just as *avoda zara* has no significance from the moment that the non-Jew no longer relates to it as a god and there is no prohibition against benefiting from it, so too with the principle of nullifying *chametz*. Among other things, *chametz* is a hint to the traits of haughtiness and self-importance. It is made from the same ingredients as matzah, but the same dough, which takes up only a small amount of space, swells to twice its size when a leavening agent is added. The *Sefer HaChinuch*[51] explains that this is why it is prohibited to offer any *chametz* on the altar the entire year. "You shall not cause smoke to go up from any leavening or fruit honey as a fire-offering to Hashem."[52] *Chametz* represents the haughty person who "swells" his own significance and is puffed up with hot air. Hashem has no interest in such an offering, because "every haughty heart is the abomination of Hashem."[53] Nullifying *chametz* before *Pesach* and declaring it as "the dust of the earth" removes the prohibition against having it in our possession, though it is still forbidden to offer "the dust of the earth" upon the altar.

Other worldly matters, such as money, can also be viewed as a form of *avoda zara*. Their ability to control us is proportionate to the significance we attach to them. When we negate them in our hearts, we rid them of any significance and they no longer exert any control over us.

The Birth Of *Avoda Zara*

Avoda zara began in the generation of Enosh and Enosh himself was among those who strayed.[54] The *pasuk* states, "And as for Shes, to him also a son was born, and he named him Enosh. Then to call in the Name of Hashem became profaned."[55] Chazal explain this verse: "Then it was begun to call the names of men, and the names of idols by the name of the Holy One Blessed is He to make them gods and to call them deities."[56]

What is the connection between Shes' naming his son Enosh and the making of idols? The first human being was named Adam. This emphasizes on the one hand that he was created from *adama* – the earth, highlighting man's insignificance. On the other hand it also comes from the word *edameh* (to liken) as in the *pasuk*: אדמה לעליון – "I liken myself to the Most High,"[57] highlighting man's significance – he was created in Hashem's image. Man rules over the creation and his actions determine the state of the world.

The name Shes, father of Enosh, is similar to the *even shesiya*, so called because "from this stone *hushsas*," – the world was founded.[58] The world is founded on man's actions – mainly those of the *tzaddikim* who sustain the world. The names of Adam and his son Shes emphasize man's power – man resembles Hashem in that he rules and is the foundation of the world.

Feelings Of Inferiority

Not only did Shes not give his son a name with the same connotation of strength, but the name Enosh implies the exact opposite. Enosh is from the same root as the expression "*makah anusha*" – "everlasting pain,"[59] which highlights man's weakness. Enosh felt insignificant when pitted against the creation at large. When a human being feels weak and insignificant, then "to call in the Name of Hashem became profaned." Suddenly there are other powerful and intimidating forces in this world – the stars, constellations, and more. As the Rambam tells us, *avoda zara* began with the worshipping of other elements of the creation. When man (adam) feels significant, when he fulfills *edameh* – "I liken myself to the Most High," there is no need for all this other foolishness, and the whole world becomes as insignificant as the dust of the earth. When man feels insignificant, however, "to call in the Name of Hashem becomes profaned."

This brings us to the critical question: How should a human being view himself? On the one hand it is necessary to be humble – Avraham Avinu said of himself, "I am but dust and ashes."[60] Moshe Rabenu asked about himself and Aharon, "For what are we?"[61] Yet, as well as humility, man must feel "his heart elevated in the ways of Hashem".[62] The same Avraham Avinu who referred to himself as "dust and ashes" was not afraid to wage war against four great and mighty kings with only one person, Eliezer, on his side.[63] Moshe Rabenu, who had said of himself and Aharon, "For what are we?" did not hesitate to confront Korach and his followers, Sichon and Og, as well as other adversaries. Man must realize that although he is a mere particle when compared to the entire world, the world also has no significance, because Hashem is the only Force in the Creation. We have nothing to fear because He is on our side.

Matisyohu understood that nothing in the world has any power or significance. The Greeks may have had a massive army of infantry and an entire division of elephants, but what were they worth? A soldier? An elephant? They are nothing! Of course an elephant is a very inflated nothing – but thousands of nothings are still nothing. Why shouldn't thirteen people be able to defeat the Greek army?[64] Perhaps if we viewed the world from this perspective, our situation would be different as well.

The war Matisyohu fought was not only against the Greeks, but also against the Hellenists, the enemies within. Perhaps today's Hellenists have to thank Hashem that Matisyohu is no longer alive. I am not advocating taking a sword and going out to battle like Matisyohu, but at least we can come to the same recognition as the Chashmonaim. We too must understand that this world is insignificant and that what sustains the Jewish people is the learning in Yeshivos, observance of *Shabbos* and all the other *mitzvos*. First and foremost, we must believe in the uniqueness of Hashem and "dedicate our hearts to Him"[65] When we arrive at this recognition, we will merit salvation speedily in our day. Amen.

Notes

1   *Bereishis* 29:2

2   Ibid. 7

3   Ibid. 8

4   Ibid. 9-10

5   See Rashi *Bereishis* 28:9.

6   Commentary on *Bereishis* 29:10

7   See Rashi *Bereishis* 28:9.

8   See *Sichos Mussar* 5731:5.

9   *Devarim* 6:4

10   See *Nefesh HaChaim Shaar* 3, Chapter 12.

11   See *Yalkut Lekach Tov* on the Torah, Volume 5, page 62.

12   *Taanis* 25a

13   See *Michtav M'Eliyahu* Volume I, page 178.

14   See *Beis Yoseph* on *Tur Orach Chaim* 670.

15   See *Rosh Hashana* 24a.

16   See *Chochma uMussar* Volume II, Article 61.

17   *Bereishis* 1:9

18   See Rashi there.

19   *Tehillim* 104:8

20   *Yirmiyahu* 13:21

21   See *Yoma* 9b.

22   See *Melachim* II 20:11.

23   *Yeshayahu* 39:1-2

24   *Divrei Hayamim* II 32:31

25 See *Sanhedrin* 104a.

26 See *Pirkei D'Rav Eliezer* 51.

27 *Yeshayahu* 39:3

28 Rashi ibid

29 *Yeshayahu* 39:3

30 Ibid. 6-7

31 *Shir HaShirim* 6:12

32 See *Sefer HaChashmonaim* 1:8 and *Avoda Zara* 8b.

33 See Rashi, *Shir HaShirim* 6:12.

34 *Bereishis* 32:5

35 *Mishle* 26:17. See *Midrash Tanchuma Parshat Vayishlach Siman* 2.

36 See Ramban's commentary to *Bereishis* 32:4.

37 *Bereishis* 31:34

38 See Rashi *Bereishis* 31:19.

39 See *Zohar* Volume I, 164:2.

40 See *Rambam, Hilchos Avoda Zara* 7:2

41 See ibid. 8:8.

42 *Tehillim* 105:37

43 *Bechoros* 5b

44 *Shemos* 11:2

45 *Shemos* 12:36

46 *Tehillim* 105:25

47 See *Avoda Zara* 42b.

48 See *Rambam, Hilchos Avoda Zara* 8:9.

49 *Shemos* 12:12

50 Rashi ibid

51 *Mitzvah* 117

52 *Vayikra* 2:11

53 *Mishle* 16:5

54 See *Rambam Hilchos Avodas Kochavim* 1:1.

55 *Bereishis* 4:26

56 See Rashi .

57 *Yeshayahu* 14:14

58 *Yoma* 54b

59 *Yirmiyahu* 15:18

60 *Bereishis* 18:27

61 *Shemos* 16:8

62 *Divrei HaYamim* II 17:6

63 See Rashi, *Bereishis* 14:14.

64 See Rashi, *Devarim* 13:11.

65   *Tefillas Geshem (Nusach Ashkenaz)*

Parshas Vayishlach

The Eternal Struggles Of Yaakov

"A Man Wrestles With Yaakov"

After many years of separation Yaakov Avinu is on his way to meet his brother Esav. The Torah relates how he journeyed with his family and belongings until he crossed Nachal Yabok and then ויותר יעקב לבדו – "Yaakov was left alone."[1] Why did Yaakov remain behind? Why did he not cross over with the others? Chazal explain, "He remained behind for פכים קטנים – 'some small flasks.'"[2] Yaakov had left some containers behind and returned to collect them. From where do we know that they were small flasks? Perhaps he left something or someone else behind. In their analysis of the *pasuk*, the *Baalei Tosafos*[3] conclude that the word לבדו – 'alone' – is superfluous. The Torah needed only to tell us that Yaakov remained on the other side; what was added by informing us that he remained alone? They explain that the Hebrew letters *beis* and *kaf* are very similar in appearance and are often interchanged in order to point up a new understanding. This means that the word לבדו can also be read as לכדו – 'for his flask.' In this word some of the commentaries find an allusion to the small flask of oil discovered by the Chashmonaim in the story of the miracle of Chanukah.

For whatever reason Yaakov remained behind, he did not manage to complete his task before "a man wrestled with him until the break of dawn."[4] Who was this man? "Our Rabbis of blessed memory explained that he was the ministering angel of Esav."[5] When the angel saw that he could not overcome him, he struck the socket of Yaakov's hip and dislocated it, causing him to limp. Scripture then dictates the prohibition of eating the *gid hanashe*, a sinew in the thigh.

In the Gemara[6] we find a difference of opinion whether only the *gid hanashe* of the right thigh is prohibited or whether both are prohibited. There are three sources for prohibiting only the right one. The first source bases his opinion in the words of the Torah commandment, "The Children of Israel are not to eat the sinew that was displaced, that is on the hip socket."[7] The definite article implies that only a specific sinew is prohibited – the one belonging to the more distinguished thigh, the right one. The Gemara states another opinion that the angel appeared to Yaakov in the guise of an idol worshipper and teaches: "If a Jew was joined by an idol worshipper on the road, he should keep him on his right side for his own security." If the need arises, the Jew will be able to defend himself with his right hand. A third view claiming that only the right sinew is prohibited explains that the angel appeared to Yaakov in the guise of a *talmid chacham*, and we know that "one who walks on the right of his teacher is a boor." Since Yaakov was standing on the left, the angel was to his right and thus struck him in the right leg. There is also an opinion that states that both sinews are forbidden. According to this view the angel attacked Yaakov from behind and displaced both the right and left sinews.

The Eternal Struggle

Chazal's discussion of how the angel attacked Yaakov goes beyond the practical question of which *gid hanashe* is prohibited. This confrontation was a cosmic event in Jewish history. As we know, the Book of Bereishis teaches *"maasei avos siman labanim"* – "The actions of the forefathers are a sign for the children." The struggle between Yaakov and Esav alludes to the struggle between Jew and non-Jew which will not end until the Final Redemption.

The confrontation can appear in different guises. At times the nations of the world may appear to us cloaked as scholars. In their attempts to influence our beliefs, they present us with beautifully packaged ideas, all very spiritual, promising culture, peace, equal rights, and many other wonderful things. What downtrodden Jew would not be interested in equality? Unfortunately, equality has produced assimilation throughout the generations. Today some people claim that the Torah discriminates against one group or another, but these are only excuses for fighting against the Torah. Other groups try to convince us of the advantages of being more cultured, promising that it will have no negative effects on our Torah values. Sadly, history has shown the opposite to be the case.

The *"talmid chacham"* of Esav often manifests himself as an *"ohev sholom verodef sholom"* – "one who loves peace and pursues peace."[8] Such a concept has been offered to us – promises of peace without compromising either Israel's security or its sovereignty over the Land. How can we take these promises seriously? As a result of peace like this, Yaakov is limping badly!

The enemy can attack from in front or it can sneak up from the rear and catch us completely by surprise, as happened during the Yom Kippur War when the experts were convinced that there was little chance of an attack.

There are instances, of course, when Esav simply flaunts his true colors, making no pretense about his desire to destroy us. The evil German tyrant, may his name be obliterated, announced at the very outset that he was planning to fight us and destroy us, God forbid.

The flasks (of oil) that Yaakov went back to retrieve symbolize the light of Torah, and it was only with the help of Torah that Yaakov was able to defeat Esav. Had Yaakov gone to retrieve other more material valuables, perhaps he would not have emerged victorious.

Cleaving to the wisdom of the Torah alone, however, is no guarantee of victory. The *menorah* lit by the flask of oil which represents the Torah's wisdom is only effective when "toward the face of the *menorah* shall the seven lamps cast light."[9] The other candles have to face the center candle, while the center candle itself must stand directly opposite the *aron*, which houses the Divine Presence. The Torah can only assure the success of an individual or the nation when we acknowledge its Godly source. Torah study as a purely intellectual pursuit can be deadly poison!

The Torah is more than a series of intellectually stimulating laws, such as the four categories of damages found in the opening Mishna of *Maseches Baba Kamma*. Other nations also have laws of liability in such cases as an ox goring a cow. When we learn Torah we must realize that these are the words of God. The learning must serve to bind our souls with the Almighty and inspire in us a commitment to keep *mitzvos*. Learning is not limited to areas of the Torah which we find relevant at a particular point in our lives. Every word we learn, even when the subject seems to have no direct practical application, brings us that much closer to the Almighty. Learning Torah is not an intellectual exercise; our learning must be in order "to learn, teach, safeguard, and perform."

The fact that the *maskilim* had a trifling familiarity with Torah ultimately proved to be deadly poison. The same may be said of today's Conservative and Reform movements whose Torah knowledge is even less. Which of today's secular Jews has even the slightest bit of Torah knowledge? Yaakov knew that the only way the Torah could save him was to understand that the light emanating from the flask of oil is part of the *menorah* which faces the *aron*. Even so, Yaakov did not enjoy a total victory and he emerged limping. The limp was only temporary, the struggle lasted until daybreak when "the sun rose for him"[10] and he was healed. Our Sages comment on this that the sun rose higher than usual,[11] but Yaakov still limped. He did not emerge unscathed from the struggle.

Yaakov Is Limping

We may have been victorious in the Yom Kippur War, but Yaakov emerged limping – thousands of Jewish lives were lost, *Rachmana litzlan*. That war also marked the beginning of all future territorial withdrawals.

Torah centers were destroyed and millions of Jews, among them giants of Torah, were killed by that German, may his name be obliterated. The devastation of European Jewry and the Yeshivos left very few survivors. The communists too succeeded in destroying centers of Torah and forbidding the practice of many *mitzvos* such as *bris milah*. Yaakov won all these struggles – Baruch Hashem, the Communist regime fell as did the evil German Empire – but Yaakov emerged limping. We clearly see the ignorance which is rampant among Russian-Jewish immigrants, not to mention the sorry state of those who remained behind.

The wounds resulting from the struggle with Esav are not only those inflicted upon us by the outside world, but from within Yaakov himself. True, the other nations are killing, destroying, burning, and humiliating us, but Yaakov is limping from within. He was left blemished and so is no longer fit to be Kohen Gadol and perform the service in the *Beis HaMikdash*. Parts of Yaakov do not adhere to the word of Hashem, such as followers of the *Haskala*, Conservative, and Reform and others.

The wound is temporary, however. It will last only until daybreak, when the sun will rise, signaling the arrival of *Moshiach*, speedily in our day, and bringing the entire nation to repentance. Even the other nations will recognize Hashem as the true God, "Let everything with a life's breath in its nostrils proclaim, 'Hashem, God of Israel, is King and His Sovereignty rules over everything.'"[12] Now, however, Yaakov is limping very badly.

One can grasp something of the gravity of the situation by a glance at the high percentage of Jews who are being educated to deny Hashem and His Torah. As deplorable as the situation is in *Eretz Yisrael*, it is far worse in the Diaspora, where the percentage of observant Jews is minuscule. Even here in the Holy Land, *Shabbos* observance is not only not what it was during the days of our ancestors; it has even declined from what it was a mere few years ago. We hear of more and more establishments being open on *Shabbos*. There are businesses that refuse to hire a Jew who does not commit to working seven days a week. Some employers give off one day a week, but it is not necessarily *Shabbos*. There was a time when all food in Jewish-owned stores had some degree of *kashrus* certification. It may not have been *Bada"tz*, but there was still some semblance of *kashrus*. Today, many establishments proudly announce that their food is not kosher. The *kashrus* of the food in the Israel Defense Forces used to be on a very high level. Recently I spoke to a *talmid chacham* who is familiar with the goings-on within the ranks of the Israel Defense Forces, who informed me that the so-called supervision is not even worthy of the name *kashrus*. I am not looking to point a finger, but the fact remains that this is but another example of how badly Yaakov is limping. Furthermore the *Baga"tz* (the Israeli Supreme Court) believes that it has the authority to decide who is a Jew and who may sit on a religious council!

Baruch Hashem, the flask of oil still burns in our holy Yeshivos and in the homes of many *yirei Shamayim*. "God fearing homes" are not only those where the father learns in Yeshiva or *Kollel* – if a person is part of the workforce and after a hard day's work, sits down and opens his Gemara rather than losing himself in the newspaper, he is creating a home with an atmosphere of *yiras Shamayim*.

Sanctifying Time

Yiras Shamayim means understanding that we are servants of Hashem and that our time is sanctified to Him. The Torah tells us, "For the children of Israel are servants to Me, they are My servants."[13] The Gemara deduces from this *pasuk* that the Jewish people are "not servants of servants."[14] The sixth chapter of Baba Metzia discusses the *halacha* that "a worker can withdraw from his employment even in the middle of the day."[15] The Gemara limits this *halacha* to a worker and not a contractor. The distinction between a worker and a contractor is that a worker is paid for his time. A contractor, on the other hand, is paid for the job. If a landowner were to hire someone to plow his field at the rate of one hundred shekels per day, he would be hiring a worker. If he were to offer him one hundred and fifty shekels for the entire job, regardless of the amount of time it takes, he would be hiring a contractor. A contractor may not suddenly decide in the middle of the job not to complete it, and if he does so, the owner is under no obligation to compensate him, even for work he has completed thus far. A worker, on the other hand, who terminates his employment in the middle of the contract, even though he had committed himself to working an additional day, week, or month must be compensated for work performed until that point. The Torah does not wish us to sell our time, for time is consecrated for service of Hashem. We are servants of Hashem and not of other servants. The Torah does not forbid earning an hourly wage, but it appears from the Gemara that it is preferable to be paid for the job, for time should be *Kodesh laHashem*.

If a businessman or even a contractor (who is not paid for his time) decided to take out a *sefer* and learn Torah while he was plowing the field or the equivalent, it would not be considered stealing. Of course, he would have to keep careful watch to make sure the ox did not stray off the path while he was deliberating the *pshat* in a difficult *Tosafos*. If he did, he would be stealing from his employer by not properly performing the job he has been hired to do. His time, however, remains *Kodesh laHashem*. A hired worker, on the other hand, who has sold his time that should have been sanctified for Hashem to the owner, is forbidden to learn Torah on the job.

The owner or contractor, who comes home after a hard day's work and opens the Gemara, understands the sanctity of time. Clearly some time is required for sleeping, eating, and *davening Maariv*, but a significant amount of time must also be devoted to learning Torah. A person who spends his day in this fashion has spent his entire day the way a Jew is required to. If, however, after a hard day's work, the only thing he can think about is the newspaper or that unmentionable appliance, then he has not sanctified any of his time. Either he feels that he is boss over his own time or that his time is totally *hefker*. In either case he has certainly not sanctified his time to Hashem! He becomes accountable for his entire day – he can no longer claim that he did not learn during the day because he needed to earn a living, for he did not avail himself of even the little opportunity he did have to learn. One who has other obligations or extenuating circumstances and thus cannot learn or perform *mitzvos*, is absolved of the requirement. If, however, the opportunity should arise later and he still does not take advantage of it, it shows that his real reason for not learning previously was because "he prefers a life without restraint"[16] – even if he had not been required to work, he would have wasted his time.

Desecrating Time

A God-fearing home means that time is sanctified there. While, as we mentioned, the flask of oil continues to burn in many homes and Yeshivos, unfortunately this is not the case in all homes. In many homes, *"pnei hador kipnei hakelevisia."*[17] The situation is deplorable. At best they watch a soccer match and are "only" guilty of *bitul Torah*, but there are far worse things to watch on that terrible box. It is well-known that Rav Kook encouraged exercise, but he was certainly not referring to developing eye muscles while viewing that cursed appliance. (In fact it is possible that prolonged viewing actually weakens the muscles rather than strengthens them).

I often wonder what Matisyohu would have done if he had lived in our generation. The mere thought fills me with trepidation, for he probably would have picked up the sword and gone into battle. How can anyone come to terms with what is taking place in *Eretz Yisrael* today? The secular public curses every step we take, using the Supreme Court and other means to put us down. If I say any more, I may be accused of incitement to violence, so let me preface my remarks by stating that Matisyohu does not live in our generation, and there is no one alive today who is worthy of fighting with a sword. I have no doubt, however, that had Matisyohu lived in our generation, he really would have gone to war. Keeping in mind that there is doubt over the credibility of the accounts in Sefer HaChashmonaim, it states that Matisyohu's initial battle was not against the Greeks, but against the Hellenists. The Hellenists had approached the king with a request to purchase the High Priesthood. Their ultimate purpose was to infiltrate the Jewish nation with Greek culture. Today unfortunately we can see that the Hellenists succeeded and our joy during Chanukah is slightly tainted – the Chashmonaim's victory was not complete. However, we celebrate that pure flask of oil which continues to burn. We are promised that ultimately victory will belong to us and not to the Hellenists. Until that day comes, however, the Jewish nation continues to limp very badly.

---

17   Editor's note: The Mishna states *"Pnei hador kipnei hakelev"* – "The face of the generation will be like the face of a dog." (*Sotah* Perek 9, Mishna 15) *Kelevisia* here is a combination of *kelev* (dog), and televisia (television).

Dispelling The Darkness

We are not worthy of achieving success using Matisyohu's methods. In order to heal Yaakov's thigh, the only options open to us are to try to strengthen our learning, and to pray with greater *kavana*. If we hope to dispel the darkness by increasing the light emanating from the flask of oil, we must pray for greater sanctity and modesty. The slightest amount of light can dispel the darkness because light is something of substance, whereas darkness is simply absence of light. By the same token, every word of Torah we learn, every proper *tefilla*, and every act of *chessed* and charity is worth far more than the secularists' many words of insubstantial darkness.

Hashem has promised us victory, because "My words that I have placed in your mouth shall not be withdrawn from your mouth or from the mouth of your offspring, nor from the mouth of your offspring's offspring."[18] There will always remain among the Jewish people those who study Torah. We must align ourselves with Yaakov's healthy thigh and pray that our brethren who do not yet see the light's rays, return to it and not wallow in the darkness.

Causing Us To Forget The Torah

The Torah begins by stating that at the time of creation there was חשך על פני תהום – "darkness upon the surface of the deep."[19] Our Sages teach us that this refers to the kingdom of Greece which darkened the eyes of the Jewish people with its decrees. The word חשך, – 'darkness,' is made up of the same letters as שכח meaning 'to forget.' One of the terrible results of the Greek oppression was that much of the Torah was forgotten. On Chanukah we recite in *Al HaNissim* that the Greeks wished להשכיחם תורתך ולהעבירם מחקי רצונך – "to make them forget the Torah and compel them to stray from the statutes of Your will."

Forgetting the Torah and straying from the performance of *mitzvos* are two separate things. The Chashmonaim and other Jews of the time sacrificed their lives and with Hashem's help, the evil Greek decrees were canceled, so the nation was able to return to observing the Torah.

When it comes to the Greeks' attempt to cause us to forget the Torah, however, I do not believe that the Chashmonaim's victory was total. The Gemara states: "From the days of Moshe until Yosef ben Yoezer, they learned Torah like Moshe Rabenu; from that time onward they did not learn Torah like Moshe Rabenu."[20] It was at this point that the Torah began to be forgotten – the first recorded dispute was between Yossi ben Yoezer and Yossi ben Yochanan. This does not imply that there were no previous disputes, but each time, a quorum convened and a decision was reached as to which opinion to follow. This period, however, marked the beginning of ongoing disputes. It began with whether or not *semicha* on offerings may be performed on Yom Tov. It was followed by the well-known disputes between Beis Shammai and Beis Hillel. In time, the number of disputes grew and grew until it appeared as if there were two Torahs.

Today we do not have only two Torahs, we have hundreds! The Rambam rules one way, the *Shulchan Aruch* another, and the Rama has a third opinion. Many Jews follow one custom, while some follow another, and a third group has its own custom. All this was a result of the Greeks causing us to forget the Torah. The Chashmonaim may have been victorious, but we are still suffering from the Greek decrees. The oil of the *menorah*, the light of Torah, is not totally pure – there is no absolute clarity as to what the Torah wants from us and what the *halacha* requires. Our task is to increase the pure oil, to make sure the Torah is not forgotten further – "You are not required to complete the task, yet you are not free to withdraw from it."[21]

The *pasuk* states: "To a foolish one, wisdom is an unattainable gem."[22] Chazal compare this to a fool who enters a house and spots a loaf of bread hanging from the ceiling. The fool wonders who could possibly take it down and finally concludes that, because no one's hand stretches the way Pharaoh's daughter's did, there is no hope of anyone reaching the loaf of bread. The wise man, on the other hand, realizes that just as somebody placed it there, there must be a way to take it down. He concludes that the person may have used a ladder. He finds a ladder, climbs up, and removes the loaf from the ceiling.[23]

The same fool enters the *Beis Midrash* and sees the people learning a particular *maseches* or perhaps *Shulchan Aruch*. The first thing he does is to note how many *dapim* the *maseches* contains or perhaps how many chapters there are in *Shulchan Aruch*. In *Orach Chaim* alone there are almost seven hundred chapters, not to mention the other three sections. He immediately asks how he can possibly hope to learn all this. The wise man, on the other hand, will realize that wise men wrote these works – Rebbe redacted the Mishna and Rav Yoseph Karo wrote the *Shulchan Aruch*, which we have with additions by Rav Moshe Isserlis. He concludes that if they could write these books, he can learn them. Even if I am unable to complete the entire *Shulchan Aruch*, I will try to learn as much as I possibly can. The same may be said for Shas. I must take upon myself to accomplish as much as I can. For the rest, "Hashem exempted one in extenuating circumstances."[24] A person who does not even attempt to do the best he can has no right to claim "extenuating circumstances." He is held accountable for everything he did not learn, regardless of whether or not he had the opportunity to do so.

We must fight against the forgetting of the Torah and master more and more pages of Gemara, as well as more and more pages of *Shulchan Aruch*. It is imperative not only that we remember what the Gemara says, but we must understand the logic behind it. We must not allow the Greeks to win! Victory must be in the hands of Yaakov and the Chashmonaim, as we read in the *haftarah* for *Parshas Vayishlach*: "The house of Yaakov will be fire, the house of Yosef a flame, and the house of Esav for straw and they will ignite them and devour them,"[25] "and saviors will ascend Mount Zion to judge the mountain of Esav and the kingdom will be Hashem's,"[26] speedily in our day. Amen.

Notes

1   *Bereishis* 32:25

2   *Chullin* 91a

3   Commentary to *Bereishis* 32:25

4   *Bereishis* 32:25

5   Rashi, ibid

6   *Chullin* 91a

7   *Bereishis* 32:33

8   *Pirke Avos* 1:12

9   *Bamidbar* 8:2

10   *Bereishis* 32:32

11   See *Sanhedrin* 95b.

12   *Shmone Esrei* of Rosh Hashana

13   *Vayikra* 25:55

14   *Kiddushin* 22b

15   *Baba Metzia* 77a

16   *Kesubos* 11a

18   Yeshayahu 59:21

19   *Bereishis* 1:2

20   *Temura* 15b

21   *Pirke Avos* 2:21

22   Mishle 24:7

23   *Shir HaShirim Rabba, Parsha* 5

24   *Avoda Zara* 54a

25 *Ovadia* 1:18

26 Ibid. 21

Acting LeShem Shamayim

ויהי ביום השלישי בהיותם כאבים ויקחו שני בני יעקב שמעון
ולוי אחי דינה איש חרבו ויבאו על העיר בטח ויהרגו כל זכר

"And it came to pass on the third day, when they (the men of Shechem) were in pain, that two of Yaakov's sons, Shimon and Levi, Dina's brothers, each took his sword and they came upon the city confidently and killed every male."[1]

Brothers

Just before he dies, Yaakov Avinu gathers his sons around him and gives each one a blessing. In his words to Shimon and Levi, he rebukes them saying, שמעון ולוי אחים – "Shimon and Levi are brothers."[2] Rashi remarks that the emphasis on their being brothers stresses that they acted בעצה אחת – "with one mind." When Scripture presents a list of different items as well as the sum total of items, (e.g. "two of Yaakov's sons, Shimon and Levi") it generally implies a similarity, a bond. For example, in the Yom Kippur service, the Torah commands the Kohen Gadol to take "two goats – one goat for Hashem and one for *Azazel*."[3] If the Torah tells us that there is one goat for Hashem and one goat for *Azazel*, do we need to be told that there are two goats? Chazal derive from here that the goats must be of the same type: "They should be alike in appearance, in height, in value, and be bought at the same time."[4]

We can contrast this with the Torah's description of the tragic deaths of Aharon's sons: ויקחו בני אהרן נדב ואביהוא איש מחתתו – "The sons of Aharon, Nadav and Avihu each took his fire pan."[5] Not only are they not referred to as brothers; they are not even referred to as "two of Aharon's sons." We can conclude from here that Nadav and Avihu did not act with "one mind" as Shimon and Levi had. Rather, each elected on his own to bring an unauthorized fire to the Mishkan. Each of them assumed that "even though the fire comes down from heaven, there is a mitzvah to bring fire from ordinary sources."[6] Had Nadav known that Avihu was bringing a fire, he would not have brought one.

Shimon and Levi, for their part, waged a battle against Shechem, in which case, "two are better than one."[7] It was in their best interest to band together and work as "brothers." Rashi explains that Shimon and Levi are referred to as Dina's brothers, "because they risked themselves for her."[8] Similarly, we find Miriam referred to as "the sister of Aharon,"[9] because Aharon had come to her aid during her time of need when she was afflicted with *tzaraas*.

The commentaries differ as to which sin the citizens of Shechem were guilty of to deserve such punishment. Some suggest that they worshipped *avoda zara*, while others are of the opinion that they were guilty of theft. It goes without saying that Shimon and Levi would not kill without justification. Obviously they had judged them and found them guilty of capital crimes under Noachide law. Whether they were justified or not, Yaakov did not condone their action: "Yaakov said to Shimon and Levi, 'You have discomposed me, making me odious among the inhabitants of the land, among the Canaanim and among the Perizzim.'"[10]

Yaakov had complete faith in their verdict, but he believed that this was not a good time to punish Shechem, for he feared that carrying out justice would result in friction between him and the local population. As he said, "I am few in number and if they band together and attack me, I will be annihilated – I and my household."[11] He opposed provoking the nations until the end of the four hundred year exile-to-come, at which time the Jewish nation would need to fight to conquer the Land. Of course the people of Shechem were guilty, but the danger that could result from punishing them outweighed other considerations.

Yaakov's Silence

Shimon and Levi argued, "Should he treat our sister like a har-lot?"[12] to which Yaakov did not respond. Did his silence imply agreement? Yaakov's parting words to his sons in *Parshas Vayechi* indicate otherwise. "Their weaponry is a stolen craft, into their conspiracy may my soul not enter; with their congregation do not join, O my honor! For in their rage they murdered people and at their whim they hamstrung an ox."[13] Although the commentaries differ regarding whether Yaakov's rebuke also included the sale of Yosef, all are in agreement that he was referring to their massacre of the people of Shechem. If Yaakov did not accept their argument, why did he remain silent? Why did he delay his reprimand for several years, when he was on his deathbed?

We can ask the same question about another incident in our *parsha* – וילך ראובן וישכב את בלהה פילגש אביו וישמע ישראל – "Reuven went and lay with Bilha, his father's concubine, and Yisrael heard."[14] Yaakov was clearly aware of what had happened and here too he saved his rebuke until he was about to die, when he said, פחז כמים על תותר כי עלית משכבי אביך – "Water-like in impetuosity, you cannot be foremost because you mounted your father's bed."[15] Rashi clarifies that Yaakov explained to Reuven, "I am telling you why I did not rebuke you all these years. It was so that you should not leave me and go join up with Esav my brother."[16] Did Yaakov really fear that a *tzaddik* of Reuven's caliber would leave the fold because of a few words of rebuke? I believe Rashi is telling us that Yaakov was concerned that being rebuked could cause Reuven great pain. While the reprimand may have been justified, the feeling of having been hurt, even at the subconscious level, could grow slightly stronger with each succeeding generation, until it reached a point where it might cause one of his descendants to abandon the house of Yaakov and join the house of Esav, God forbid. We can derive an important lesson from this incident: before reprimanding someone, we must weigh all the potential consequences carefully. The punishment may not be worth the resultant damage, in which case it is better to remain silent. Perhaps this explains why Yaakov elected not to rebuke Shimon and Levi immediately after the incident.

The Gemara relates an incident: "There is a town in Bavel called Birta DeSatin and today the residents of that town have strayed from Hashem. This is because one *Shabbos* the fishpond in that town overflowed with fish. The residents of the town went and caught the fish on *Shabbos*, and Rav Achai ben Rav Yoshiah excommunicated them for doing this and they became apostates."[17] There is a difference of opinion among the Rishonim regarding the Gemara's point. One view claims that in this particular case, excommunication was not the proper course of action, as is clear from the result that people abandoned the faith. Others see the reverse side of the coin – even when anticipating a negative reaction one may not sit idly by and witness *chillul Shabbos*.

Rashi's commentary on the incident involving Reuven favors the first interpretation – at times it is better to remain silent.

An Inconsistency

We find an inconsistency of style in Yaakov's words to Shimon and Levi. He reprimands them: "For in their rage they murdered people and at their whim they hamstrung an ox. Accursed is their rage for it is intense, and their wrath for it is harsh; I will separate them within Yaakov, and I will disperse them in Israel."[18] The general style of his parting words to his sons is poetic, with parallel expressions linking the beginning and end of each sentence. For example, the sentence which begins "Accursed is their rage for it is intense," ends with "and their wrath for it is harsh." 'Rage' and 'wrath' are similar, as are the words 'harsh' and 'intense' – the phrases at the beginning and end of the sentence convey a similar message. Similarly, the next sentence begins with "I will separate them within Yaakov," and ends with "I will disperse them in Israel." If so, how does the phrase "For in their rage they murdered people and at their whim they hamstrung an ox" fit this pattern, if 'rage' and 'whim' do not have the same implication?

Perhaps the ideas we have just developed can help explain this. Their decision was the right one, yet there was an inherent danger in implementing it at this point. True, they were driven by family honor, but the potential danger should have led them to think twice before acting so boldly. Yaakov's silence meant that he approved their decision in principle but he believed that the time was not ripe. They should have waited. Then there was the sale of Yosef. What happened to that strong family bond? Even if Yosef really was a *rodef*, which appears preposterous, was he not part of their family? Had they not just demonstrated that family ties take precedence over avoiding potential danger? Conversely, if avoiding potential danger and carrying out justice against Yosef takes precedence over family honor, they should have waited before destroying Shechem! Yaakov saw the contradiction in their behavior. He was unable to reprimand them at the time of their action against Shechem, because the inconsistency did not become apparent until after the sale of Yosef. It was only in his later years that Yaakov was able to rebuke them: "For in their rage they murdered people ..." On the one hand, Shimon and Levi killed the people of Shechem for family honor, while at the same time, "... at their whim they hamstrung an ox." Here family honor was not such an important consideration. The two halves of this statement combined, comprise Yaakov's rebuke; he was not criticizing them for a specific act, but for their inconsistency!

The commentators differ on whether Yaakov Avinu knew about the sale of Yosef. What we have just said concurs with the view that he was aware of the sale. If we subscribe to the view that he was not aware of the sale and therefore the rebuke does not refer to their inconsistent behavior, how do we explain why Yaakov did not immediately respond to Shimon's and Levi's wiping out the city of Shechem?

"Our Sister!"

The answer is that there was no need for Yaakov to respond at the time. Shimon and Levi themselves became aware of their mistake at the moment when they justified their actions to Yaakov. "Should he treat our sister like a harlot?" They began by claiming that Shechem "had committed an outrage in Israel by lying with a daughter of Yaakov – such a thing may not be done!"[19] Why should such a thing not be done? "The nations of the world renounced sexual immorality because of the flood."[20] What a terrible sin, what a terrible affront to the honor of heaven – we must fight to uphold the honor of Hashem! This sounds very noble, but what does "our sister" have to do with it? Would they have been any less concerned with the honor of heaven had it been someone else's sister? The sincerity of their zeal was now slightly compromised. Their motivation was no longer purely in defense of the honor of Hashem and the Torah; they also wished to avenge the terrible act committed against their own sister. Yaakov had no need to criticize, for they said it all themselves. They were at least partly driven by personal bias. Perhaps at the time of their act, they were not fully aware of their feelings, but by the time they made that statement, they certainly were.

A Time Of Jealousy

The brothers judged Yosef as a *rodef*. Far be it for us to criticize the holy tribes, yet we are obligated to try to understand, within our own limitations, what the Torah is teaching us. The brothers felt threatened by the stories Yosef was telling their father. They feared that perhaps Yaakov would take away their spiritual inheritance and give it all to Yosef. Where did they go wrong? How could they even entertain the notion that a *tzaddik* such as Yosef was a *rodef*?

The Torah relates, "Now Israel loved Yosef more than all his sons, since he was a child of his old age, and he made him a fine woolen tunic. His brothers saw that it was him whom their father loved most of all his brothers so they hated him."[21] Chazal tell us, "On account of two *selaim* of fine wool that Yaakov gave to Yosef in excess of what he gave to his other sons, his brothers became jealous of him and the matter evolved until Yosef was sold by his brothers, and our forefathers went down to Egypt."[22] Look at what the brothers' jealousy over this garment led to! They were certainly not aware of it, for if they had recognized their bias against Yosef, they would definitely have disqualified themselves from judging the case against him. There were other options. They could have had Yosef judged in Shem's *Beis Din* as was done later with Tamar. Perhaps they could have asked Yaakov for his view on the matter. They believed that they were driven purely by *ruach hakodesh* and that they did everything *leShem Shamayim*. The measure of the brothers' spiritual level is clear from the fact that Hashem shared their silence on the matter. It did not dawn on people of such stature that they were motivated, even slightly, by jealousy.

Similarly, Shimon and Levi believed that their zeal was purely *lishma*, that they had a mitzvah to defend the honor of the Torah. They were not aware that within this *lishma* was intertwined even the slightest bit of *lo lishma* which skewed their normally straight way of thinking. They came to the realization that their zeal was not pure only when they found themselves referring to Dina as "our sister."

Performing *Chessed* For A Guest

The *pasuk* states: כי הלל רשע על תאות נפשו. The simple interpretation is: "When the wicked man glories (הלל) in his personal desire."[23] Some explain that the word הלל does not refer to the verb "to glory" but refers to the Tanna Hillel. Chazal relate that when Hillel took leave of his students in the *Beis Midrash*, he would walk out with them. His students would ask, "Rebbe, where are you going?" He would reply: "To perform a kindness for a particular guest in my home." Day after day, Hillel would respond in this fashion to this question, until finally his students asked him, "Do you really have a guest in your house every day of the year?" He replied: "Is not this unfortunate soul a guest within my body? It is here today and gone tomorrow."[24] The guest for whom Hillel performed an act of *chessed* was his own soul! If his soul needed lunch, then he would have to feed it, just as he would feed a stranger staying in his house. This act of *chessed* in fact is even greater than one done for a stranger, for if I don't invite the stranger into my home, we can assume he has another place to go. This guest, however, has nowhere else to go, and therefore takes precedence over all other guests. Hillel viewed eating as an act of *chessed* for his soul. As the *pasuk* states: גומל נפשו איש חסד – "A man of kindness brings good upon himself."[25]

The *pasuk* כי הלל רשע על תאות נפשו teaches us that a *rasha* who eats for his own enjoyment may claim that he is no different from Hillel – Hillel eats and so do I! There is one major difference – Hillel eats *leShem Shamayim* while the *rasha* eats only to fulfill his personal desire. Few of us are on Hillel's level, in that we consider eating an act of kindness towards our soul.

This of course was said in fun and is not the true intent of the *pasuk*. There is however a place in Tanach where we find a more explicit reference to such behavior. Amos said of the people of his generation, "They sing along to the tune of the lute, considering themselves like David with their musical instruments."[26] How are they different from David? David played music and they too play music! David's music, however, is *leShem Shamayim* – his music brings honor to the Almighty and is the basis of the book of *Tehillim*. His music was inspired by *ruach hakodesh* and was imbued with holiness. A *rasha* plays music solely for pleasure and claims that he is emulating David HaMelech. He may even delude himself into thinking that he is acting *lishma*, without realizing that for every ounce of *lishma* there is plenty more *shelo lishma*. How can he possibly compare himself to Dovid HaMelech?

The prophet teaches us, "The heart is the most deceitful of all, and it is fragile – who can know it?"[27] The heart is very perverse – it deceives us into thinking that all our actions are *leShem Shamayim* when in fact they are very far from that.

Delusions Of *LeShem Shamayim*

In *Pirke Avos* we learn, "Let all your deeds be for the sake of heaven."[28] The Kotzker Rebbe asks, "What is the extra emphasis on all?" He explains that all of one's actions, even a person's *leShem Shamayim* must be *leShem Shamayim*. A person can always delude himself into believing that whatever he does is for the sake of heaven. Why does he hate a particular person? *LeShem Shamayim*! In this way he justifies speaking *loshon hara*, being lenient in a case where the Torah dictates that he should act stringently, and acting stringently when the Torah instructs him to be lenient. Everything is purely *leShem Shamayim*. "The heart is the most deceitful of all, and it is fragile: who can know it?" What is the answer to this question? Who truly knows a person's heart? The very next *pasuk* tells us: "I, Hashem, plumb and test the innermost thoughts."[29] When a person reaches the heavenly court, he will have no excuses for his actions. A human judge can be fooled, but it will not work in the *Beis Din Shel Maala*.

"A man's soul is the lamp of Hashem, which searches the chambers of one's innards."[30] The *baalei mussar* call attention to the fact that Hashem's candle is required to penetrate the darkness, which means that there must be enormous darkness within a person. Another interpretation has the opposite emphasis – the candle must be very powerful if it is able to penetrate such darkness. In fact both approaches are correct – the candle is powerful and there is tremendous darkness. We all constantly fool ourselves into thinking our motives are sincere.

In the *haftarah* for *Parshas Toldos* we read how the prophet Malachi rebukes the nation. "'I loved you,' says Hashem, but you say, 'How have You loved us?'"[31] This phrase, "but you say," repeats itself throughout Malachi's prophecy. Time and again, Malachi rebukes the Jewish nation and each time the nation responds that they do not know what he is referring to: "... the Kohanim who scorn My Name, yet you say 'How have we scorned Your Name?' You present on My altar loathsome food and you say 'How have we loathed You?'"[32] "'Your words have become harsh against Me', says Hashem, 'but you say, 'How have we spoken against You?'"[33] How are we to understand this? If Malachi's charges are correct, why do the Jewish people respond, "What do you want from us?" A person caught red-handed with stolen goods can try to justify his actions, but he cannot deny the fact that he stole!

Malachi is chastising the nation about violations of which they themselves are not even aware. "But you say ..." is not a lie, it is not mere lip service, it is the truth! They are not attempting to deceive the prophet – they truly do not understand why they are being rebuked. Their wrongdoings are so deep inside them that they are not conscious of them at all. We can compare this, *lehavdil*, to when Hashem asks Avraham, "Why did Sarah laugh, saying, 'Shall I in truth bear a child, though I have aged?' Is anything beyond Hashem?"[34] Sarah denies it all, claiming, "I did not laugh."[35] Did the prophetess Sarah, who had attained a higher level of prophecy than Avraham Avinu, truly believe that she could deceive Hashem?

Certainly not! Her laughter was so internal, so deeply unconscious, that she convinced herself that there was no lack of faith on her part. Hashem, however, Who knows a person's innermost thoughts, spotted a hairsbreadth of a lack of faith on her part, not in our terms, of course, but in terms appropriate for someone on her level. Similarly, Malachi accused the people of his time of things buried so deep in their hearts that they themselves did not know they were there, so they did not understand what he was referring to.

Malachi's final allegation against the nation is, "Your words have become harsh against Me, says Hashem, but you say, 'How have we spoken against You? Are we speaking against Hashem?'" God forbid! Says Malachi, "You are! You have said, 'It is useless to serve Hashem.'"[36] Malachi, as we have said, is not accusing them of openly making such a claim. They did not form a political party with the slogan, "It is useless to serve Hashem! Vote Meretz!" All the people were devout observers of Torah and *mitzvos*. However, the prophet is alleging that in the depths of their hearts, they did not value serving Hashem sufficiently. One with a true desire to serve Hashem will search for *hiddurim*, for ways of fulfilling the mitzvah in the best way possible. One who feels that serving Hashem is a burden will search for the easy way out, for *kulos*, for ways to avoid having to perform this particular mitzvah.

A Tree Of Life

The Torah is "a tree of life for those who grasp it."[37] It is like a log of wood floating upon the water, a log which a person drowning in the river can grab hold of to be saved. Will a person in such a state search for *kulos*? Will he start to calculate that perhaps holding on to the tree with one hand is sufficient? Will he reason, 'Maybe I can save my life by holding on with only three fingers?' Certainly not! Such a person will grab the log with both hands and hold on with all his might! If possible, he will wrap his legs around it as well! He understands that his life depends on it. The Torah is our tree of life! Malachi is stating that deep in their hearts, people do not realize that it is the Torah that gives us life. They feel "It is useless to serve

Hashem!" When someone does not understand that without Torah, there is no life, his mitzvah observance becomes lax.

The people said: "It is useless to serve Hashem. What gain is there for us that we have kept His watch, and that we walk submissively before Hashem, Master of Legions so now we praise the wicked, evildoers are built up."[38] They did not appreciate the good life of the *tzaddik*. All they saw was צדיק ורע לו רשע וטוב לו – "Misfortune befalls the righteous, while the wicked prosper."[39] Because that was all they perceived, they concluded that "it is useless to serve Hashem." The prophet then said in the Name of Hashem, "Your words have become harsh against Me" – you are fooling yourselves. You ask, 'How have we spoken against You?' You certainly have! Deep inside your hearts lies this feeling of "It is useless to serve Hashem."

Purity Of Heart

To purify our hearts and to rid ourselves of such feelings is a formidable task. How do we keep our thoughts and feelings pure? One way is to follow the words of the prophet: "Those who fear Hashem spoke to one another."[40] We can help each other. If we are not aware of where we are guilty, perhaps our friend or neighbor is, and we can consult him.

Despite being fewer in number, the Chashmonaim managed to defeat the Greeks, with Hashem's help. What was the secret of the success of the Chashmonaim, who were no greater in number than others who challenged the ruling authority of the time? Later battles were doomed to fail, such as the revolt at the time of the destruction of the *Beis HaMikdash* and the Bar Kochva revolt. While the Romans destroyed the *Beis HaMikdash* and other holy sites and objects, that period cannot be classified as a *shaas hashmad*, because mitzvah observance was not banned until after the Bar Kochva era.

What characterized the Chashmonaim was that they fought with purity of heart. They were not fighting for independence. Despite their heavy tax burden, they never rebelled against Greek rule. Their fight was purely for the honor of the Almighty. They fought because the time was a *shaas hashmad* – the Greeks wished to convert the Jewish people to their religion and they defiled the *Beis HaMikdash*.

It was the Chashmonaim's sincerity, the fact that their cause was purely *leShem Shamayim* that accounted for their victory. Perhaps those involved in the other rebellions also fought with "the lofty praises of God in their throats, and a double-edged sword in their hand."[41] Perhaps they too were sincere. They claimed that their revolt against the Romans was completely for Hashem's honor, yet in reality it was not completely *lishma*. Yet, as long as there was a personal interest as well, as long as they also wished, even subconsciously, to rid themselves of the unfair tax burden or of the Roman oppression, their fight could not be classified as purely *leShem Shamayim*. Because there were some personal interests intertwined with their noble intentions, their war could not end in victory.

This may not have been the only reason for their failure. The generation as a whole was guilty of causeless hatred and they also lacked *tzaddikim* on the level of the Chashmonaim. First and foremost, however, their *lishma* was not pure and their zeal was therefore of no value.

The Chashmonaim not only battled the Greeks but they fought the enemy from within as well – the Hellenists. People have often asked why we do not wage a similar war today, a battle to protect the honor of Heaven, the honor of the Torah, and the honor of our *gedolim*. Firstly, today cannot be classified as a *shaas hashmad*, but even if it were, we would never be able even to approach the purity of the *lishma* that characterized the Chashmonaim, when they waged their war. We may think that our motives are sincere, but we are only fooling ourselves. At best our actions are comparable to "considering themselves like David with their musical instruments."

The miracle of the flask of oil involves the essence of purity. There were other oils available, but Hashem performed a miracle specifically with oil that was completely pure. Today, rather than waging war, "It is preferable to sit and refrain."[42] We should sit in the *Beis Midrash* and strengthen our Torah learning. We must also strengthen our level of *tefilla* and increase our acts of *chessed*. This is what will help to bring about a true *Kiddush Hashem*, and a fulfillment of the *bracha* recited by the Kohanim, and of course the Chashmonaim who won the war against Hellenism were Kohanim:

יאר ה' פניו אליך ויחנך. ישא ה' פניו אליך וישם לך שלום – "May Hashem illuminate His Countenance for you and be gracious to you, and May Hashem lift His Countenance to you and establish peace for you."[43]

Notes

1 *Bereishis* 34:25

2 *Bereishis* 49:5

3 See *Vayikra* 16:5.

4 *Yoma* 62a

5 *Vayikra* 10:1

6 *Yoma* 53a

7 *Koheles* 4:9

8 Rashi, *Bereishis* 34:25

9 *Shemos* 15:20

10 *Bereishis* 34:30

11 Ibid.

12 *Bereishis* 34:31

13 *Bereishis* 49:5-6

14 *Bereishis* 35:22

15 *Bereishis* 49:4

16 Rashi, *Devarim* 1:3

17   *Kiddushin* 72a

18   *Bereishis* 48:6-7; see *Devarim* 33, where Yosef is compared to an ox.

19   *Bereishis* 34:31

20   Rashi

21   *Bereishis* 37:3-4

22   *Shabbos* 10b

23   *Tehillim* 10:3

24   Vayikra *Rabba* 34:3

25   *Mishle* 11:17

26   Amos 6:5

27   *Yirmiyahu* 17:9

28   *Pirke Avos* 2:17

29   *Yirmiyahu* 17:10

30   *Mishle* 20:27

31   *Malachi* 1:2

32   Ibid. 6-7

33   *Malachi* 3:13

34   *Bereishis* 18:13-14

35   Ibid. 15

Parshas Vayeshev

Yosef Hatzaddik
And Chanukah

Deep Pits

Yosef's brothers, believing him to be a *rodef*, throw him into a pit. והבור רק אין בו מים – "The pit was empty; no water was in it."[1] The Gemara comments, "From the plain meaning of what is stated, 'the pit was empty,' do I not know that there was no water in it? What teaching does the Torah mean to convey when it states, 'No water was in it'? Water was not in the pit, but snakes and scorpions were."[2]

There was no danger of Yosef's drowning in the pit, yet if not for Hashem's Providence, he might have met his death through a snake bite or a scorpion's sting. Immediately before this passage, the Gemara cites a saying attributed to the same *amora*, Rav Nosson bar Minyumi in the name of Rav Tanchum: "A Chanukah light that one placed above twenty *amos* from the ground is invalid."[3] Rashi explains, "Because the eye cannot see that which is above twenty *amos* and thus this lighting does not publicize the miracle." What connection is there between the fact that the pit was filled with snakes and scorpions and the fact that the Chanukah light must be placed within twenty *amos* of the ground?

One possible explanation is that the Gemara, as it often does, grouped together these two sayings because they were spoken by the same person. In fact these are the only two citations attributed to Rav Nosson bar Minyumi in the name of Rav Tanchum in the entire Shas.

Perhaps because *Shabbos Parshas Vayeshev* always falls either immediately before or during Chanukah, Rav Tanchum was delivering a *drasha* at that time of year in which he combined these two ideas.

Some commentaries point to a deeper connection. The brothers' plan to kill Yosef was forestalled by Reuven who said, "Shed no blood! Throw him into this pit in the wilderness, but lay no hand on him!"[4] How would throwing Yosef into a pit full of snakes and scorpions prevent bloodshed? It may be true that Hashem protected Yosef in the pit, yet the brothers, with the possible exception of Reuven, did not anticipate that, since they did not feel he deserved special protection, what would have been the difference if he had been killed by snakes and scorpions rather than by the sword?

The juxtaposition of these two quotes teaches us that the pit was twenty *amos* deep. Just as we learn that one who lights his Chanukah lights at that height has not fulfilled his mitzvah of publicizing the miracle because a person does not notice what is twenty *amos* above him, so too the brothers were unaware that there were snakes and scorpions at the bottom of the pit twenty *amos* below. We can find support for this explanation in the fact that Torah describes Yosef as being "cast into the pit." Casting implies being flung a minimum of twenty *amos*.[5]

Snakes ...

I would like to suggest another explanation. Of course, we are not permitted to speak this way of the holy tribes, yet we are obligated to do our utmost to understand what the Torah is teaching us, as far as we can with our limited comprehension. From a certain perspective, Yosef deserved to be bitten by a snake. By speaking *loshon hara*, by telling tales to his father about the terrible sins of which he suspected his brothers,[6] he was following in the footsteps of the serpent, which was the first of Hashem's creations to speak *loshon hara*. The serpent suggested to Chava that the only reason Hashem forbade her and Adam to eat from the Tree of Knowledge was that He feared that they would become like Him. The serpent insinuated that Hashem was unable to create the world until He ate from the tree and that He had no interest in sharing this ability with anyone else, since "every craftsman hates others of his craft."[7] It is symbolic that Yosef's punishment would be at the hands of the precursor of *loshon hara* in the world.

Yosef, of course, had no negative intentions when he told these stories to his father, but he assessed the situation wrongly. He should have understood that although he may have been "the wise son," according to Onkelos' interpretation of the description "*ben zkunim*," the brothers were not "reed cutters in a swamp"[8] – an expression used by Chazal to refer to someone whose rulings are ignored. If ten *tzaddikim* argued with him, might they not have been in the right, and he have been mistaken? Perhaps we can draw a comparison between the disputes between Yosef and his brothers and those between Beis Shammai and Beis Hillel. On the one hand, "Beis Hillel were the majority,"[9] while on the other, "Beis Shammai were sharper."[10] Yosef, being the "wise son," believed that the *halacha* should follow his understanding, yet the brothers, who were the majority, felt that they were in the right. Regardless of who was ultimately right, should Yosef not at least have considered the possibility that his assessment might be mistaken? At the very least he should have asked his father for a ruling.

Pirsumei Nisa

We have just learned that, on the one hand, Yosef deserved to be bitten by a snake, God forbid, while on the other hand, Hashem protected and saved him. What did he do to merit the Almighty's protection? By relating his dreams to others, he was publicizing Hashem's Divine Providence. As a reward, Hashem prevented him from sinning with Potiphar's wife and protected him in Pharaoh's jail. Throughout his ordeals, Yosef continued publicizing Hashem's Providence and guidance. While he was in Potiphar's house, we are told, "His master perceived that Hashem was with him."[11] This means that every time he spoke, he would preface his remarks with "*be'ezras Hashem*" or "*beShem Hashem*." He attributed everything to Hashem. When the butler and the baker had no one to interpret their dreams, Yosef came along and said: "Do not interpretations belong to Hashem?"[12] He gave all the credit for his special ability to interpret dreams to Hashem, taking none for his own wisdom and insight. When Pharaoh turned to Yosef for assistance, he answered: "It is Hashem Who will respond with Pharaoh's welfare."[13] What do I know? I have no wisdom of my own. it all comes from Hashem. Yosef's entire life was one of *pirsumei nisa* – publicizing Hashem's miracles and providence in this world.

Not only did Yosef believe deeply that Hashem was running the world, but he did his best to convey this message to others. The connection between the two sayings discussed above is that the requirement of *pirsumei nisa*, which requires that the Chanukah candles be lit in an area where passersby will notice them, was introduced to the world by Yosef HaTzaddik.

We learn from the story of Yosef that the concept of *pirsumei nisa* is not limited to Chanukah, but is the ultimate purpose behind man's creation. The Ramban writes that Hashem created the world so that man will acknowledge and recognize Him as the Creator. He adds that the reason we raise our voices in prayer and pray in the public setting of a synagogue, is to give people a place to gather together and publicly thank Hashem for having created them, and to declare, 'We are Your creations.'[14] (As an aside I would like to add – "raising our voices" in prayer does not refer to speaking on cellular phones in the *Beis Midrash*!). The Ramban continues that this was in fact the entire purpose behind the many miracles performed in Egypt, as Hashem Himself stated: "And Egypt shall know that I am Hashem."[15] "And you shall know that I am Hashem."[16] The miracles in Egypt as well as every facet of our daily lives should lead us to the crystal-clear realization: *"Ein od milvado"* – "There is none beside Him."[17]

Chanukah Miracles

The Chanukah story comprises two miracles. The first was the victory of the Chashmonaim over the Greeks: "You delivered the strong into the hands of the weak, the many into the hands of the few." The Greeks had an arsenal of the most modern weapons of the time, as well as being reinforced by a troop of elephants, while the Chashmonaim fought with little more than their bare hands. The second miracle was that they found a flask containing sufficient oil to burn for one day which in fact burned for eight days. The more significant of these two miracles was the victory in the war, for that freed us from the evil decree להשכיחם תורתך ולהעבירם מחקי רצונך – "To make them forget the Torah and compel them to stray from the statutes of Your will," and allowed us to resume learning Torah, observing *mitzvos* and serving in the *Beis HaMikdash*. On the other hand, the victory in the war did less to reveal Hashem's glory to the world than did the miracle of the flask of oil. Because history has witnessed other weaker and smaller nations defeating greater and stronger ones, the victory in the war was not clear evidence of "*Ein od milvado.*" It could be argued that perhaps Yehuda HaMaccabee and Matisyohu were simply more adept at military strategy.

There is no way, however, to attribute to any laws of nature the reality of a flask with one day's supply of oil that burned for eight days. The fact that the oil burned for eight days proves that the entire story, including the victory in the war, was a miracle from Hashem. This may explain why Chazal chose to enact lighting candles as our way of expressing our gratitude to the Almighty for the miracles of Chanukah and for the fact that "the kingdom was returned to Israel for more than two hundred years."[18] It is interesting to note that although Hallel is recited on several occasions, the Rambam chose the laws of Chanukah to elaborate on the *halachos* of Hallel. I would like to suggest an explanation based on the Rambam's emphasis that "the kingdom was returned to Israel for more than two hundred years." Among the reasons suggested by the Gemara for not reciting Hallel on Purim is that even after the great miracle of Purim, "We are still servants of Achashverosh,"[19] and we therefore cannot declare "Hallelukah, Give praise, you servants of Hashem."[20] The Rambam is teaching us that Chanukah, unlike Purim, was a total redemption; we were no longer subjects of Antiochus. On Chanukah, as on Pesach, we went from servitude to complete freedom and can thus declare, "Give praise, you servants of Hashem."

Two Redemptions

We find a similar idea in the *halachos* of Purim. The Gemara discusses whether during a leap year Purim should be observed in the first or the second Adar.[21] The Gemara tells us that the rule of "We do not pass over the opportunity to perform *mitzvos*,"[22] would dictate that the first Adar takes precedence. Yet we delay our observance of Purim until the second Adar, which is adjacent to the month of Nisan, because "the juxtaposition of the redemption of Purim to the redemption of Pesach is even more worthwhile."[23] Why is it so crucial that we link these two redemptions, so that it takes precedence over the rule of "We do not pass over the opportunity to perform *mitzvos?*"

I would like to suggest an answer along the lines of what we have just discussed. The miracle of Purim can easily be viewed as having come about through natural means. A drunken king kills his wife, takes himself a new wife, and then appoints as chief minister an evil Jew-hater who wishes to destroy the Jewish people, God forbid. The king's new wife then convinces the king that the evil minister should be replaced by Mordechai the Jew. Nothing in this story appears beyond the limits of nature. We know that Hashem decreed that a wicked Jew-hater rise to power in accursed Germany and it was Hashem who decreed his downfall, even though his defeat could be attributed to the fact that the entire world fought against him. We might understand this, but there are people who attribute everything to the laws of nature. To prevent us from entertaining these heretical thoughts, the miracle of Purim is celebrated right before the anniversary of the exodus from Egypt. There can be no denying that Hashem took us out of Egypt. There is no natural way to explain how the Egyptians' water turned to blood while the Jewish people were able to drink pure water. The same may be said about all the other plagues. The observance of Purim close to Pesach teaches us that just as it was Hashem who took us out from Egypt, it was He who brought salvation to the Jewish people in Shushan. By the same token, the miracle of the oil's burning for eight days teaches us that the victory in the war against the Greeks was not due to any law of nature or to Matisyohu's strategic ability (We have no record of his having undergone officer training.) The victory came about because it was Hashem's will that this war should defy the laws of nature and that the few and the weak defeat the many and the strong.

Present It To Your Governor

When Chazal instituted the observance of Chanukah, they ordained three levels: basic observance, *mehadrin*, and *mehadrin min hamehadrin*. We do not find such gradations when it comes to keeping other *mitzvos*. Why are there not three levels of fulfilling the mitzvah of eating matzah on the first night of Pesach, the basic mitzvah being a *kezayis*, while the *mehadrin* eat twice that, and the *mehadrin min hamehadrin* eat three *kezeisim*?

The mitzvah of lighting Chanukah candles was chosen to institute the requirement of *hiddur* in order to make amends for the days of Malachi when the people did not beautify the service of Hashem sufficiently. As we mentioned[24], Malachi chastised the people: "When you present a blind animal for sacrifice, is nothing wrong? And when you present a lame or sick animal, is nothing wrong? Present it, if you please, to your governor: would he be pleased with you or show you favor?"[25] If you had to bring an animal to the Persian governor, you would not even consider bringing one that is blind or sick. Only when an offering must be brought to the *Beis HaMikdash*, do you bring such animals. Why? "It is as if you said ... 'The Table of Hashem is repulsive.'" Your service is only a show; in the depths of your hearts, you do not see any value in the *Beis HaMikdash* service or in bringing offerings. As a result you see no reason why you should offer a beautiful animal.

The idea of "Present it, if you please, to your governor," applies to us as well. When we *daven* we must dress as if we are standing before a King or senior officer.[26] Would you appear before the governor with your shirt sticking out? You would take your appearance more seriously. How much more so must we take care to dress properly when standing in prayer before the King of kings!

Of *Pilim* And *Tilim*

The lack of respect for the service which was prevalent during the period of the second *Beis HaMikdash*, when Malachi prophesied, was responsible for the phenomenon of Hellenism. The Hellenists saw no beauty in the *Beis HaMikdash*. When they watched the service being carried out without beauty or enthusiasm, they thought, 'Why not join the Greeks? They have so much beauty and glory!' Along came the Chashmonaim who were able to see beyond superficial beauty. The Greeks had thousands of soldiers and thousands of elephants, yet the Chashmonaim understood that the entire Greek army is actually nothing. Compared with the will of Hashem, nothing has any significance. From this perspective we can understand how thirteen people waged war against the entire Greek army. Others joined them later, but it all began with the members of the Chashmonaim family.[27] We must understand that "Nothing prevents Hashem from saving, whether through many or through few."[28] What can the greatest army do against the will of Hashem? Nothing! If so, thirteen people cleaving to Hashem can overpower the entire Greek army with its thousands of soldiers and elephants. Today instead of elephants (*pilim*) our enemies have missiles (*tilim*), but there really is no difference!

External Vs. Internal Beauty

If a major aspect of the Chanukah lights, as we have just discussed, is the concept of *hiddur* mitzvah, we would expect this idea of *hiddur* to express itself on another level as well. Chazal might have decreed that the basic mitzvah could be accomplished with a tin *menorah*, that the *mehadrin* use one made of silver, and that the *mehadrin min hamehadrin* use a golden *menorah*. Yet we find that the *menorah* has the same status as other *mitzvos* when it comes to the idea of *hiddur* – a person need not spend more than a third above the basic price. If a tin *menorah* can be purchased for ten shekels, we need not spend more than fifteen shekels on fulfilling this mitzvah. (The additional five shekels is a third of the total of fifteen.) Why is this so? This was the nature of the Chanukah miracle. There were two items missing that prevented the Chashmonaim from kindling the *menorah* in the *Beis HaMikdash* – pure oil and the *menorah*, for in addition to defiling all the oils, the Greeks had plundered all the vessels of the *Beis HaMikdash.*[29] Hashem miraculously allowed the people to find pure olive oil as well as causing one day's worth of oil to burn for eight days. This left sufficient time for the people to become ritually pure and able to produce their own oil. Why was there no miracle for the *menorah* itself? Why did they have to light on bronze sticks plated with tin? Why was it that only later, when *Klal Yisrael* had more means, that they were able to purchase a *menorah* of silver, and as their wealth increased even more, they obtained one made of gold?[30] "Is the hand of Hashem limited?"[31] Was He unable to produce a golden *menorah* for them, just as He had produced that little bit of oil that defied all the laws of nature and burned for eight days?

We can reinforce this question by noting that the *menorah* was made from gold not for esthetic considerations alone. It had *halachic* ramifications as well. Although it was preferable for all the vessels in the *Beis HaMikdash* to be made of gold, there was a special *halachic* preference for a golden *menorah* which did not apply to the other vessels. This means that if there was a limited amount of gold available, first the *menorah* must be constructed out of gold, with the remainder going to the other vessels. *Halacha* regards a golden *menorah* very differently from one made of other materials. For example, Chazal tell us, "If the *menorah* is produced out of gold, then it must be produced with goblets, knobs, and flowers. If the *menorah* is not produced out of gold then it does not have to be produced with goblets, knobs, and flowers."[32] If a golden *menorah* is so significant, why did Hashem not provide the Jews at the time of the Chashmonaim with a miracle *menorah* to enable them to observe the mitzvah in the best possible manner?

It appears to me that this is the explanation: Hashem wished to teach us an important concept. It is true that the external beauty of *mitzvos* must be maintained. An animal which is blind, lame, or sick should not be brought to the *Beis HaMikdash*, as Malachi reminded the nation in his rebuke. It is true that not caring about the appearance of the offerings led to Hellenism. Even so, what is inside is of greater significance than all these externalities. The essence of the battle of the Chashmonaim against the Greeks was the clash between internal beauty and external beauty. Our Torah is the spiritual essence of the world, while Greek culture is physical and external. Rav Yehuda HaLevi compares Greek culture to a flower whose beauty is only external. It does not possess any fruits which can provide satisfaction.

The gold of the *menorah*, as opposed to tin, is an external distinguishing mark which even a non-Jew can detect. Pure olive oil symbolizes that which is internal. The best microscope in the world cannot identify the difference between *tahor* and *tamei* oil; only the *halacha* can distinguish between the two. As much as Hashem wishes us to serve Him with external beauty, what is inside counts more. For this reason Hashem did not send *Am Yisrael* a golden *menorah*. The miracle occurred specifically with the oil to give us the message that the principal service of Hashem is spiritual, not physical. The fire itself symbolizes both Torah and the enduring flame of the Jewish soul.

A synagogue must also be beautiful and well cared for, but this is not enough. In the Talmud Yerushalmi, Chazal relate the story of two people who passed a synagogue. One said to the other, "Look at how much money my forefathers invested in this synagogue." His friend turned to him and said, "Look at how many souls your forefathers invested in this synagogue."[33] The friend was protesting that rather than beautifying the synagogue, the money would have been better spent teaching Torah and supporting Torah scholars. First and foremost, we must emphasize the internal aspects of a mitzvah and make sure that they are taken care of. Only then may we spend money on external *hiddurim*.

Destroying One's Property With His Own Hands

Shlomo HaMelech, the wisest of all men, teaches us "One who grows lax in his work is also a brother to the master of destruction."[34] The *Mesilas Yesharim* points out that there is little difference in the end result between one who intentionally destroys and one who is not destructive, yet neglects his business.[35] Shlomo HaMelech illustrates this point with an example: a person can enter his vineyard and chop down his vines with an axe, thus destroying his property with his own hands, or he can accomplish the same act of destruction by neglecting to prune and water the vineyard.[36] There is a very small difference between being lazy and being destructive.

Let us return to the two sayings of Rav Tanchum. Perhaps we can use this idea to reach another understanding of their juxtaposition. Yosef HaTzaddik, on his level, was guilty of *loshon hara*. The Greek decrees came about because of *loshon hara* – wicked people from within the Jewish camp informed on their own people to Antiochus and his reaction was to slap evil decrees on the Jewish nation. Eventually salvation came about through the miracle of Chanukah. By juxtaposing these two sayings, the Gemara is teaching us that one who is lax in his fulfillment of the mitzvah and does not place the *menorah* in the proper position, has failed to publicize the good that Hashem has done for us. Refraining from publicizing Hashem's good is tantamount to having spoken *loshon hara*: "One who grows lax in his work is also a brother to the master of destruction."

The Gemara asks a question: "Rav Yitzchak says: 'What is alluded to by the verse, 'Is there indeed silence? Righteousness should you speak; with equity should you judge people?'[37] What is a person's vocation in this world? He should render himself silent like a mute. It might be thought that this pertains even to matters of Torah. Scripture therefore states: 'Righteousness should you speak.'"[38] We cannot remain totally silent; it is imperative that we speak, but we should limit our speech to "righteousness" – to words of Torah. Perhaps the principle of "One who grows lax in his work is also a brother to the master of destruction" can be applied here. It is highly commendable to refrain from speaking *loshon hara*, but if a person stops there and does not use the power of speech to learn Torah, he is not far from having spoken *loshon hara*. It is our obligation to spread the light of Torah and to spread the word of Hashem's miracles. It is not enough to refrain from speech even if it means never saying anything forbidden.

Chazal established eight days in which we praise Hashem and thank Him for our salvation. The Rama[39] mentions the *minhag* of eating dairy foods, which commemorates the miracle of Yehudis, who made the Greek ruler drowsy with milk and killed him when he had fallen asleep. There is also the popular *minhag* of eating foods fried in oil to commemorate the oil which burned for eight days instead of one. I am not saying that we should not enjoy our *latkes*, but our primary obligation during Chanukah is to praise and thank Hashem for the miracle He performed for us.

The Gemara asks, "What is the remedy for a speaker of *loshon hara*? ... He should engage in the study of Torah, as it says, 'The cure of a tongue is the Tree of Life.'[40] Tongue refers to *loshon hara* ... and the Tree of Life refers to Torah."[41] The remedy for the sin of *loshon hara* which, as we mentioned, led to the Greek decrees, is to speak words of Torah.

When "the voice is the voice of Yaakov,[42] then "the hands of Esav"[43] cannot rule over us. Strengthening the voice of Torah can save us not only from Esav but also from Yishmael, our current enemy: קול ה' חצב להבות אש – "The voice of Hashem cleaves with the shafts of fire."[44] Perhaps we can say that the voice of Hashem cleaves with the shafts of fire caused by the Molotov cocktails and the explosions.

קול ה' יחיל מדבר יחיל ה' מדבר קדש – "The voice of Hashem convulses the wilderness; Hashem convulses the wilderness of Kadesh."[45] The wilderness of Kadesh refers to Yishmael, for the angel of Hashem revealed himself to Yishmael's mother between Kadesh and Bared.[46] With the help of the voice of Hashem, we will be able to overcome the explosions and even the nation referred to as *"pereh adam"* – a "wild man."[47] May we merit once again to fulfill, "וטהרו את מקדשך והדליקו נרות בחצרות קדשך" – "They cleansed Your Temple, purified the site of Your Holiness and kindled lights in the Courtyard of Your Sanctuary," or perhaps in the Sanctuary itself, speedily in our day. Amen.

Notes

1   *Bereishis* 37:24

2   *Shabbos* 22a

3   Ibid.

4   *Bereishis* 37:22

5   See *Meila* 11b – *Tosafos*: *"Dishun"* and *Tosafos* Yom Tov on *Tamid Perek* 1, Mishna 4.

6   See Rashi, *Bereishis* 37:2 for an elaboration.

7   Rashi, *Bereishis* 3:5

8   *Sanhedrin* 33a

9   *Yevamos* 14a

10   Ibid.

11   *Bereishis* 39:3

12   *Bereishis* 40:8

13   *Bereishis* 41:16

14   Ramban's commentary to *Shmos* 13:16

15   *Shemos* 7:5

16   *Shemos* 6:7

17   *Devarim* 4:35

18   Rambam, *Hilchos* Chanukah 3:1

19   *Megilla* 14a

20   *Tehillim* 113:1

21   See *Megilla* 6b

22   Ibid.

23   Ibid.

24   See *Parshas Toldos.*

25   Malachi 1:7-8

26   See *Shulchan Aruch, Orach Chaim* 91:5.

27   See Rashi, *Devarim* 33:11.

28   Shmuel I 14:6

29   See Rashi *Avoda Zara* 43a.

30   See *Avoda Zara* there.

31   *Bamidbar* 11:23

32   *Menachos* 28a. See also Rambam, *Hilchos Beis HaBechira* 3:2-4.

33   Yerushalmi *Peah, Perek* 8, *Halacha* 8

34   *Mishle* 18:9

35   *Mesilas Yesharim,* Perek 6

36   See *Mishle* 24:30-34

37   *Tehillim* 58:2

38   *Chullin* 89a

39   *Orach Chaim* 670:2

40   *Mishle* 15:4

41   *Erchin* 15b

42   *Bereishis* 27:22

43   Ibid.

44   *Tehillim* 29:7

45   Ibid. 9

46   See *Bereishis* 16:14

47   *Bereishis* 16:12

When Man Judges His Fellow

Who's The Bad Guy?

It is very difficult to discuss the saga of Yosef and his brothers. It is never easy to understand the true meaning behind the Torah's description of the shortcomings and sins of personalities in the Tanach, but one thing was always clear until this incident. We knew who was the "good guy" and who was the "bad guy." There was no question in our minds whether we should identify with Kayin or Hevel, Avraham or Lot, Avraham or Amrafel, Yitzchak or Yishmael, Yaakov or Esav. When speaking of Yosef and his brothers, however, the distinction between "good" and "bad" becomes more complex, for both sides of the dispute were *tzaddikim gemurim*! "*Kulam ahuvim, kulam berurim*" – "all are beloved, all are flawless,"[1] all are giants of the world. All of their names are inscribed on the shoulders and heart of the Kohen Gadol[2] "in order that the Holy One Blessed is He, should see the names of the Tribes written before Him and give thought to their righteousness."[3] At the same time, we cannot ignore the terrible feud between them, the senseless hatred, their ganging-up against their own brother with intent to kill him and in the end selling him into slavery. How can we begin to understand?

The truth is that these events are well beyond our comprehension. We have no grasp of who these giants were, not of their righteousness, nor of their shortcomings. However, this section is included in the Torah for us to study and analyze as best we can. At the same time we must realize our own limitations and inability to comprehend such matters fully.

At face value, the very idea of trying to kill such a *tzaddik* and in the end selling him into slavery seems preposterous. What could

Yosef possibly have done that his brothers felt deserved such a punishment?

The Torah tells us: "Then they took him, and cast him into the pit ... and they sat to eat bread."[4] Why does the Torah stress that they sat down to eat? The Torah wishes us to gain some insight into what exactly took place. The *halacha* states: "A *Sanhedrin* who carried out a death penalty cannot eat the entire day."[5] This is one of the many *halachos* derived from the *pasuk*, "You shall not eat over the blood."[6] How can they sit and eat when they have just sentenced their brother to death and have carried out the sentence by casting him into a pit filled with snakes and scorpions? Furthermore, after the brothers judge Yosef, Yehuda stands up and says, "What gain will there be if we kill our brother and cover up his blood? Come let us sell him to the Ishmaelites – but let our hand not be upon him."[7] If Yosef is truly guilty of a capital crime, they cannot sell him to the Ishmaelites or punish him in any other way in place of the death penalty. The Torah instructs us clearly: "You shall not accept ransom for the life of a murderer who is worthy of death."[8]

Conversely, if they believed that he did not deserve the death penalty, what right did they have to throw him into the pit? Chazal, after all, comment on the *pasuk*: "'The pit was empty; no water was in it.'[9] ... 'Water was not in the pit, but snakes and scorpions were in it.'"[10] Even if Yosef did not meet his death through the bite of a snake or the sting of a scorpion, he would eventually have died of starvation, God forbid! Without a clear *psak* from the *Sanhedrin* that a person must be put to death, it is forbidden to kill him.

A *Rodef*

The brothers were not sentencing Yosef to death for involvement in an ordinary capital crime. They were judging him as a *rodef*, a person who is perceived as dangerous and liable to kill someone else. The Torah permits killing such a person, however, the *halacha* mandates that if there is an alternative way to foil the *rodef*, it is forbidden to kill him.[11] For this reason, as soon as Yehuda proposed selling Yosef into slavery as a means of ridding themselves of the *rodef*, they all accepted his suggestion and agreed to follow his advice. If they could accomplish their goal of getting rid of him without actually killing him, then why kill him? Rather sell him into slavery!

What brought the brothers to such a monstrous conclusion? Even if "Yosef would bring evil reports of them to their father,"[12] is that a reason to suspect him of planning some sinister plot? The brothers feared that history was repeating itself, that this was just another chapter in the story of the previous two generations. Avraham Avinu had many sons, yet only one of them was chosen, not only as heir to the Holy Land, but to continue Avraham's legacy as well – Yishmael and the sons of Ketura were shunted aside. The same thing happened in the following generation – of Yitzchak's two sons, only Yaakov was chosen to inherit *Eretz Yisrael* and to be the spiritual heir; Esav was rejected. Although Esav cried out in protest,[13] it did not help him. It was Yaakov who received the Land of Israel and the entire spiritual legacy of Avraham Avinu, while Esav was told "Your brother you shall serve."[14]

Yosef's brothers believed that, in the same way, he was planning to oust them from the spiritual legacy of their forefathers, leaving him to inherit alone, and to take for himself the blessing that Yaakov had received from his father: "Be a lord to your brothers."[15] This would mean that at best, the brothers would be his slaves, as appears from the dreams he related to them, and at worst, they would be sent away from *Eretz Yisrael* to a faraway land, as Avraham had done with his sons from Ketura.[16] The brothers thus viewed Yosef as a very dangerous *rodef* who "wished to take their lives, to remove them from this world, the Next World, or both."[17]

Their allegations were unfounded, of course. Yosef meant no harm. The brothers may have hated him, but he harbored no hatred towards them. He loved them. The reason Yosef brought reports to his father about his brothers was not to persecute them, but for their own good. Yosef mistakenly thought that his brothers were guilty of eating *eiver min hachai* – portions from a live animal, as well as other sins.[18] He felt compelled to report this to his father, not, God forbid, to inflict harm upon them, but so that Yaakov would set them on the proper path, so that they would merit life in the Next World. Remember, Yaakov was not only their father, he was also one of the *gedolei hador.* (Yitzchak Avinu was still alive at this point.) However, just as Yosef erred in his assessment of his brothers' actions, so they erred in their assessment of Yosef's – they interpreted his behavior as a wish to persecute them. Thus they believed they had the right to kill him.

Judging Favorably

The Mishna teaches us "Judge every man favorably."[19] This was where Yosef and his brothers failed, if we are permitted to speak in such terms. Each side did not give the other the benefit of the doubt. Yosef should have said to himself, "If ten of the greatest *talmidei chachamim* declared that this food is not *eiver min hachai*, then perhaps I am the one who is mistaken. Perhaps it is permissible to eat the meat in this fashion." Although he is not permitted to concede to their opinion without clear proof, he should at least judge them in a more favorable manner. A possible course of action would have been to ask his father. Our father is one of the *gedolei hador*; let him rule for us. If he is not sure, we can ask our grandfather Yitzchak. Yosef should not have rushed to accuse his brothers of eating *eiver min hachai*.

The brothers, for their part, should have judged Yosef favorably. Where did they get the idea that he was a *rodef*? Perhaps he intended quite the opposite, to prevent them from sinning, so that they too would have a share in *Eretz Yisrael* and the entire spiritual legacy of the holy forefathers.

The Rishonim teach us that the requirement to judge others positively does not extend to wicked people.[20] Does this imply that any time we wish to view someone in a negative light, all we need do is declare him evil and we are now permitted to judge him negatively? We must be careful; unless we are certain that someone is a *rasha*, we must judge him favorably. We must always try our best to find the good in others. The brothers assumed that Yosef was a *rasha* and therefore that they had the right to judge him unfavorably, but what gave them the right to assume that he was a *rasha*?

Life would be so much better if we learned to judge others positively. This applies especially to married couples. Perhaps if people did not interpret the actions of their spouses negatively, there would be fewer divorces than we are seeing today. When a man comes home and his food is burnt, why must he assume that his wife burnt it intentionally? Perhaps while the food was on the fire she went to answer the telephone or to attend to a crying baby? In such circumstances, it is very easy to lose track of time. The story is told of a woman who came to the Rav with a question. She had salted her meat and then rinsed it as the *halacha* requires, but she could not remember whether or not she had waited the requisite amount of time prior to the rinsing. The Rav asked her what she was doing while the meat was being salted, to which she replied: "I was speaking to my neighbor." The Rav's response was, "In that case it is definitely kosher!"

Obviously what I am saying regarding judging others positively applies to women as well – they too must take care not to interpret their husbands' actions in a negative light.

A Tale Of Wafers …

There are countless stories told of people who misjudge others when they should have given them the benefit of the doubt. A woman was once waiting at the airport for her flight. (Let us judge her favorably and assume she had a valid reason for flying to *chutz la'aretz* and was not simply vacationing there!) Feeling a little hungry, she went to the newsstand and purchased a package of wafers to eat while she was waiting. As she was sitting in the transit lounge and eating her wafers, she heard her name being called over the loudspeaker, instructing her to come to the counter to straighten out some paperwork. She duly took care of her business, and returned to her seat. To her horror, she noticed a total stranger sitting there, quite calmly eating her wafers! Inside she was very angry, but she decided to do her best to avoid publicly embarrassing him. What did she do? She sat herself down right next to him and proceeded to eat the wafers from her package – the same package the man was helping himself to. Between them, they managed to finish off the entire package of wafers, yet neither said a word to the other. Many hours later when the plane was well on its way, she opened her handbag to take out her *siddur*, only to discover a package of wafers! She realized that, in her haste to get to the counter, she must have put the wafers in her bag. It was now clear that it was not the stranger who was eating her wafers, but she who was eating his! She had thought he was stealing from her, when in fact she was stealing from him. She could only imagine what must have been going through the poor man's mind when some strange woman sat herself down next to him and demolished his wafers one after another. Perhaps he judged her favorably and assumed that she had spent her very last penny on the flight and had nothing left to eat, but could she not at least have asked his permission?

In His Place

Chazal teach us how to judge others positively: "Do not judge your fellow man until you find yourself in his place."[21] My father z"l once explained that "his place" can at times be taken literally. We cannot compare a person raised in one environment with one raised in another. Baruch Hashem we merited being raised in *Eretz Yisrael*, in Yerushalayim or one of many other wonderful cities. We cannot compare ourselves to a Jew raised in Moscow, where the value system is so different from ours. In each place there are different opinions and different ways of speaking.

I would like to point out that all of Chazal's adages regarding judging others favorably apply only when it is necessary to judge the other! For example, when a *shidduch* is suggested, a person must know whether or not the family is suitable for him to marry into. If someone suggests a *chavrusa*, he must also inquire whether it is a good match. In such circumstances Chazal instructed us to do our utmost to judge the other favorably and to try to put ourselves in his place. When there is no pressing need to judge another, then better not judge him at all! "The judge of all the earth, He will do justice."[22] Why must you be the judge?

One of the laws of Chanukah stresses how important it is to judge others favorably. The *halacha* states that if a person's house has two doors, he must light a *menorah* by each entrance to avoid *mar'is ayin* – in case a person who passes one of the entrances could suspect that he did not light. If all of mankind were to judge each other favorably, no one would suspect any such thing and there would be no need for such a *halacha*, but unfortunately this is not the case. (Today, some *poskim* rule that one may be lenient with regard to this *halacha*. This is not because the situation has improved, but since most people light inside their houses in any case, not lighting by the door will not arouse suspicion that the person has not lit.)

When we judge others favorably, Hashem will grant us a favorable judgment "*mida keneged mida*" – "measure for measure." May we all have a happy and enjoyable Chanukah and merit the kindling of the *menorah* in the *Beis HaMikdash* speedily in our day. Amen.

Notes

1   Weekday *Shacharis*

2   See *Shemos* 28:12 and 28:29.

3   Rashi, *Shemos* 28:12

4   *Bereishis* 37:24-25

5   *Sanhedrin* 63a

6   *Vayikra* 19:26

7   *Bereishis* 37:26-27

8   *Bamidbar* 35:31

9   *Bereishis* 37:24

10   *Shabbos* 22a

11   See Rambam *Hilchos Rotzeach uShmiras HaNefesh* 1:7.

12   *Bereishis* 37:2

13   See *Bereishis* 27:34-38.

14   Ibid. 40

15   Ibid. 29

16   See *Bereishis* 25:6, and Rashi there.

17   *Sforno* on *Bereishis* 37:18

18   See Rashi, *Bereishis* 37:2 and *Sifsei Chachamim* there, who explains what brought Yosef to this erroneous conclusion.

19   *Pirke Avos* 1:6

20   See Rambam and Rabenu Yonah's commentary to *Avos* 1:6.

21   *Pirke Avos* 2:5

22   See *Bereishis* 18:25.

Parshas Miketz

"Foolishness Corrupts"

Foolishness

Sefer Mishle states אולת אדם יסלף דרכו ועל ה' יזעף לבו – "A man's foolishness (אולת) corrupts his way, and his heart rages against Hashem."[1] How does the word אולת imply foolishness? In Hebrew we find many cases of synonyms which are similar not only in meaning but in spelling as well. For example, סכלות and כסילות each imply foolishness. I would like to suggest that the word אולת is similar to the word אולי which means 'perhaps.' The fool in this *pasuk* invents doubts where they do not exist. Certainly there are times when expressions of uncertainty are called for. For example, *Tosafos* phrase a question with ... ואם תאמר – "If you were to say ..." When the Gemara has a question, it often uses the term איבעיא להו which also implies a degree of uncertainty. These uncertainties, however, express humility – perhaps the question is not such a strong one. The fool, however, expresses doubt at completely inappropriate times.

The Gr"a teaches us that the word אולי – 'perhaps' is a form of wishful thinking. When Avraham instructed Eliezer to bring back a wife for Yitzchak, Eliezer hopefully replied, אולי – "Perhaps the woman will not wish to follow me."[2] Rashi[3] comments, "Eliezer had a daughter and he was searching for a pretext so that Avraham would tell him to turn to himself, to marry his daughter to Yitzchak."

An אולת is when a person convinces himself that the highly improbable is true. A person who purchases a lottery ticket thinking that perhaps he will win, must realize that he has no greater chance of winning than anyone else.

The *pasuk* states, "If you crush a foolish person in a mortar with softened grain and pound him with a pestle, you will not remove his foolishness from him."[4] The scenario is a foolish person sitting in a mortar containing grain and being pounded by a pestle. As long as the mortar contains grain, the fool insists that אולי, perhaps, the pounding of the pestle is not directed at him but rather at the grain.

There are of course instances where considering the אולי – the highly unlikely – is commendable. A person in a desperate situation, even when there appears to be but little hope, should have confidence that Hashem will save him. Similarly, a person who is wronged should search for ways to judge his fellow in a positive light, however unlikely they are to be true. I once saw in the name of a great *chacham* that the reason that Hashem created twisted logic was to allow us to judge our fellow Jew favorably.

Chazal relate, "Rav Yochanan encountered the young son of Reish Lakish as he was sitting and reciting the verse, 'A man's foolishness corrupts his way, and his heart rages against Hashem.'[5] Rav Yochanan sat and pondered this and asked: 'Is there anything written in *Kesuvim* that is not alluded to in the Torah?' The boy said to Rav Yochanan: 'Is this verse not alluded to in the Torah? Does it not say ויצא לבם ויחרדו איש אל אחיו לאמר מה זאת עשה אלקים לנו – "Their hearts sank, and they turned trembling one to another, saying: 'What is this that Hashem has done to us?'"[6] Rav Yochanan appears to have accepted this explanation.[7]

The *pasuk* which the boy quoted is in this week's *parsha*. After accusing the brothers of being spies, the Egyptian viceroy sends them to their father to bring their youngest brother back with them. In the inn on the way home, one of the brothers opens up his sack and is amazed to find that the money they had paid for their produce is in his sack! ויאמר אל אחיו הושב כספי וגם הנה באמתחתי – "And he said to his brothers, 'My money has been returned and behold! It too, is in my saddlebag!'"[8] This then is the reaction of the holy tribes: ויצא לבם ויחרדו איש אל אחיו לאמר מה זאת עשה אלקים לנו – "Their hearts sank, and they turned trembling one to another, saying: 'What is this that Hashem has done to us?'" According to the above Gemara, their reaction can be described as an אולת – "A man's foolishness corrupts his way."

In what way did the tribes behave foolishly? My father-in-law zt"l, HaGaon HaRav Chaim Zev Finkel, explained that their foolishness was in their not checking their sacks on leaving Egypt. They should have checked to see whether the Egyptians had really filled their sacks with grain as they had promised. Perhaps they planted rocks instead, or if not rocks – for that would have been too heavy a load for the donkeys – perhaps they filled the sacks with feathers rather than grain. If they had checked their bags, they would have discovered the money immediately. Not only didn't they check, but they did not learn their lesson and the same thing happened a second time! Had they checked their bags after finding the money, they would have discovered the goblet in Binyomin's sack. Instead they agreed with the viceroy's accusation that Binyomin must have stolen the goblet. It stands to reason that men accused of spying would check their bags to make sure that there were no maps or other things planted in their sacks to frame them. It is this misplaced confidence that Chazal refer to as אולת.

Strange Goings-On

In my humble opinion, there is more going on here than we can even begin to understand. When Chazal describe the actions of the brothers as אולת, they had much more in mind. The brothers appear to be completely blind to what is happening! Did it not even enter their minds that the viceroy before them might be Yosef? Had Yosef not told them years earlier of his dreams that he would rule over them? Surely they knew there was a possibility that Yosef was still alive.

Perhaps they were confused by the fact that the viceroy was called Tzofnas Paneach and not Yussuf, but this does not justify their total blindness to the viceroy's true identity. Throughout history there have been many people who were known by more than one name – Avraham's name used to be Avram, Yaakov was also known as Yisrael, Yisro had seven names, and Nebuchadnezzar referred to his servants by other names. Even the fact that the last time they had seen Yosef twenty-two years earlier, he was a seventeen year old lad without a beard, is not enough of an excuse.

Despite the rationalizations for their not recognizing him, the viceroy's actions demand an explanation. Is it not obvious that something quite unusual is happening here? Let us analyze the sequence of events: here is a group of *tzaddikim* who are probably deeply engaged in a Torah discussion when they are suddenly accused of being spies. Even if we venture to say that they realized that entering Egypt through ten different gates would arouse suspicion, did they not think it was odd that an Egyptian viceroy, Pharaoh's second-in-command, constantly spoke about fearing Hashem? Perhaps they thought that he was one of the people Avraham Avinu converted, who Rambam tells us numbered in the tens of thousands.

Let us go further. Shortly after their arrest, the viceroy proclaims, "I fear Hashem"[9] and releases them out of concern for the plight of their families in Canaan. Is it conceivable that captors would release accused spies because they are worried about the families they left behind? Even if we assume that the Egyptian authorities had a guilty conscience, could they not have dispatched some messengers with a few food parcels from Egypt?

Then the viceroy decides to send home all the brothers except one. Real spies would rejoice at being able to leave with whatever secrets they had stolen, without worrying about the life of the one they left behind. A life is expendable for the good of the cause. Does the viceroy not realize this? Furthermore, is the viceroy not worried about being court-martialed for releasing spies who may have discovered Egyptian military secrets?

Before leaving, they discover the money in their bags. Even if they assume that it was placed there by mistake, is it conceivable that the Egyptians would make the same mistake ten times? Yosef's steward reassures them that they are not accused of stealing, but rather, "Your God and the God of your father has put a hidden treasure in your sacks."[10] Do they not find it odd that they suddenly receive ten treasures as gifts? Did the possibility that the man might be their brother not even enter their minds?

Many, Many Questions

I am unsure whether I am permitted to say this, but in my humble opinion Yaakov Avinu's behavior is also very difficult to understand. At the time of Yosef's disappearance, the brothers produce a blood-stained coat and request of their father, "Identify it, if you please. Is this your son's tunic or not?"[11] Is "A savage beast devoured him"[12] the only logical conclusion? Could he not have been taken captive by a band of terrorists who took off his blood-stained coat during the struggle? I am not a *dayan*, but I find it very hard to believe that a blood-stained coat would be considered sufficient evidence to permit a man's wife to remarry. Perhaps Yaakov realized deep down that Yosef was still alive, for "he refused to be comforted."[13] "A person does not accept consolation over a living person whom he believes to have died, for a Heavenly decree has been issued over one who has died, that he be forgotten from the heart, but this decree has not been issued over one who is alive."[14] On the other hand, perhaps Yaakov did not understand why he was unable to accept consolation.

When Yosef related his dreams, the Torah says, "But his father kept the matter in mind."[15] Yaakov had hoped in his heart that the dreams would come true. Did it not enter his mind that Yosef was still alive and that the dreams were now being fulfilled? I have great difficulty understanding how Yaakov Avinu did not even consider the possibility that the strange viceroy might actually have been Yosef.

The brothers then return to Egypt with Binyomin, whereupon Yosef immediately blesses him: "God be gracious to you, my son."[16] Is it conceivable that the leader of a nation blesses a suspected spy? The Egyptians were not known for their kindness. A fly in the wine or a stone in the bread was punishable by incarceration or hanging. Suddenly we see them handling suspected spies with kid gloves! Furthermore, the moment the spies set out on their journey back to their father, Shimon is released from jail and given food and drink. Is Shimon not suspicious? Does he not realize that something strange is going on?

When the spies return, they are invited to dine with their accuser and seated in order of age. How does the viceroy know the relative ages of ten strangers? Since when are suspected spies invited to dine with their accuser? In all probability Shimon, who had been detained, also described to them the good treatment he had received. In addition, they are given a lunch which adheres to the strictest levels of *kashrus* – the *gid hanashe* had been removed, and the meat was slaughtered to the highest standards.

On their departure, Yosef accuses them of stealing his goblet and orders that their bags be searched. "He began with the oldest and ended with the youngest."[17] Do they not think that something strange is going on when once again money is discovered in their sacks? Perhaps Hashem gave them another gift! Could Hashem not have given Binyomin the goblet as a gift as well? Why do the brothers accuse Binyomin of stealing the goblet? They tell him, "You are a thief, the son of a thief. Your mother stole her father's idols and now you have stolen the goblet."[18]

When the goblet is discovered, the brothers offer themselves as slaves. "Here we are, ready to be slaves to my master."[19] The viceroy seems to concur that this is an appropriate sentence, yet he responds, "The man in whose possession the goblet was found, only he shall be my slave, and as for you – go up in peace to your father."[20] Why is the viceroy so concerned with the welfare of their father? True, Yaakov was a prophet of Hashem and he may have been well-known, but this does not mean that the Egyptian viceroy should concern himself with his welfare.

A "Magic Goblet"

In my opinion the greatest difficulty lies in explaining how Yosef is able to use his goblet to tell them about their past. Firstly, it determined the respective ages of the brothers: "The firstborn according to his seniority and the youngest according to his youth."[21] Rashi tells us that the goblet was even able to divine what they spoke about in the privacy of their bedroom. How incredible, a magic goblet! What a mind reader! Let us suppose that they believe this to be the influence of idols and spirits. Perhaps the goblet contains some *ruach tumah* that knows how to read minds. Do they not realize that the power of the goblet ceased the day Yosef was sold! The goblet was able to relate details of every event prior to the sale of Yosef, such as Shimon and Levi's action of annihilating Shechem, and so on. Suddenly the goblet's power ceases, and it is unable to reveal anything that occurred subsequent to the sale of Yosef, such as the incident involving Yehuda and Tamar. Are they not curious about this? Why must Yosef ask whether their father is still alive? Why does he not ask the magic goblet?

The questions are endless ... Eventually, after all the accusations, Yosef suddenly reduces Binyomin's sentence. He tells the brothers that the sentence should be "Anyone among your servants with whom it is found shall die,"[22] yet he decides to act לפנים משורת הדין – "not by the letter of the law" and declares: "The man in whose possession the goblet was found, only he shall be my slave, and as for you – go up in peace to your father."[23] Suddenly all the spies, with the exception of the thief, are freed and sent home!

Even if all this does not prove that the viceroy is indeed Yosef, should it not at least have crossed their minds? We are not dealing with fools here; these were some of the wisest men of the generation! How is it that they were unable to solve the puzzle? Granted, it does not take any great genius on our part to solve the puzzle, because we have all studied the book of *Bereishis* and have learned from the ending that the viceroy was indeed Yosef HaTzaddik. Nevertheless, I ask myself, how is it that wise people such as these could not have figured out the truth?

Please Don't Confuse Me With The Facts ...

The brothers were unable to recognize the Egyptian viceroy as their brother Yosef even when the facts were staring them in the face, because to do so would mean a denial of everything they believed! They would rather accept any other explanation, or even be left with unanswered questions, than admit that they had erred. This is what Chazal meant when they attributed the verse, "The foolishness of a man perverts his way," to Yosef's brothers. Far be it for us to speak this way about the holy tribes, but the explanation uttered by Reish Lakish's young son was accepted by Rav Yochanan.

The brothers were so envious of him, their jealousy was so deep-rooted, that they were willing to believe any far-fetched answer rather than accept the fact that Yosef was now Egypt's second-in-command. They had believed that the dreams were all lies based on Yosef's visions of power and grandeur. "Would you then reign over us, would you then dominate us?"[24] The obvious answer, that Yosef's dreams had come true and they really had bowed down to him, was impossible. Yosef had related his dreams to them: "Behold! We were binding sheaves in the middle of the field, when, behold! My sheaf arose and also stood: then behold! Your sheaves gathered around and bowed to my sheaf."[25] Is it not obvious that these events actually came to pass? For the brothers, deep as they are in the morass of denial, this cannot be! Any other explanation is possible, just not this one!

When a person's mind is made up, he doesn't want to be confused with the facts! The story is told of a Bible critic who refused to accept that Moshe Rabenu wrote the Torah. He would hear of any other suggestion besides Moshe. Finally, when 'his back was to the wall', he conceded, "Maybe it was Moshe but it must be referring to my cousin Moshe." On a different note, a Jew in Russia once needed to travel to a far-off city, for which he needed a passport. He didn't have his own so he decided to borrow his neighbor's. Of course the passport was in his neighbor's name, so he needed to borrow his neighbor's identity for a few hours as well. As he was traveling he kept reminding himself, "My name is not Abramowitz; it is Rabinowitz; my name is not Abramowitz, it is Rabinowitz." He arrived at the point of entry where the clerk asked him, "What is your name?" to which he responded: "Not Abramowitz."

The man cannot be Yosef! How does he know everything that has gone on in our lives? He must be a magician! What about the fact that he is God-fearing? We have an explanation for that as well. This is what envy can do. It can totally distort facts. This is the foolishness Chazal are referring to. Of course we ourselves are not permitted to speak in such a fashion about the holy tribes and we cannot judge them. I am only basing this discussion on what is written in the Torah, using our limited ability to comprehend.

When one has a particular mindset, it is impossible to change it. If one feels the pestle pounding at the grain, he will remain convinced that the blows are not directed at him – it is merely a coincidence.

Denying The Hand Of God

A wise person who witnesses the prescribed order of the world on a daily basis knows that there is no mere coincidence but that there is someone "Who forms night and creates darkness."[26] There is a delicate balance between opposing forces. If the pulling force would be greater than the pushing force, we would all be pulled towards the sun, God forbid. In the opposite case we would be pushed into the ground. One can say the same about the delicate balance within our own bodies. Without the proper sense of counterbalance, we would be compressed into a tiny entity, or we could be split apart and pulverized into tiny particles.

Hashem created the world and "fashioned man with wisdom."[27] He provided us with a way to circulate air and to digest food and even with a way to expel waste. With all of man's wisdom, the Big Bang Theory still flourishes. A great explosion was responsible for the creation of the world. Were there witnesses present during the explosion? Has anyone in the history of mankind ever witnessed such neat, clean, and beautiful results from an explosion? Certainly not, but it is the same element of אולי, – 'perhaps,' that accounts for believing in such an explosion. Why should one observe six hundred and thirteen *mitzvos*, when it is more convenient to claim that there was an explosion, despite its lack of even the most basic element of logic?

Miracles are certainly strong evidence for the existence of a Divine Plan, yet the fool is never convinced. Chanukah celebrates the delivery of "the many in the hands of the few;" the nation with experience and weaponry loses to the few and the weak. The fool encourages the notion that the Chashmonaim had superior military knowledge or perhaps they possessed strong leadership abilities and managed to unify the nation to fight the mighty Greeks. They will stop at nothing to deny the Hand of Hashem in this victory. We have no record of Yehuda and Matisyohu undergoing any military training, and Rashi even teaches us that Matisyohu began with a mere twelve soldiers.

We believe that the Greek decrees came about because Hashem was angry with us for tolerating the phenomenon of Hellenism. Nevertheless Hashem had mercy on us in the merit of Matisyohu and those who sacrificed themselves in the Name of Hashem and His Torah.

In my youth, I once came across a publication of the Israeli Communist youth movement which contained a picture of one of their members kindling the Chanukah lights. What possible connection could Communists have with Chanukah? They explained that the Chanukah lights represented the Jewish victory over Greek imperialism! Chanukah is not a victory over imperialism, but a victory over anyone who believes in any foolishness other than the hand of Hashem. Those who refuse to believe will always find rationalizations and justifications.

How do they explain the fact that a flask containing sufficient oil for one day burned for eight days? Perhaps it was all a lie, after all, only those who were present in the *Beis HaMikdash* witnessed it. Maybe they fabricated the entire story.

The Fool Sees Everything As A Natural Phenomenon

One of the greatest miracles in world history was Noach's Flood. "All the fountains of the great deep burst forth; and the windows of the heavens were opened."[28] Practically the entire world was destroyed. Even so, the *dor hahaflaga* invented a natural explanation for this phenomenon. According to their theory, the Flood proved that once every one thousand six hundred and fifty years the world is destroyed. They decided that they must prevent this from happening again by constructing a massively tall building to support the heavens! Just as we know that in every year there is one very short day and one very long day, they were convinced that every certain number of years a flood occurs.

Why should the world be destroyed by a flood every one thousand six hundred and fifty years? Because that is the way it is – 'Mother Nature.' The fool does not understand that nature, just like miracles, is ordained by Heaven.

The Gemara[29] teaches us that at the End of Days Hashem will ask the other nations, "With what did you occupy yourselves?" They will respond, "Master of the Universe, we have constructed many bridges, conquered many cities, and waged many wars. And all these we did only for the sake of the Jews, so that they should be able to occupy themselves in Torah study." Hashem will then berate them: "Whatever you have done has been for your own sake! You constructed bridges to collect taxes, you conquered cities in order to press their inhabitants and livestock into the service of the king. And as to the wars that you waged, I, in fact, am the one who has waged war,"[30] as it is stated: 'Hashem is the Master of war.' The fact that the many were defeated by the few is only because wars are fought under the direct supervision of Hashem. Yehuda HaMaccabee did not attend any officers' training course. The only military strategy he employed was that he shouted מִי לַה' אֵלָי! – "Whoever is for Hashem, join me!"

May we learn from the miracles of Chanukah to discern the Hand of Hashem in everything.

Notes

1   *Mishle* 19:3

2   *Bereishis* 24:5

3   See *Bereishis* 24:39.

4   *Mishle* 27:22

5   *Mishle* 19:3

6   *Bereishis* 42:28

7   *Taanis* 9a

8   *Bereishis* 42:28

9   *Bereishis* 42:18

10   *Bereishis* 43:23

11   *Bereishis* 38:32

12   Ibid. 33

13   *Bereishis* 37:35

14   Rashi

15   *Bereishis* 37:11

16   *Bereishis* 43:29

17   *Bereishis* 44:12

18   *Midrash Aggada Bereishis* 44

19   *Bereishis* 44:16

20   Ibid. 17

21   *Bereishis* 43:33

22   *Bereishis* 44:9

23   *Bereishis* 44:17

24   *Bereishis* 37:8

25   *Bereishis* 37:7

26   First *brocho* of *Krias Shma* of *Shacharis.*

Debts Of Gratitude

Who Is The Old Man?

The twelve brothers come down to Mitzrayim. There they are taken prisoner, on suspicion of being spies. Discussing their fate among themselves, they conclude, "Indeed we are guilty concerning our brother, in that we saw his heartfelt anguish when he pleaded with us and we paid no heed; this is why this anguish has come upon us."[1] The brothers accept the blame for selling Yosef and understand that Hashem is punishing them for it. We then read: "Reuven spoke up to them, saying, 'Did I not speak to you, saying, Do not sin against the boy'? But you would not listen! And his blood as well, behold, is being avenged.'"[2] What is Reuven telling them here? Is he trying to say that they are to blame for their current trouble; is he telling them "I told you so"?

Reuven seems to emphasize that they are being punished for someone else's blood as well as Yosef's. Rashi comments that Reuven is referring to "his blood as well as the blood of the old man." For many years I believed that the "old man" referred to their father Yaakov. Reuven was admitting to his brothers that even if his attempt to save Yosef exonerated him from guilt towards Yosef, he had not sufficiently taken into account how saving him from the clutches of his brothers and throwing him into the pit, as he had suggested, would adversely affect his father. He was thus now being punished for this together with them.

I eventually concluded, however, that this cannot be what Rashi is referring to. We already learned in *Parshas Vayeshev* that Reuven was indeed concerned about the effect the incident would have on his father, for when he returned to the pit and realized that Yosef was missing, he said, "The boy is gone and I, where can I go?"[3] Rashi explains: "Where can I flee from father's grief?"

Perhaps the "old man" refers to Reuven's grandfather Yitzchak, for after the sale of Yosef, the Torah tells us, "And his father cried for him."[4] Rashi comments that the 'father' refers to Yitzchak who "would cry because of the agony of Yaakov." Reuven realized that he was being held accountable for the suffering he had brought upon his grandfather Yitzchak. If this explanation is correct, the Torah is teaching us a very valuable lesson. Hashem brings exact punishment for a misdeed; for the direct consequences and, in addition, its ramifications. The brothers were being punished not only for the effect their act had on Yosef or even on Yaakov, but also for the fact that Yitzchak shed tears because his son Yaakov was mourning. This principle applies to any deleterious effects resulting from one's behavior, as they impact on an ordinary person. How much more so for having brought grief to a *tzaddik* like Yitzchak Avinu! Reuven's intentions in saving Yosef were noble, yet he should also have taken into account the consequences of his actions on his father and his grandfather. When it comes to *tzaddikim* such as Reuven, "Hashem, deals strictly with those around Him, even to a hairsbreadth."[5]

Mass Murderer

Kayin was the first murderer. After the killing of his brother Hevel, Hashem rebuked him: "The voice of your brother's blood cries out to Me from the ground."[6] The word 'blood' is written דמי, in the plural form, as opposed to the singular דם. Chazal observe that Kayin was accountable for destroying not only Hevel, but his potential descendants as well.[7] For instance, if Hevel had had ten children and each of their children had had ten children, then in six thousand years, Hevel's descendants could have numbered in the billions. Kayin was punished for all the unborn souls which he destroyed.

The *pasuk* takes Achav to task for spilling "the blood of Navot the Yizraelite and the blood of his children."[8] The Gemara cites two opinions: one asserts that Achav "killed Navot and his children;" while the other proposes that it refers to "children who could potentially have issued from him"[9] – the killing of Navot affected future generations. This principle applies not only to murder but also to one who causes another undue suffering; he is causing anguish to the victim's family as well. A person who suffers cannot run a happy household and will very likely raise unhappy children. It is highly probable that his children will also raise unhappy children. Today we are well aware of the effects the Holocaust had on the victims' children. Hashem will bring retribution on the wicked Germans both for the suffering of their victims and for its effects on the victims' descendants, for the spiritual as well as the emotional and physical anguish. The wanton murder of Rabbanim and the uprooting of Torah learning produced a generation of ignoramuses and *apikorsim* and Hashem will settle that account with the Germans and other enemies of Israel. By the same token, we cannot even begin to measure the amount of Torah lost because the Romans slaughtered Rabi Akiva. Hashem will punish them for this as well as the loss to all future generations who would have benefited from his scholarship.

The Effects Of One Smile

If Divine retribution takes into account the negative effect on future generations, how much greater is the reward for the impact of positive behavior. Chazal teach us: "A measure of good is greater than a measure of retribution."[10] The Gemara states: "It is better to show one's white teeth (by smiling affectionately) to his friend than to give him a glass of milk."[11] How are we to understand this adage? Is it not better to provide someone with a cool, nutritious glass of milk than simply to smile at him? The answer is that the effects of a glass of milk are short-lived. The effects of a smile, however, are everlasting. A simple smile can bring the recipient closer to Hashem. If a person were to enter the Yeshiva and be greeted by smiling, happy faces, he would more likely want to learn in the Yeshiva and provide his children and grandchildren with a Yeshiva education as well. That one smile can produce many years of a Torah-filled life and can affect many future generations. I am not saying that we should deprive someone of a glass of milk; rather we should keep in mind that a smile is worth far more. If a person visiting a Yeshiva is not greeted with a smile, he may walk away with a negative feeling and be less than enthusiastic about giving his offspring a Torah education.

Moshe Rabenu's *Hakaras Hatov*

We mentioned above that a person is judged for incidental suffering which he brings upon others, beyond the intended victim himself. By the same token, the incidental and unintentional benefit a person bestows on another is also rewarded. Moshe Rabenu's gratitude was boundless. The Torah narrates that when Moshe came to the rescue of Yisro's daughters and saved them from the shepherds, they related the incident to their father, saying, "An Egyptian man saved us from the shepherds."[12] What did they mean by saying that an Egyptian man saved them? Moshe was Jewish! Chazal offer several interpretations of why Moshe was referred to as an Egyptian man. One of the explanations is that "the Egyptian man" does not refer to Moshe Rabenu at all. When Yisro's daughters wished to thank Moshe for having saved them, Moshe answered, "It was not I who saved you, but the Egyptian man whom I killed. It was because of him that I had to flee to Midian. He is the one who saved you."[13] You owe me no thanks; any debt of gratitude you may have is to that Egyptian.

When that evil Egyptian hit the Jewish man, it was clearly not with the intention of rescuing Yisro's daughters. He must have been unaware that Yisro even had any daughters. He had evil in mind – the killing of a Jewish man as well as the many other sins he was guilty of.[14] Even so, because he was responsible for Moshe's having to flee Egypt, ultimately ending up in Midian and being in the position to rescue the young women from the shepherds, they owed him a debt of gratitude. We see how far this obligation of *hakaras hatov* extends. I am not sure how far I am really obligated to take this. Must I be thankful to the Germans that my parents were forced to leave Germany and therefore came to *Eretz Yisrael*?

Similarly, the Torah tells us that immediately after Moshe Rabenu was born, he was placed in a little floating basket and hidden in the River Nile for three months and was thus saved from the clutches of Pharaoh. As a result, when he had to smite the Nile in order to bring about the plagues of blood and frogs, Moshe Rabenu gave the task to Aharon. He felt a debt of gratitude to the Nile and thus would not hit it. Did the Nile have any desire to save him? We can assume that the Nile did not know the difference! Actually, we learn that even inanimate objects have some will as is demonstrated by the many stones vying for Yaakov's head to be placed upon them, so what would the Nile say if we were to ask it whether it wished to be smitten by Moshe Rabenu? It would certainly reply in the affirmative, because the Egyptian worship of the Nile was in defiance of Hashem's wishes. The water's turning to blood as retribution was a great Kiddush Hashem. Surely the Nile would desire to be a part of this Kiddush Hashem. Even so, because of the *hakaras hatov* which Moshe owed the Nile, it was inappropriate for him to be the one to strike it.

The same applies to the plague of lice, which was set in motion by striking the ground. Since the Egyptian earth had helped Moshe Rabenu by burying the Egyptian whom Moshe killed, his *hakaras hatov* precluded his striking the earth.

Later, when Moshe Rabenu is commanded to wage war against Midian, he sends Pinchas to lead the nation in battle. Moshe felt he owed a debt of gratitude to the people of Midian because they had provided him with a safe haven when he ran away from Pharaoh, and it was there that he met his wife. Certainly, making war against Midian was the right thing to do, as we see from the fact that Moshe sent his own soldiers. He simply felt that he himself should not be the one to carry out the action.

Of Bathhouses And Bushes

The Shita Mekubetzes[15] relates that the Rif, Rav Yitzchak Alfasi, was once a guest at the home of a very wealthy individual. His host owned a bathhouse and invited the Rif to make use of it. The Rif did so and thoroughly enjoyed it. After a period of time, the wealthy Jew lost all his possessions and had to sell his bathhouse in order to pay off his creditors. Both buyer and seller asked that the Rif assess the value of the bathhouse and preside over any required *halachic* litigation. The Rif refused, arguing that he could not rule about a bathhouse that had given him such pleasure. One may note that he did not refer to the *hakaras hatov* he had towards the owner but to the bathhouse itself. Following in the footsteps of Moshe Rabenu, the Rif would not involve himself in a case regarding an inanimate object from which he had derived benefit.

We find a similar story in our own generation as well. HaGaon HaRav Yisrael Zev Gustman zt"l, Rosh Yeshiva of Yeshivas Netzach Yisrael here in Yerushalayim, would personally water the bushes in the front garden of the Yeshiva. As great a *talmid chacham* as he was, he always found the time to water the plants. I am not sure if he watered them while reviewing *Tosafos'* question or their answer, but he always made sure to do so. Why did the Rosh Yeshiva need to do it himself? Could the gardener who took care of the rest of the grounds not have done as good a job? This was his *hakaras hatov*. When he fled from Vilna (either from the Communists or the Nazis), he hid behind bushes in order to evade his pursuers. Those bushes, in fact, saved his life, and to show gratitude he watered them himself. Were these the same plants that saved him? No! Those bushes were in Vilna and these are in Yerushalayim! It was the kind of plant that saved him, and he felt *hakaras hatov* towards all of them.

Going To The Dogs

The Torah commands us that *tereifos* should be given to the dogs. Chazal teach us that they were rewarded for not barking in Egypt during the plague of the slaying of the firstborn.[16] Do the dogs appreciate the reward? Not only are these not the same dogs that were in Egypt, but it is highly unlikely that any dog you see today is descended from a dog which was present at the time. Yet, the Torah commands us to have gratitude to dogs as a species.

All these are examples of people and objects we must have gratitude to, even though they had no intention of benefiting us. The dogs did not intend to help *Am Yisrael*, nor did the water or sand of Egypt. Certainly the evil Egyptian, whose only aim was to harm a Jew, had no such intentions. How much more so are we obliged to have gratitude to Hashem. He gives us everything, though He owes us nothing. He not only gave us life but He gave us the Torah which is eternal life. Throughout the generations He has saved us from so many oppressors. One of the periods of the year when we commemorate this is Chanukah, the time when Hashem saved us from the Greeks who forbade us to learn Torah and keep *mitzvos*.

Thanksgiving

The Americans have one day of Thanksgiving; on Chanukah we have eight days of thanksgiving. Although we must be thankful to Hashem every day, the days of Chanukah are set aside especially for this. Similarly, while we accept upon ourselves עול מלכות שמים – 'the yoke of the Kingdom of Heaven' – every day of the year, Rosh Hashana is the day specifically designated for declaring Hashem as our King. The entire year we are required to remember the exodus from Egypt, yet *Seder* night is especially designated for elaborating on the story. Although we are obligated to thank Hashem all year long, Chanukah is the special time nominated for this, as we mention in *Al Hanissim*:

וקבעו שמונת ימי חנוכה אלו להודות ולהלל לשמך הגדול

"And they established these eight days of Chanukah to express thanks and praise to Your great Name."

The *halacha* states that if one has sufficient funds to purchase either wine for Kiddush or a candle for Chanukah, but not both, he must purchase the candle for Chanukah.[17] The Steipler Gaon, HaRav Yaakov Yisrael Kanievsky zt"l wondered how the Rabbinic commandment to kindle the Chanukah lights can take precedence over Kiddush, which, according to some authorities, is a Torah obligation. He solved this by answering that when a person goes to the store before *Shabbos*, he is not yet obligated to make Kiddush, so he can purchase oil rather than wine. When *Shabbos* enters, he is exempt from making Kiddush because he has no wine.

---

17   He may not purchase more than the bare minimum of one candle at the expense of Kiddush.

Kiddush Hashem

Why did Chazal stipulate that the mitzvah of Chanukah lights takes precedence over Kiddush on wine? Kindling the lights involves sanctifying Hashem's Name. Our entire obligation in this world is to sanctify His Name, as we recite daily, "Blessed is He, our God, Who created us for His glory." Hashem created us to honor His Name and this is what the Chanukah lights accomplish. One may ask, does Kiddush not testify that Hashem created the world in only six days? Does this not also sanctify His Name? Perhaps we can explain that Kiddush is a private mitzvah carried out in a person's home, whereas the Chanukah lights are to be seen by all.

The order of precedence of these *mitzvos* is hinted at in the *pasuk* which lists the seven species:

ארץ חטה ושעורה וגפן ותאנה ורמון ארץ זית שמן ודבש

"A Land of wheat, barley, grape, fig, and pomegranate; a Land of oil-olives and date-honey."[8]

'Wheat' is next to the first ארץ, 'olives' is right next to the second ארץ, while 'grapes' is not next to either ארץ. According to *halacha*, which ascribes precedence to the species closest to the word ארץ, this means that one with limited funds must first purchase bread for his *Shabbos* meals, then comes the Chanukah light, followed by wine.

It is interesting to note that the light from the oil symbolizes wisdom, while wine is associated with getting drunk and forgetting. The aim of the Greeks was to cause us to forget the Torah. The word for 'darkness' – חשך is composed of the same letters as שכח – 'to forget', while the Aramaic word for 'light' is נהיר which also means 'to remember.' These eight days of Chanukah are designated for thanking Hashem for defeating the Greeks, whose goal was to cause us to forget the Torah. We certainly also owe a debt of gratitude to the Chashmonaim for their *mesirus nefesh* because of which we are able to study Torah and observe *mitzvos* today. This debt of gratitude increases with every page of Gemara we learn and every *Shabbos* we observe.

The idea that our debt increases with every mitzvah we observe applies to *kibbud av va'em* as well. We owe a tremendous debt of gratitude to our parents. Our parents, after all, are Hashem's partners in bringing us into the world. If so, just as we must thank the Almighty for each breath we take,[19] for the air He gives us to breathe, for our supper and our breakfast, and for the infinity of things he has given us, to a certain extent we must also thank our mothers and fathers for these things. Had it not been for my father and mother, I would not have anything to be grateful for, I would not breathe, I would not have supper, or breakfast, or anything else. They raised me with great dedication, they cared for all my needs, and got up in the middle of the night to take care of me. How much more should we be grateful to them for allowing us entry into the Next World by educating us in the way of Torah and *mitzvos* and by sending us to Yeshiva. There is no limit to the gratitude we owe our parents.

The Gemara tells us, "Scripture puts the honor due to one's father and mother on the same level as the honor due to the Omnipresent."[20] Rav Shimon bar Yochai is of the opinion that the obligation to honor our parents goes even beyond the obligation to honor Hashem. Regarding Hashem's honor we read, "Honor Hashem with your property."[21] If you have assets you must honor Him; if you do not, you are absolved from doing so. This means that if you do not have the means to purchase the items required, you are not required to observe the *mitzvos* of *tefillin*, *lulav*, *sukkah*, and many other *mitzvos* that involve expenditures. About *kibbud av va'em*, however, it simply states, "Honor your father and your mother."[22] – "Whether you have assets or whether you do not have assets, you must honor your father and mother, even if it means knocking on doors!"[23] According to Rav Shimon bar Yochai, this means that if necessary, a person is obligated to raise the funds necessary to honor his parents properly. Although the *halacha* does not concur with this view,[24] Rav Shimon's opinion demonstrates how much importance the Torah attaches to this mitzvah.

How can we pay back the massive debt we owe our parents? Of course, being at home presents many opportunities for doing so. Even in Yeshiva, however, we have wonderful opportunities to fulfill the mitzvah of *kibbud av va'em*. If the time in Yeshiva is utilized to advance one's learning, all the credit goes to the parents. What greater respect can a person give his parents? This is true honor! If his parents are no longer alive, then any *chiddush* in Torah provides them with great honor in Gan Eden.[25] This is one way in which a person can pay back part of the great debt he owes his parents.

Paradoxically, it seems to me that the more we try to pay off this debt, the more it increases. Why? Because each time we fulfill the mitzvah of *kibbud av va'em*, our debt to our parents grows, because we now owe them *hakaras hatov* for having afforded us the opportunity to fulfill this mitzvah and so on and so on ... Practically speaking, it is impossible to pay back the debt completely. Of course, Hashem would never demand that we pay a debt which is impossible to pay. However, we must try to at least scratch the surface, as much as possible.

Let us pray that soon we will be at the stage when we can thank Hashem for the redemption, for the building of the *Beis HaMikdash*, and for the rekindling of the *menorah* with olive oil speedily in our days. Amen.

Notes

1   *Bereishis* 42:21

2   Ibid. 22

3   *Bereishis* 37:30

4   Ibid. 35

5   *Yevamos* 121b

6   *Bereishis* 4:10

7   See *Avos D' Rav Nosson* Chapter 31.

8   *Melachim* II 9:2.

9   *Sanhedrin* 48b

10 *Sanhedrin* 100b

11 *Kesuvos* 111b

12 *Shemos* 2:19

13 *Shemos Rabba* 1:32

14 See *Tanchuma, Shemos* 9.

15 On *Baba Kamma* 92b

16 See Rashi *Shemos* 22:30.

18 *Devarim* 8:8

19 See *Bereishis Rabba* 14:9.

20 *Kiddushin* 30b

21 *Mishle* 3:9

22 *Shemos* 20:12

23 Yerushalmi *Peah Perek* 1, *Halacha* 1

24 See *Shulchan Aruch, Yoreh Deah* 240:65.

25 See *Zohar Chadash, Rus* 84:3.

Parshas Vayigash

More Precious Than Pearls

Honor For Pharaoh's Priests

Towards the end of *Parshas Vayigash*, Yosef purchases land for Pharaoh from the Egyptian people. The Torah then narrates:

רק אדמת הכהנים לא קנה כי חק לכהנים
מאת פרעה ואכלו את חקם אשר נתן להם פרעה על כן לא מכרו את אדמתם

"Only the land of the priests he did not buy, since the priests had a stipend from Pharaoh, and they lived off their stipend that Pharaoh had given them; therefore they did not sell their land."[1]

A few *psukim* later, the Torah repeats,

רק אדמת הכהנים לבדם לא היתה לפרעה

"Only the priests' land alone did not become Pharaoh's."[2]

Why does the Torah inform us of this detail and why is it emphasized by repetition? One explanation is that the Torah wishes to stress a *kal vachomer*: "If Pharaoh accords such honor to his idol-worshipping priests, by providing them with food and not confiscating their land, how much more so must we honor our Kohanim who serve Hashem in the *Beis Hamikdash*!"[3] The way we provide for our Kohanim is by giving them *matnos kehuna* – the priestly gifts.

The Gemara[4] tells us, "Kohanim, Leviim, and the poor, who help in the house of the shepherds, the threshing floor, and in the slaughterhouses, we [the owners] do not give them *trumah* or *maaser* as a reward. If they do so, they have desecrated them. Regarding them the *pasuk* states, 'You have corrupted the covenant of Levi,'[5] and another *pasuk* further states, 'Sanctities of the Children of Israel you shall not desecrate, so that you shall not die.'"[6] Conversely, a Kohen may not offer any form of assistance to the one who has given him *trumah*; doing so incurs the death penalty.

A Yisrael may suggest that his fellow Yisrael give his *matnos kehuna* to a particular Kohen, and the Yisrael who gives the priestly gifts is permitted to accept compensation from the Yisrael who asked him to do so. The Kohen or Levi himself, however, is forbidden under any circumstances to give any form of compensation to the Yisrael who gave him *trumah* or *maaser*. According to the above Gemara, payment may not even be made discreetly, such as by assisting the owner with some of his tasks.

Why is this so? Does Judaism not encourage a person to have *hakaras hatov* – recognition and gratitude – for the good another has done for him? With so many Kohanim to choose from, should the recipient Kohen not be grateful that he was chosen above all the others? He may even have received a large share which otherwise would have been divided among many Kohanim. Is some show of appreciation not called for? *Hakaras hatov* is such an intrinsic part of Judaism that Chazal tell us that one who lacks *hakaras hatov* toward his fellow human being will eventually have no gratitude to Hashem. As the Torah tells us, Pharaoh at first "did not know Yosef,"[7] and eventually proclaimed, "I do not know Hashem!"[8] If *hakaras hatov* is so basic to our belief, why should the Kohen or Levi who wishes to express it be punished?

The Torah provides us with the reason why the Kohen and Levi are given gifts. "For it is a wage for you in exchange for your service in the Tent of Meeting."[9] The Kohanim and Leviim are not being given handouts; they are salaried employees of the *Beis HaMikdash*! If they were to show appreciation to those who gave them *matnos kehuna*, for example by assisting them, that would be like declaring that working in the *Beis HaMikdash* was not sufficient cause for compensation! This amounts to disdain for their work, and it is said of one who does so: "You have corrupted the covenant of Levi."[10]

Recently I came to the understanding that perhaps this explains the nature of the sin committed by Korach and his followers. Moshe Rabenu asked them, "Is it not enough for you that the God of Israel has segregated you from the Assembly of Israel to draw you near to Himself, to perform the service of the Tabernacle of Hashem, and to stand before the Assembly to minister to them? And He drew you near, and all your brethren, the offspring of Levi, with you – yet you seek priesthood as well!"[11] Should Korach not have been praised for yearning for a higher degree of spirituality and wishing to serve as a Kohen? His method of demanding it – by publicly degrading Moshe Rabenu and his prophecy – may leave much to be desired, but what is wrong with the actual wish to serve alongside the Kohanim? Is this just cause for punishment?

Based on what we have just discussed, the answer is clear. The work of the Leviim was of great significance, as we can deduce from the Rambam's words: "Just as the Leviim are warned against performing the work of the Kohanim, so too the Kohanim are warned against performing the work of the Leviim."[12] Korach was in fact declaring that being a Levi was not honorable enough for him and he wished to climb one step higher and become a Kohen. Holding the tasks of the Leviim in contempt amounts to "corrupting the covenant of Levi," an offense punishable by death.

The *matnos kehuna* as compensation for services rendered is not just a mere philosophical idea. The Ktzos HaChoshen[13] claims that it has legal implications. The Gemara[14] tells us that *trumah* may be given to a Kohen who is under age. How is this possible? After all, a child does not *halachically* take possession of gifts which are given to him, so how does a person who gives *trumah* to a child Kohen fulfill the mitzvah of giving *trumah*? The Ktzos HaChoshen explains that although a child may not make an ordinary acquisition, he may be compensated for a job done.[15] Given that the Kohanim are compensated for tasks performed in the *Beis HaMikdash*, the child may receive and legally acquire *trumah*. Although a child does not perform any actual function in the *Beis HaMikdash*, he is given these priestly gifts as compensation for work performed by other family members and Kohanim in general.

Although, as we have said, the Kohanim earn a salary for their work, the Torah did not intend them to work only for the purpose of receiving compensation. The Kohen's motives must be *leShem*

Shamayim, for the purpose of performing Hashem's mitzvah. Now, one may ask if there is really a difference whether we view the payment as compensation for a job performed or as a gift. There is a major difference! The recipient of a handout is embarrassed, which is why charitable gifts should be given in the most inconspicuous way possible. However, there is no *halachic* requirement for an employer to compensate his employees discreetly. The Kohen and Levi have no reason to be embarrassed. They are employees of the *Beis HaMikdash* and as such have earned whatever compensation they may receive.

"Digging Into The Torah"

In the same way as we view gifts for Kohanim and Leviim as compensation for services rendered, so too must we view financial support of those who study Torah. Stipends given by the Yeshiva or *Kollel* are not a gift but a salary – they are earned. The Jewish nation is in need of people who spend their days studying Torah, just as it is in need of Kohanim to serve in the *Beis HaMikdash*.

Although learning only for the sake of receiving a salary transforms the Torah into "an axe with which to dig (for food),"[16] it is preferable to study Torah *shelo lishma* than not to learn at all. "One should always be involved with Torah and *mitzvos* even if not with the proper intention, for doing it without the proper intention will lead to doing with the proper intention."[17] We find a similar notion regarding Balak. Chazal[18] tell us, "In reward for the forty-two sacrifices that Balak king of Moav offered, he merited that Ruth descended from him and Ruth was the ancestress of Shlomo HaMelech, of whom it is said, 'Shlomo offered up a thousand offerings on that Altar.'[19]" Balak's base intention in bringing the offerings was to help him curse the Jewish nation, yet despite his negative intentions, he was rewarded for having brought them. There is value in learning and performing *mitzvos* even *shelo lishma*.

A person whose whole desire is to learn, who accepts a stipend in order to be freed from the burden of having to earn a living, is not learning "for the sake of receiving a reward"[20] but rather *lishma*. The compensation enables him to learn, for we know "If there is no bread, there is no Torah."[21] The fact that the Yeshiva provides him with three meals a day and, if he is married, also provides assistance in supporting his family, does not turn the Torah into an axe with which to dig for food, rather the food becomes the axe with which to "dig" into the Torah.

Just as the Kohen and Levi are obligated to value their work and to recognize that they deserve compensation, so too is it incumbent on one who studies in Yeshiva and receives any sort of compensation to realize that he is earning his wage. The Torah he learns is worth far more than what he is receiving, "For wisdom is better than pearls and all desires cannot compare to it."[22] Not only is he not being given a handout, but he is making an enormous contribution to the Jewish people. There is a tremendous need for Torah scholars and an even greater need for *gedolei Yisrael*. The Gemara relates how the Tzdukkim incited Yannai to kill all the sages of the time. Yannai asked: "But the Torah, what will become of it?" They responded, "Behold the Torah scroll is rolled and it rests in the corner. Anyone who wishes to study it, let him come and study."[23] The Tzdukkim's retort was that killing the sages would make no difference because the Torah is always available for people who wish to learn it. The Gemara continues, "This answer is satisfactory for the Written Torah, but what of the Oral Torah?"[24] The Written Torah may be placed in a corner, but without sages and Torah giants to interpret it and explain it to us, we cannot possibly understand it. This did not bother the Tzdukkim, because they denied the existence of the Oral Torah in any case. We, however, understand that without Torah sages, there can be no one to teach the Torah. Having people devote their lives to the study of Torah is of the utmost importance, and it is up to us to ensure that there will be a next generation of *gedolim*.

Raising Future *Gedolim*

In a similar vein, the Gemara tells us, "If either he or his son can study, he takes precedence over his son."[25] In other words, if at any particular time it is impossible for both the father and son to learn Torah, if, for example, there is urgent work to be done in the house, the father's obligation to learn takes precedence. Rav Yehuda qualifies this: "If his son is diligent, bright, and retains that which he has studied, his son takes precedence over him."[26] In fact, this is the *halacha*. Why? Although the son cannot fulfill his father's obligation of Talmud Torah by his own learning, we have an additional obligation to produce *gedolei Yisrael*. Rav Yehuda is of the opinion that this obligation is greater than one's personal obligation to learn. Thus, if the son has the potential to become a *gadol*, his obligation takes precedence. Where would we be without *gedolei Yisrael*? What would have become of *Shabbos* observance without the *Mishna Brura* and *Shmiras Shabbos Kehilchasa*? A person can master the entire *Shulchan Aruch* and still not know whether or not he is permitted to answer his telephone on *Shabbos*. New situations arise in each generation, and without *gedolim*, there would be no one to rule on such issues. One can argue, "When in doubt follow the more stringent view," but this is not always a practical approach. Only *gedolim* can guide us in these areas and teach us what is permitted under extenuating circumstances and what is forbidden even in such situations.

We are in need not only of *gedolei Torah*, but also of other holy vocations such as Rabbonim, *soferim*, *mohalim*, etc. Such people will certainly not arise from the secular element of our population unless they become *baalei tshuva*, speedily in our day. Until the *Baga"tz* (Israeli Supreme Court) rules that there can be secular Rabbonim, we will have to produce them from within our own ranks! The same goes for *soferim*, *mohalim*, and *shochatim*. Furthermore, the Gemara states that one who says, "Of what use to us are the Rabbis? They study Scripture only for themselves, and they study Oral Law only for themselves,"[27] denies the explicit words of the Torah: "I would spare the entire place on their account."[28] Had there been righteous people in Sodom, Hashem would have pardoned the entire population in their merit. People who study Torah are not simply fulfilling their own needs; they are providing for the entire Jewish people.

אם לא בריתי יומם ולילה חקות שמים וארץ לא שמתי

"If My covenant with the night and with the day would not be; had I not set up the laws of heaven and earth."[29] – they are sustaining the entire world.

Grab The Tree Of Life With Both Hands!

Today, we are unfortunately witness to the fact that those who do not engage in Torah study often descend to the depths of depravity, sometimes becoming involved in drugs, satanic cults, etc. כי הם חיינו – "for they are our life" is not simply a figure of speech; it is to be taken literally! The Torah is "the tree of life for those who grasp it."[30] A drowning man can survive only as long as he can keep his head above water. If he spots a log floating above the water, will he begin searching for *kulos*? Will he ponder whether holding on with one hand is sufficient to save his life, or perhaps only with three fingers? Certainly not! He will grab the tree with both hands and with all his strength. If possible he would wrap his legs around it as well! He understands that his life depends on that log and once he relinquishes his hold, he will drown.

Ideally we should study Torah non-stop, for learning is our life. Would anyone contemplate ceasing to breathe for the next fifteen minutes? Torah is oxygen – we cannot stop learning for even one moment. The only reason we cannot learn non-stop is that "the Torah was not given to ministering angels."[31] We are human beings and must live our lives accordingly. The only stipulation is that we do not waste time unjustifiably. A person who takes advantage of every available moment will never be asked why he did not learn more. Eating and sleeping are necessities and valid reasons for not learning – "Hashem exempted one in extenuating circumstances."[32] Not only is such a person not punished for the time spent not learning but he is rewarded: "Even if a person contemplated fulfilling a mitzvah and was unavoidably prevented from performing it, Scripture credits him as if he had fulfilled it."[33] How much greater is his reward for eating and sleeping if it was with the intention of gathering more strength to enable him to learn! Yet someone who squanders his time by involving himself in purposeless pursuits has shown where his true priorities lie – he is not eating and sleeping out of necessity, but out of choice. He will be accountable for every moment he did not learn, even when such moments are justified.

We can learn an interesting principle in Torah study from a particular distinction in the laws of *Shabbos*. One of the thirty-nine categories of prohibited acts on *Shabbos* is to pick up objects in a private domain and put them down in a public one. The Talmud asks, what would happen if a person were to pick up an object in a private domain, walk outside, and then stands still, without placing the object on the ground? Is he liable as if he had put the object down? The Gemara distinguishes between עומד לכתף – one who stops in order to rearrange his load, thereby easing the remainder of his journey, and עומד לפוש – one who stops in order to rest. The former is not considered as having put the object down, because he paused only for the sake of the continuing journey; it is as if he did not stop. The latter, however, is considered as having put the object down and is thus liable for having violated *Shabbos*.[34]

The same distinction applies to בטול תורה – the prohibition of wasting time which should have been spent learning Torah. A person who truly yearns to spend every available moment learning and wishes he did not have to break for eating, drinking, and sleeping is עומד לכתף; he interrupts his learning only in order to be able to continue and is therefore rewarded even for the time he does not learn. If, on the other hand, he proclaims, "Baruch Hashem, my learning *seder* is over and I can finally sit down to a good meal and get a good night's sleep," his sleeping and eating are viewed as time wasted that should have been spent learning. Two people may do the identical act, yet its value is determined by their intention.

Hashem Did Not Forgive *Bitul Torah*

Bitul Torah is a very severe offense indeed. Regarding the destruction of Yerushalayim, Chazal teach us, "Hashem forgave them for *avoda zara*, adultery, and murder, but did not forgive them for *bitul Torah*."[35] The primary reason for the *churban* of Yerushalayim was *bitul Torah*. To this was added the nation's guilt for transgressing the three cardinal sins, but the underlying cause of all their sins was *bitul Torah*. On Pesach we are all extremely meticulous not to allow even a minuscule amount of *chametz* into our possession. Are we all aware that just as the minutest quantity of *chametz* may not be consumed, so too is the smallest amount of *bitul Torah* also prohibited? (barring extenuating circumstances, as we mentioned above.)

The Torah commands us: ושננתם לבניך ודברת בם – "You shall teach them thoroughly to your children and you shall speak of them,"[36] not only בשבתך בביתך – "while you sit in your home,"[37] but even בלכתך בדרך – "while you walk on the way."[38] Travel does not exempt a person from his obligation to learn Torah. There is no reason not to keep a pocket-sized *sefer* handy so that whenever the occasion arises, one can learn, for example, while waiting at the bus stop. The Gemara teaches that for reasons of safety, a person may not study in-depth while traveling, but he is permitted 'to recite.'[39] Everyone knows something which he can recite by heart – perhaps the *psukim* of the *Shma* or *Ashrei*.[40] We must remember that the Jewish people are depending on our learning – this is our oxygen.

Honoring The Torah

While we are on the subject of Talmud Torah, I would like to make an additional point. The Gemara[41] implies that giving honor to the Torah takes precedence over actual Torah study. We are obligated to treat our holy books with the respect they deserve. The *halacha* instructs us as to which books may be placed on top of others – Neviim and Kesuvim may not be placed on top of Chumashim, and books of the Oral Law may not be placed on top of Neviim and Kesuvim, and certainly not on top of Chumashim. Although our printed Chumashim do not have the same sanctity as *Sifrei Torah*, nor do the Names of Hashem contained therein, they still are considered as the Written Torah, so books of the Oral Law may not be placed on top of them.

We must take extreme care not to place the books upside down. A human being would not take too kindly to being turned upside down, with his head down and his feet sticking up in the air! Just as we would never consider placing a *Sefer Torah* upside down inside the *Aron HaKodesh*, so must we view our books in the same manner. Just as, "Those who write Torah scrolls, *tefillin*, and *mezuzos* are not allowed to turn the parchment face down,"[42] we may not place our open books face down. If one has to leave the *Beis Midrash* and

---

40   One should first make sure the area is clean, otherwise it is forbidden to recite any words of Torah.

feels he will not be able to find the page he is on, he should close the book leaving a marker in the page. Piling up large stacks of books in such a way that one touch will send them all flying off the shtender or table is certainly disrespectful. How can it be that the Raavad worked so hard to knock down the words of the Rambam, and with one wave of a hand we manage to knock down six volumes of his works!

Honoring the Torah is not only an obligation in itself, but it helps us to learn better. Valuing our books properly, and certainly the living *Sifrei Torah* – our *talmidei chachamim*, affords us the opportunity to learn so much more from them.

The Gemara relates that Rav Chisda was unsure of the *halacha* in the case of זה נהנה וזה לא חסר, where an individual benefited from something which belongs to another at no cost to the owner. For example, someone slept in another's yard: the man benefited by not having to rent a room, while the owner did not incur any loss.[43] Rami bar Chama informed him that he could prove from a particular Mishna what the *halacha* would be. When Rav Chisda inquired which Mishna he was referring to, Rami bar Chama's response was: "I will answer this 'as soon as you perform a personal service for me.'"[44] It was only after Rav Chisda folded Rami bar Chama's cloak that he was given the answer.

Did Rami bar Chama really need Rav Chisda to fold his cloak? Furthermore, Rav Chisda was not only Rami bar Chama's Rebbe, he was also a Kohen,[45] in addition to being his father-in-law. It seems Rami bar Chama should have been honoring Rav Chisda, not the other way round. One way of understanding Rami bar Chama's behavior is that he feared that Rav Chisda would not take his words seriously. For Rav Chisda's sake, he first demanded that Rav Chisda perform some task for him, causing him to feel a certain subservience, thus making him more open to accepting what Rami bar Chama said. Later we read that Rava indeed challenged Rami bar Chama's proof and there is no record that Rava served him. Had Rav Chisda not initially served Rami bar Chama, perhaps he too would have questioned Rami bar Chama's proof.

We find a similar story involving the relationship between Avimi, Rav Chisda's rebbe, and Rav Chisda.[46] The Gemara relates that Avimi went to Rav Chisda to learn *Maseches Menachos*. The Gemara asks how that could be. Should it not be Avimi teaching Rav Chisda? The Gemara answers, "Avimi forgot *Maseches Menachos* and he came before Rav Chisda to be reminded of his own teachings." The Gemara goes on, "But Avimi should have sent a message to Rav Chisda requesting that Rav Chisda come to him." Why did Avimi go to his student? Rav Chisda would have considered it a privilege to go to Avimi. The Gemara responds: "Avimi thought that by behaving in this way, he would be more likely to succeed." Avimi felt that by making the extra effort to go to Rav Chisda, he would appreciate Rav Chisda more as a true "source of living waters"[47] and he would feel more receptive to learning from him. Rav Chisda's *shiurim* would have been the same in either case. This is tremendous *mussar* for us – it teaches us how to respect and value our books properly as well as those who learn Torah. "A poor man's wisdom is despised."[48] If we wish to learn from them, our seforim and *talmidei chachamim* must be valuable in our eyes.

Segulos As Protection

This principle applies at all times, but especially now that עת צרה היא ליעקב. – "It is a time of trouble for Yaakov."[49] We are witness to endless terrorist acts and other tragedies, Yerushalayim is on the negotiating table and they are begging Yasser Arafat, to be so kind as to concede that the Jewish people have even a minor religious connection to *Har HaBayis*. I suppose the fact that this connection is documented in the Torah, Neviim, Rashi, the Rambam, and all other authorities is not sufficient. We require the *psak* of Rabenu Yasser as well! We would never, God forbid, ask him to relinquish his claim to *Har HaBayis*; that would be far too much to ask for, but he should at least acknowledge that we have some claim to it as well. What a terrible disparagement of the Torah and the Jewish people! Who knows what they will decree next? Perhaps they will announce

49 *Yirmiyahu* 30:7 – This *sicha* was delivered during the second Intifada in 5761.

that from now on we must pray towards Mecca or some other location, God forbid!

During these difficult times, we must strengthen our learning. If there is to be even a chance of these terrible decrees being rescinded, we must first enhance the glory of Torah. During the Chmielnitzki years, in the mid-seventeenth century, there lived a great *mekubal* by the name of Rav Shimshon Ostropoler who eventually died *al Kiddush Hashem*. He tried his utmost to have some of the decrees placed upon *Klal Yisrael* rescinded. Suddenly the Satan appeared to him, informing him that he was willing to cancel some of the decrees on one condition; he would permit observance of *Shabbos* and other *mitzvos* but learning Torah must be banned. Rav Shimshon refused to pay such a price under any circumstances. We must realize that learning Torah is the best merit we have to withstand these decrees.

Talking of *segulos* for helping us during these difficult times, my Rebbe, HaRav Gedalia Eisman shlit"a is fond of quoting Chazal: "If someone responds אמן יהא שמי-ה רבא – 'Amen, may His great Name be blessed' with all his might, the evil decree in judgment against him is torn up."[50] Some claim that "with all his might" refers to shouting loudly, literally with all his might, while others maintain that it refers to a person's *kavana* – to proclaim that one's entire purpose in life is that the Great Name of Hashem be blessed throughout all the worlds! If we strengthen our belief in the Almighty, give *tzedaka* and perform other acts of *chessed*; if we strengthen our *Shabbos* observance, *shmiras halashon*, and whatever else requires strengthening, then Hashem will help us and protect our holy sites. May we then merit seeing the rebuilding of our true connection to *Har HaBayis*, speedily in our day. Amen.

Notes

1   *Bereishis* 47:22

2   Ibid. 26

3   See *Bereishis Rabbasi Parshas Vayigash.*

4   *Bechoros* 26b

5   *Malachi* 2:8

6   *Bamidbar* 18:32

7   *Shemos* 1:8

8   *Shemos* 5:2; see *Shemos Rabba* 1:8.

9   *Bamidbar* 18:31

10 *Malachi* 2:8

11 *Bamidbar* 16:9-10

12 Rambam *Hilchos Klei HaMikdash* 3:10

13 243:4

14 *Yevamos* 99b

15 See *Tosafos Sanhedrin* 68b "*katan*".

16 *Avos* 4:5

17 *Pesachim* 50b

18 *Sotah* 47a

19 *Melachim* I 3:4

20 *Avos* 1:3

21 *Avos* 3:17

22 *Mishle* 8:11

23 *Kiddushin* 66a

24   Ibid.

25   *Kiddushin* 29b

26   Ibid.

27   *Sanhedrin* 99b

28   *Bereishis* 18:26 – referring to the possibility of *tzaddikim* in Sodom.

29   *Yirmiyahu* 33:25

30   *Mishle* 3:18

31   *Kiddushin* 54a

32   *Avoda Zara* 54a

33   *Berachos* 6a

34   See *Shabbos* 5b.

35   *Yalkut Shimoni*, Yirmiyahu 282

36   *Devarim* 6:7

37   Ibid.

38   Ibid.

39   *Taanis* 10b

41   *Megilla* 3b

42   *Eruvin* 98a

43   *Baba Kama* 20a

44 *Baba Kama* 20b

45 See *Berachos* 44a.

46 See *Menachos* 7a.

47 *Yirmiyahu* 2:13

48 *Koheles* 9:16

49 *Yirmiyahu* 30:7 – This *sicha* was delivered during the second Intifada in 5761.

50 *Shabbos* 119b

Remembering And Forgetting

"You Shall Not Bear A Grudge"

The Torah commands us: לא תקם ולא תטר את בני עמך – "You shall not take revenge and you shall not bear a grudge against the members of your people."[1] Although it is often quite difficult to restrain ourselves from taking revenge, it is within man's ability to do so.[2] But how can we be expected to refrain from bearing a grudge? A grudge is an emotion. How much control can we assert over our emotions?

Not bearing a grudge is related to not remembering the way others have slighted us. While memory is also a function of the heart and mind, we avail ourselves of certain aids to assist us in fulfilling *mitzvos* which require us to remember. For example, there is a positive commandment to remember the exodus from Egypt. We fulfill this commandment by mentioning it every morning and evening, and elaborating on it further at our Seder table. The Rambam writes that when we recite Kiddush, we fulfill the mitzvah of remembering *Shabbos*.[3] According to the Ramban, we also fulfill this mitzvah when we announce the day of the week (היום יום ראשון בשבת ...) before reciting the Psalm of the Day. We remember what Amalek did to us by reading the relevant *psukim* from a Sefer Torah once a year and many have the custom of reading it daily from their *siddur* at the conclusion of *Shacharis*.

How are we expected to forget what another person did to us? How can a person be expected not to bear a grudge in his heart for an injustice perpetrated against him by his fellow man? What should he do – should he repeat over and over "Hashem has commanded me to forget"? Not only would he not succeed in forgetting, but the memory of the act would become more deeply ingrained!

We can pose a further question: Hashem says of Himself, "For I am the Beneficent One – the word of Hashem – and I will not bear a grudge forever."[4] Does this mean that Hashem forgets? Do we not declare on Rosh Hashana, "There is no forgetfulness before Your Throne of Glory"?[5] Not only does Hashem not forget, but with Him the whole concept of forgetting has no meaning. We affirm every day: שמע ישראל ה' אלקינו ה' אחד.

One interpretation of the word אחד – 'One' – is that Hashem never changes. He always was and always will be the same One; no information is new for Him and not a single piece of knowledge escapes Him. The verse "I will not bear a grudge forever" certainly cannot mean that the Almighty will forget a person's sin!

The implication of the *pasuk* is not that He will forget our sins, but that He will not act on that knowledge. When man repents, Hashem will act as if the sin did not occur and He will therefore not punish him. In the same way we can understand the verse, "Preserver of kindness for thousands of generations."[6] It goes without saying that Hashem remembers forever. The meaning of the *pasuk* is that He will respond to acts of *chessed* and reward them for many generations with precious gifts such as the Land of Israel. When we praise Hashem in our daily *Shmone Esrei* as being One "Who recalls the kindnesses of the patriarchs," we do not mean that He recalls in the way a human being does, but rather that He acts on this memory by promising "a redeemer to their children's children for His Name's sake, with love," may it occur speedily in our day.

This gives us some insight into fulfilling the mitzvah of not bearing a grudge. We are neither required nor expected to forget the wrongs done to us. We are forbidden to act in response to them or to allow them to affect negatively our relationship with the person involved.

"It Was Hashem Who Sent Me Here"

A classic example of this definition of not bearing a grudge is to be found in this week's *parsha*. Yosef explicitly tells his brothers that he has not forgotten what they did to him. "I am Yosef your brother – it is me, whom you sold into Egypt."[7] Our Sages teach us that after Yosef and his brothers buried their father in Hebron, Yosef visited the pit into which he had been cast as a young man and recited the *bracha*, שעשה לי נס במקום הזה – "Who has performed for me a miracle in this place."[8] The *Midrash* relates that it was on witnessing this that "Yosef's brothers perceived that their father was dead, and they said, 'Perhaps Yosef will nurse hatred against us.'"[9] His return to the scene of the crime was a clear indication that he had not forgotten. The brothers saw this and feared what he would do to them. Yosef, of course, had no intention of harming them. He remembered everything but did not intend to act upon this memory.

How does a person reach such a level? Yosef HaTzaddik endured terrible suffering. First his brothers wished to kill him, then they threw him into a pit filled with snakes and scorpions. After that they sold him into slavery and eventually he ended up in jail. Can we imagine a person having all these offenses perpetrated against him and not bearing a grudge? Yosef himself explains: "It was not you who sent me here, but Hashem."[10] Anything that happened to me was not through your doing. You did not have the power to sell me into slavery or the power to kill me. As the author of *Chovos HaLevavos* writes, "Benefit and harm are not in the hands of the creations, nor within their power, without permission of the Creator."[11] No creature can help or harm me in any way without it being so decreed by Divine Providence. This can be compared to a dog which is hit by a rock. The incensed dog now goes and bites the rock which hit him! He does not think of blaming the person who threw the rock with intent to hurt.

Yosef understood this quite clearly. He realized that Pharaoh could not determine whether or not he would be king, just as his brothers had no say in whether or not he would become a slave. What we see is only a façade. The ultimate truth is that life and death, slavery and freedom, are all in Hashem's hands. It is He Who decrees who shall live and who shall die, who will be a slave and who will be a free man. "When it was Hashem's will that I become king, I became a king, and when it was His will that I be a slave, I became a slave. It is true that I remember it all – but that is no cause for me to be angry with you. It is all in Hashem's hands and everything that happened to me was decreed from Heaven."

In fact, Chazal inform us: "Yaakov Avinu was destined to descend to Egypt in iron chains, however, his merit caused him."[12] This means that the decree to Avraham: "Know with certainty that your offspring shall be aliens in a land not their own – and they will serve them, and they will oppress them – four hundred years,"[13] included being brought down to Egypt in iron chains, perhaps by the Midianites or one of the other nations who would have taken Yaakov captive and brought him down to Egypt as a prisoner. It was Yaakov's merit that caused this detail to be omitted and instead Yaakov made the journey in a royal chariot sent to him by Pharaoh. It would appear that these words of Chazal applied not only to Yaakov himself but also to his entire family. Yosef apparently did not have the merit to be spared this decree, and he therefore descended to Egypt as a captive. It was not the actions of the brothers that brought Yosef to Egypt, but the decree foretold to Avraham Avinu of "Your offspring shall be aliens." Had the brothers not been responsible for sending Yosef to Egypt, Hashem would have found another messenger to carry out His wishes. Yosef had no cause for anger, for indeed "It is not you who sent me here but Hashem."

Free Choice

Yeshayahu the prophet beseeched Hashem: "Hashem, arrange peace for us, even as You brought about whatever happened to us."[14] It is ultimately Hashem Who is responsible for everything – there can be no peace if that is not His will. Man's free choice enables him only to choose one path or another. He cannot determine the realization of his wishes. Usually בדרך שאדם רוצה לילך בה מוליכין אותו – "In the way that a man wishes to go, in that way they lead him,"[15] but there are times when Hashem prevents this from happening. Were there not many good Jews who were determined to observe *mitzvos* and perform good deeds, yet Hashem placed them in Siberia where it was "withheld from them all they proposed to do" ?[16] On the other hand, often throughout history, evil people wished to destroy the

Jewish nation, God forbid, but Hashem's will was that they drown in the deep waters of the Yam Suf or be hanged from a tree fifty *amos* high. Although in the majority of cases man is led along the path he desires for himself, Hashem can determine otherwise.

What we have just said, however, does not fully explain the events that transpired in our *parsha*. It may be true that what happened to Yosef was Hashem's will and without the Almighty's decision, the brothers would not have been able to carry out their wishes, yet they are not entirely out of the picture. Did they not intend to harm their brother?

A "Partnership With Hashem"

In *Hilchos Shabbos* we learn, "If this one was able, but this one was unable, the able one is liable while the unable one is not."[17] If two people together carried out an act that was in violation of the *Shabbos*, the one who was unable to carry out the prohibition on his own is not liable, because he was nothing more than an assistant, and "assisting is insignificant."[18] The *halacha* views the combined action of these two people as if the "able" one carried everything out on his own.

One way of viewing the story of the brothers is as such a partnership. Hashem obviously is the "able" one who needs no assistance in running the world. He could have carried out whatever He had decreed for Yosef on His own – He had no need of the brothers' assistance. The brothers were "unable" – without Hashem's will, they would have been unable to harm Yosef on their own.

However, although the assistant may not be punishable for violation of *Shabbos*, he was still involved in the act. For example, two partners wished to transport a heavy object weighing one hundred kilograms from a private domain to a public domain. The able one may have been able to carry it on his own, but with his friend's assistance, he need only exert the effort required to carry eighty kilograms. Should the brothers not be held at least somewhat responsible for "assisting" Hashem? Why did Yosef ascribe responsibility to Hashem for all that had taken place? The answer is that man's role is even less than that of the "unable" partner. "Assisting is insignificant," but man's assistance is even less than insignificant. We received from Hashem any tools we may avail ourselves of; it is He alone Who is responsible. Man cannot assist Hashem even one iota. Why should Yosef be angry with his brothers?

This is one of the fundamental principles of the Torah. The Ramban writes that there is no natural order of the world, because Hashem decrees everything and whoever does not understand this has no share in the Torah of Moshe Rabenu. The brothers had absolutely no involvement in this case. The Midianites, although they will be punished for their role, were ultimately not responsible for the sale; it was the will of Hashem from beginning to end.

The fact that Hashem is responsible for everything is not limited to the incident involving Yosef and his brothers. We must realize that any time someone wrongs us, it is the will of Hashem. The other person's role is illusory – can we bear a grudge against an illusion? Yosef reassured his brothers that they had not done anything to him and therefore they need not fear that he would take revenge or bear a grudge.

Hakaras Hatov

We may then ask, 'Does this also mean that a recipient of *chessed* does not owe his benefactor a debt of gratitude? As we cited from the *Chovos HaLevavos*, "Benefit and harm are not in the hands of the creations, nor within their power, without permission of The Creator." Certainly not! It is our obligation to feel gratitude towards anyone who acts kindly towards us. In the words of Chazal, "The wine belongs to the master; the good is attributed to the one who pours it."[19] In addition to the owner of the wine, I must thank the one who poured it. If Hashem sends someone to aid me in any way, I may not think, 'Hashem has no need for assistance. If it was His will that this good be brought upon me, He could have done so without the messenger. The messenger therefore deserves no credit for any of the good deeds he has performed.'

If Hashem chooses to bestow His kindness upon me through the good deeds of a fellow human being, I must acknowledge what the person has done for me. This obligation of *hakaras hatov* applies even to inanimate objects that have no free choice. As we discussed in *Parshas Miketz*[20] a classic example of this was Moshe Rabenu. He was told to instruct Aharon to strike the river in order to bring about the plagues of blood and frogs. Moshe himself was not commanded to strike the river because he owed it a debt of gratitude for having protected him as an infant.[21] Did the river know that it was protecting Moshe? In fact, if I were to ask the river if it wished its water to be transformed into blood, it would have been overjoyed at the prospect. For its entire existence, the river had suffered by being used for Egyptian *avoda zara*. Finally it had a golden opportunity to perform a *Kiddush Hashem* – to provide water for the Jews while at the same time supplying the Egyptians with blood! Even so, striking the river would not be a respectful way to act towards something which had bestowed such good.

Similarly, as we explained in *Parshas Miketz*, when Moshe Rabenu comes to the rescue of Yisro's daughters, they relate, "An Egyptian man saved us from the shepherds."[22] Why is Moshe Rabenu referred to as an Egyptian? One of Chazal's explanations is that the "Egyptian man" was not Moshe Rabenu. When the daughters came to thank him, Moshe responded, "It was not I who saved you, rather the Egyptian man whom I killed. It was because of him that I had to flee to Midian; he is the one who saved you".[23] This is how far the obligation of *hakaras hatov* extends.

Foundation Of Our Belief

Gratitude is the very foundation of our belief! A person who lacks *hakaras hatov* towards another human being will ultimately fail to recognize the good that Hashem has done for him.[24] Such a person may come to argue that all the good Hashem has given him, his wealth, his food and clothing, the gift of *Eretz Yisrael*, does not make a dent in Hashem's pocketbook. Why should Hashem not give? He has nothing to lose. We must therefore practice the *middah* of *hakaras hatov* – towards one another, even to those who had evil intentions. Only when we accustom ourselves to feeling gratitude towards Hashem's messengers, will we be able to feel gratitude to the One towards Whom we really must have *hakaras hatov* – the Almighty.

Chazal teach us, "One is obligated to become intoxicated on Purim until one does not know the difference between 'cursed is Haman' and 'blessed is Mordechai.'"[25] What does it mean not to know the difference between '*Arur Haman*' and '*Baruch Mordechai?*' HaGaon HaRav Yitzchak Ezrachi shlit"a explained that a person is obligated to attain the level of recognition that there is ultimately no difference between Haman and Mordechai in terms of the ability of their actions to influence our lives. It was not really Haman who wrought evil upon the nation and it was not Mordechai who brought about our salvation. *Am Yisrael* brought the trouble on themselves by bowing down to an image or by benefiting from the feast of Achashverosh.[26] It was the people as well who ultimately brought about the salvation – by doing *teshuva*.

All this is true, and it ties in with what we just quoted from the *Chovos HaLevavos*, yet that does not absolve us of our obligation of *hakaras hatov* towards Esther and Mordechai. In the case of Haman, however, although we have just learned that we do not attribute bad to the one who carried it out, the prohibition of "You shall not take revenge and you shall not bear a grudge" does not apply. It only applies "against the members of your people."[27] Not only does Amalek not fall under this category, but there is an explicit commandment to "Remember what Amalek did to you."[28] We are permitted to hold a grudge against Haman and his wife for their sinister plans and we are allowed to say "Cursed be Haman" and "Cursed be Zeresh," even though the decree was from God. *Nekima* and *netira* are forbidden only with regard to our fellow Jews.

Everything Hashem Does Is For Our Good

Yosef HaTzaddik teaches us an additional reason why a person should not be angry when someone wrongs him. "Although you intended me harm, Hashem intended it for good."[29] Not only are you not the correct address for any grievances, but why should I be angry? If Hashem did it, then it must be for the good. Can we be angry with someone who is good to us? It may be that you intended me harm, but Hashem, Who runs the world, intended it for good. "Whatever the Merciful One does, He does for the good."[30] If Hashem decreed that I be a slave in Egypt, then it was for my own good. I must have *hakaras hatov* to Hashem even when things appear bad. I must be grateful for being thrown into a pit filled with snakes and scorpions – it was all for my good. We can compare this to a doctor who saves his patient's life by amputating his leg. Would the patient be angry? Not only would he not be angry, but he would be willing to compensate the doctor for services rendered. Any difficult and painful operation which Hashem puts us through is ultimately for our own benefit. Rashi[31] explains that Yosef was thrown into the pit and then sold into slavery as a *tikkun* for the damage he had caused by bringing bad reports about his brothers to their father. The suffering that he underwent served to cleanse him of these sins until he became worthy of being king in Egypt and becoming the savior of the Jewish people, who also suffered through an exile that was for their own good – "that a vast people be kept alive."[32] Had Yosef not undergone this "operation," he would not have been able to rule over Egypt.

In Yosef's case, the outcome showed clearly how ultimately it was all for the good – he became viceroy in Egypt, bringing salvation to the Jewish people. It is not always obvious to us that "whatever the Merciful One does, He does for the good,"[33] yet we must understand that nothing happens to us that is not for our own good. "Hashem is our God, Hashem is the One and Only," whether He invokes the Attribute of Mercy or the Attribute of Justice. In fact, justice stems from the Attribute of Mercy – Hashem punishes us in order to set us on the path of Torah and *mitzvos*, to enable us to earn a share in *Olam Haba*. We pray that there no longer be a need for the Attribute of Justice and that we be worthy of *chessed* without punishment. None of us desires to suffer the way Yosef and many other *tzaddikim* did. The *halacha* is, however, that "a man is obligated to recite a blessing on bad news, just as he does on good news."[34] What appears to us as bad is in fact for our own good, even if in this world we have difficulty discerning it.

We pray that we remain healthy and do not have to undergo any 'operations.' If we are destined to suffer, then may our sufferings be with mercy. The Talmud asks, "At what stage does Divine retribution commence? ... Where one intended to take out three (coins) and took out two."[35] He must now go to the trouble of putting his hand in his pocket a second time in order to retrieve the third coin. A further example of suffering cited by the Gemara is "If his shirt gets turned inside out."[36] If someone did not put his shirt on properly, he must take the time to remove it, turn it the right way around, and put it on again. What terrible and unimaginable suffering these people are enduring! May we too endure only this sort of suffering!

If a slight nudge from above like this awakens us to *teshuva* then the "minor operation" is sufficient. However, if we persist in our ways and do not repent, Hashem will have to give us punishments that involve a greater degree of suffering. Everything Hashem does is for our good. He would rather act with us in a sweeter manner. When there is no choice, He employs harsher means.

For The Sake Of His Name

The *pasuk* states: "Everything Hashem made He made for His sake."[37] Everything Hashem does is for the purpose of sanctifying His Name, "... even the evildoer for the day of retribution"[38] – even punishment of the wicked produces a *Kiddush Hashem*. Of course, Hashem would rather dispense with this form of *Kiddush Hashem* and have all His creations follow in the ways of the *tzaddikim*. The *Midrash* states: "'And the earth was astonishingly empty.'[39] This refers to the actions of the wicked. Hashem said, 'Let there be light.'[40] This refers to the actions of the righteous. I cannot know which of the two He prefers. Since it states: 'Hashem saw that the light was good,'[41] we know that it is the actions of the righteous that He desires, and not those of the wicked."[42] Hashem would prefer that all His creatures benefit from this world rather than having to suffer plagues and punishment.

We Are All Brothers

We discussed Yosef's belief that he had no cause for anger, since ultimately Hashem was responsible. He knew that it was all for the best, because everything Hashem does is for our good. Yosef furnishes us with a third reason why he bore no resentment, why there was no room for any revenge or grudge – "I am Yosef your brother."[43] אח – 'brother' – comprises the first two letters of the word אחד, one. We are one body, one unit. How can I take revenge on myself? A grudge against you is a grudge against me. The Yerushalmi illustrates the prohibition of taking revenge and bearing a grudge: if a person were to hold a piece of meat in one hand and a knife in the other, but instead of cutting the meat, he accidentally cut his hand, would he then transfer the knife to the injured hand to take revenge upon the healthy hand? Both hands belong to the same person! The one who caused the damage is also the victim![44] Can a person take revenge and bear a grudge against himself? Should he punish the right hand by declaring, "Let my right hand forget its skill"[45]? He will continue to wash his right hand and care for it as he did before. The brothers are all sons of Yaakov, "All sons of one man are we."[46] They are all one body – one 'self.' The self in the guise of Reuven, Shimon, and Levi sold the self in the guise of Yosef into slavery. Yosef reassures them that any harm brought upon him is similar to one hand harming the other. There is no one to take revenge against.

Intertwined

In his work *Tomer Devorah*,[47] Rav Moshe Cordovero uses this idea to explain Chazal's adage: כל ישראל ערבים זה בזה – "All Jews are responsible for one another."[48] To be an ערב implies being intertwined with the other and responsible for his actions and welfare. In fact a guarantor on a loan is referred to as an ערב because with regard to the loan, the assets of the borrower and guarantor are intertwined. Each Jew contains within him a spark of every other Jew. We are one body. If the left hand hurts the right hand, or the right hand hurts the left, there is no one to be angry with. Is there jealousy among our various body parts? When there is hard work to do, I use my hands, when there are long distances to journey, my feet bear the brunt.

However, when there is delicious food available, my mouth eats it! Is this justice? Is this a fair distribution of tasks? It is neither the hands that work, nor the feet that walk nor the mouth that eats and enjoys the food. They are all part of one body, which functions as one complete unit – it works, walks, and eats. The body parts are the specific organs set aside for carrying out these various tasks – they cannot be interchanged with each other. The entire Jewish nation is one individual, and we are all intertwined.

The Talmud discusses the division of the Land of Israel and questions whether a city could be divided up among more than one tribe.[49] *Tosafos* ask, 'Is Yerushalayim, which is divided among the tribes of Yehuda and Binyamin, not an example of a city whose jurisdiction is divided between two tribes?'[50] *Tosafos* explain that Yerushalayim was an exception because Hashem expressly commanded that it be divided in this fashion. I would like to suggest another explanation. Why was Yerushalayim shared specifically by Yehuda and Binyamin? Because they are in effect one tribe! Before taking Binyamin down to Egypt, Yehuda promised his father אנכי אערבנו "I personally will guarantee him."[51] The word אערבנו comes from the same root as מעורב – mixed in, intertwined. The tribes of Yehuda and Binyamin are in effect one tribe.

The Shita Mekubetzes relates a fascinating *Midrash*. During the time of Shlomo HaMelech, there lived a person who was born with two heads. When the man's father passed away, he charged that he had the status of two people and he therefore claimed a double portion of inheritance. The other brothers maintained that he was only one person. The case was brought before Shlomo HaMelech. The wisest of all men covered one of the heads with a thick blanket so that he could not see, and poured hot water over the other head. Both heads screamed in anguish, proving that "they" were only one person – one head felt the pain of the other. *Klal Yisrael* is גוי אחד בארץ – one nation on earth. We feel the pain of our fellow Jews more than any other nation feels the pain of their brethren. The pain of a Frenchman living in Syria or Lebanon means little to the people in France, yet when a Jew suffers anywhere in the world, the entire Jewish nation cries out.

The Torah commands us: ואהבת לרעך כמוך – "Love your fellow as yourself."[52] This does not mean to love him "as if he were you," but to understand that he really is a part of you and you are a part of him. Your soul contains a spark of him, while a spark of your soul is in him. Would you ever say of yourself, "I would like myself if not for these few faults I have?" How then can you go and say that about your fellow Jew? (Of course this does not include those whom the Torah commands us to hate.) Just as you love yourself despite any faults you may have, so too must you love your friend despite anything negative you discover in his character.

Perhaps we can suggest a fourth way to understand the mitzvah of not taking revenge or bearing a grudge. The Torah commands us, "You shall not covet."[53] According to the Ibn Ezra's understanding, the prohibition is to covet in one's heart something which belongs to another. (Other Rishonim are of the opinion that this prohibition involves an action.[54]) The Ibn Ezra asks if it is really possible to fulfill this commandment. What if we truly desire what the other person has? We can demand of someone not to steal from another, but to have no desire for something that belongs to another ...? The Ibn Ezra explains that if a commoner were to glimpse at a beautiful princess, he would realize the futility of coveting her, for the king would never agree to let him marry her. The king would choose someone very wealthy or an important minister or a successful army officer. The notion "Do not covet" does not even apply here! Says the Ibn Ezra, we must view the possessions of others in this fashion – like an unattainable princess. There is nothing to talk about: she is not and cannot be yours. Once we understand this, we will have no desire for the possessions of another.

"Remember Always You Stood Before Hashem"

I thought of another way to answer the Ibn Ezra's question. The *Midrash* recounts that when the Jewish people stood at Har Sinai, their souls departed from them.[55] The people were drawn to such spirituality that their only wish was to cleave to Hashem. They no longer had any connection to this world. It was only the dew of resurrection that returned their souls to them. At that moment, if they had been asked: "Are you interested in your friend's house?" they would have responded: "I am not even interested in my own house, for my only wish is to cleave to Hashem." The Torah demands that we carry the memory of *Maamad Har Sinai* with us forever. "Only beware for yourself and greatly beware for your soul, lest you forget the things that your eyes have beheld and lest you remove them from your heart all the days of your life ... the day that you stood before Hashem, your God, at Horeb."[56] Just as on that day, you received the Torah "with awe, with dread, with trembling,"[57] so must you receive the Torah all the days of your life. This is a very difficult task to fulfill, yet the Torah commands us that the impression of *Maamad Har Sinai* should remain with us always. Just as at Har Sinai we were not interested even in our own house, and certainly in houses belonging to our fellow Jews, we must view others' possessions in the same way.

The Ibn Ezra's question is no longer difficult. If we were to live our lives under the influence of the great assembly at Har Sinai, we would never covet the property of others. In the same way, we would never violate the commandment, "You shall not take revenge and you shall not bear a grudge." When we live our entire lives as if we are still at Sinai, cleaving to Hashem, there is no room for revenge and grudges. Our only concern is how we can better serve Hashem. It is Hashem's wish that I love every Jew. This must be my goal – I cannot bear any grudges.

What we have said is easy to say, but very difficult to practice, for we do not really live under the influence of Har Sinai – we lead a life that requires us to eat, sleep, and take care of other bodily needs. But we should make it our goal to live our days cleaving to Hashem the way we did at Har Sinai. If we do so we will have no difficulty avoiding the prohibition of "You shall not take revenge and you shall not bear a grudge against the members of your people," and we will have no trouble fulfilling "Love your fellow as yourself."

Notes

1   *Vayikra* 19:18

2   See *Mesilas Yesharim* Chapter 11.

3   See *Shemos* 20:8 and Rambam *Hilchos Shabbos* 29:1.

4   *Yirmiyahu* 3:12

5   From the *Zichronos* section of Rosh Hashana *Musaf.*

6   *Shemos* 34:7

7   *Bereishis* 45:4

8   See *Tanchuma*, end of *Parshas Vayechi.*

9   *Bereishis* 50:15

10   *Bereishis* 45:8

11   *Yichud HaMaase*, Chapter 2 – the fifth topic.

12   *Shabbos* 89b

13   *Bereishis* 15:13

14   *Yeshayahu* 26:12

15   *Makkos* 10b

16   *Bereishis* 11:6

17   See Rambam *Hilchos Shabbos* 1:16.

18   *Shabbos* 93a

19   *Baba Kamma* 92b

20   *Sicha* II

21   See Rashi, *Shemos* 7:19 and 8:12.

22   *Shemos* 2:19

23   *Shemos Rabba* 1:32

24   See *Shemos Rabba* 1:10.

25   *Megillah* 7b

26   See *Megillah* 12a.

27   *Vayikra* 19:18

28   *Devarim* 25:17

29   *Bereishis* 50:20

30   *Berachos* 60b

31   *Bereishis* 37:2

32   *Bereishis* 50:20

33   *Berachos* 60b

34   *Berachos* 54a

35   *Erchin* 16b

36   Ibid.

37   *Mishle* 16:4

38   Ibid.

39   *Bereishis* 1:2

40   Ibid. 3

41   Ibid. 4

42 *Bereishis* Rabba 2:5

43 *Bereishis* 45:4

44 See *Nedarim* 9:4.

45 *Tehillim* 137:5

46 *Bereishis* 42:11

47 1:4

48 *Sanhedrin* 27b

49 See *Sanhedrin* 111b.

50 See *Tosafos Yeshanim Yoma* 12a.

51 *Bereishis* 43:9

52 *Vayikra* 19:18

53 *Shemos* 20:14

54 See Rambam *Hilchos Gezela Va'aveda* 1:9 and *Chinuch* Mitzvah 38.

55 See *Shir HaShirim Rabba* 6:3.

56 *Devarim* 4:9-10

57 *Yoma* 4b

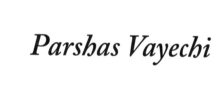
Parshas Vayechi

"Tiny Details, Tremendous Impact"

וירא ישראל את בני יוסף ויאמר מי אלה

"Yisrael saw Yosef's sons and he said 'Who are these?'"[1]

A Matter Of A Marriage Document

What did Yaakov mean by "Who are these?" Surely this was not his first encounter with Yosef's sons! Our Sages explain, "Yaakov wished to bless them, but the *Shechina* departed from him because Yeravam and Achav were destined to come from Ephraim, and Yehu and his sons from Menashe."[2] When Yaakov asked "Who are these?" he meant, "From where did these who are unfit for blessing emerge?"

The Torah then relates:

ויאמר יוסף אל אביו בני הם אשר נתן לי אלקים בזה

"And Yosef said to his father, 'They are my sons whom God has given me here.'"[3]

On this Rashi comments: "Yosef showed Yaakov a document of marriage and a *kesuva*. Yosef prayed for mercy over the matter and *ruach hakodesh* rested upon Yaakov." Rashi's commentary is based on a *midrash*.[4] How does the *midrash* arrive at the conclusion that Yosef showed these documents to Yaakov? Perhaps the *midrash* was struck by the fact that Yosef used the term בזה – which generally refers to something tangible, that one can point to with a finger.

For example, we are all familiar with the Haggadah which states: בעבור זה – לא אמרתי אלא בשעה שיש מצה ומרור מונחים לפניך – "Because of this, I learn from it that the ceremony does not begin until the time when matzah and maror are set before you." In this case the word זה refers to the matzah and maror which are on the table before us. When Yaakov saw these documents, he responded: "Bring them to me, if you please, and I will bless them."[5]

This seems puzzling. How does viewing these documents solve Yaakov's dilemma of whether or not he should bless the children? Perhaps Yaakov suspected Yosef of adopting the Egyptian custom of fathering children outside the confines of marriage. The marriage certificate and the *kesuvah*, which Yosef showed his father, dispelled these suspicions.

The Chasam Sofer sees the matter in a different light. When the Divine Presence suddenly departed as he was preparing to bless the children, Yaakov wondered what blemish they could possibly possess that would cause this to happen. Yosef then brought out his marriage contract. He showed his father that the children's only fault was that their father's marriage contract was made out in the name 'Tzofnas Paneach' rather than 'Yosef.' On seeing this, Yaakov was satisfied that that was their only fault, and said, "Bring them to me, if you please, and I will bless them."

Notwithstanding that Yaakov foresaw that Yeravam would descend from Ephraim, and Yehu from Menashe, he was also able to identify the *tzaddikim* destined to descend from these two tribes. The Torah relates that Yaakov placed his right hand on Ephraim, the younger son. Yosef was troubled by this, and thinking that his father had erred, he tried to remove Yaakov's right hand from Ephraim and place it on Menashe, the firstborn. Yaakov responded: "I know, my son, I know. He too will become a people, and he too will become great. However his younger brother shall become greater than he."[6] Rashi comments here that although Gidon, one of the Shoftim, was destined to descend from Menashe, Yehoshua, who would lead the Jewish people into the Land of Israel and would teach them Torah, was destined to come forth from Ephraim. Regarding Ephraim, Yaakov added: וזרעו יהיה מלא הגוים – "His offspring's fame will fill the nations."[7] Rashi comments that this refers to Yehoshua's acquiring great fame when he caused the sun to stand still at Givon and the moon to stand still in the Ayalon Valley. Yaakov was aware that Yosef's sons would each produce good and bad offspring. However, at this point he was unsure whether the effect of the good would outweigh the effect of the bad or God forbid, the opposite. The Divine Presence then returned to Yaakov and he proceeded to bless the children. Rashi interprets the *pasuk*: "I led Ephraim and he took them upon his arms,"[8] to mean "I led My Spirit into Yaakov for the sake of Ephraim until he took them upon his arms to bless them." The spirit of prophecy returned to Yaakov, so that he might bless Ephraim, whereupon Yaakov realized that the good which would emanate from them would outweigh the bad, making them indeed worthy of blessing.

The Minutest Flaw Can Invalidate A Sefer Torah

This little incident can teach us so many things – we can learn from here that something as seemingly trivial as whether the marriage certificate contains the name 'Yosef' or 'Tzofnas Paneach' can have a major influence on who descends from the marriage! The future of two of the tribes of Israel appears to have rested on this. We cannot begin to comprehend the importance of these details. A *Sefer Torah* in which a letter *yud* is missing just the point of its tip may be invalid (to read) even if the damaged letter is in *Parshas Bereishis* while the current *keriah* is *Parshas Vayechi*. The unfit *Sefer Torah* is still considered holy for it contains the Name of Hashem, yet it does not have the same level of sanctity as a perfect, unblemished *Sefer Torah*.

If a person uses a *mezuzah* or *tefillin* with an invalid letter, not only has he not fulfilled the mitzvah, but he has made a *bracha levatala* – a blessing for no reason. Minor details that to us may appear trivial can have major implications.

מלא כל הארץ כבודו – "The whole world is filled with Hashem's Glory,"[9] and man was created in His image. Man therefore has the potential to reach tremendous heights. A person may appear insignificant – he takes up only four *amos* of space – yet in reality he is "*bezeir anpin*," a 'miniature version of God', whose Glory fills the whole world. The slightest fault in man creates a blemish in the entire universe.

Chazal teach us the principle: מדה טובה גדולה ממדת פורעניות – "A positive trait is greater than a negative trait." This means that if a slight flaw in man can blemish the entire universe, how much more so can the slightest improvement in man improve the entire universe! Just as one detail of the *kesuvah* can affect the world negatively, so it can also influence the world positively. We cannot begin to comprehend the potential influence of man and his actions.

While on the one hand, Yehoshua, who played a major positive role in Jewish history, descended from Yosef, on the other hand the blemish in the *kesuvah* was responsible for the births of Yeravam and Achav, who brought great destruction. A person must realize that although he is a סלם מצב ארצה ... – "a ladder whose foot is planted on earth ...", yet ראשו מגיע השמימה ... – "... its top reaches heavenward."[10] He has the potential to reach the heavens. As the *pasuk* describes man: ותחסרהו מעט מאלקים – "You have made him but slightly less than Elokim."[11] We have the potential to come very close to Hashem.

Raising Or Lowering Our Spiritual Barometer

The wisest of all men tells us:

אורח חיים למעלה למשכיל למען סור משאול מטה.

"A path of life waits above for the intelligent one, so that his soul will turn away from the grave below."[12]

Every step we take can bring us closer to Hashem or take us further away from Him. Man cannot remain static – he either ascends or descends. A person who speaks words of Torah is busy creating worlds, while a person who is engaged in idle conversation is destroying worlds or at best creating worlds of nothingness.

There is a world of difference between a person who eats kosher food and one who eats non-kosher food. The smallest ant in a person's food can prove very destructive to his soul, while a person can be raised to tremendous heights by adhering to the strictest standards of *kashrus* and making sure all the necessary tithes have been taken. We know that eating non-kosher food has the effect of obstructing a person's heart[13] – a person who learns Torah or *davens* after eating non-kosher food will not be as open to absorbing the holiness as one who has just eaten kosher food.

It is not just our actions, such as what we eat, that influence us and our future generations, but our thoughts can have the same effect. Thoughts of Torah and *chessed* have a radically different effect on us from thoughts of heresy. The Torah contains many *mitzvos* relating to what is in a person's heart and mind, such as לא תשנא את אחיך בלבבך – "You shall not hate your brother in your heart"[14] and לא תטר – "You shall not bear a grudge."[15] We can ascend or descend spiritually according to our thoughts and feelings.

Even something as seemingly passive as resting can raise or lower our spiritual barometer. If the purpose of our rest is to gather strength in order to learn Torah, then even that short nap will raise us to higher levels. Otherwise it will lower us. There is no option of remaining static.

As we mentioned, both our actions and our thoughts impact on us. To many people, being a good Jew means observing the *mitzvos*, while *hashkafa*, outlook, is of secondary importance. It is possible for a person to be meticulous in his observance of the laws of *Shabbos*, yet lack the required basic belief that Hashem created the world in six days and rested on the seventh. What purpose is there in observing the *Shabbos* without the foundation of belief in Hashem's ability to create the world?

A person can go through the motions of fulfilling many *mitzvos* while remaining a complete non-believer. The foundation of our belief and practice must be rooted in the Thirteen Principles of Faith. Without this there is little value in observing *mitzvos*.

Then of course, some people take the opposite approach – as long as one's heart is in the right place, they maintain, adhering to the specific mitzvah requirements is less significant. This is certainly untrue; the Torah guides us in every step we take and we already mentioned the repercussions which one movement can cause. If a person is not careful, while in an ecstasy of singing beautiful *zemiros* on *Shabbos*, his hands can be busy violating the prohibition of *borer*.

The mitzvah of *tefillin* symbolizes this dual aspect of *mitzvos*. The Torah commands us to wear *tefillin* on our arms as well as on our heads. The *tefillin shel yad* signify that our actions should be for the sake of Heaven, while the *tefillin shel rosh* signify that our thoughts should be for the sake of Heaven. Both are essential components of the mitzvah.

Navi Or Political Analyst

When a person starts splitting *hashkafa* from observance of the *mitzvos* he can reach extreme conclusions. Bible critics first invented the notion of two Yeshayahus. Now, all of a sudden, two are not sufficient – they require three! They maintain that differences in style in certain sections of the *sefer* point to different authors. Stylistic differences can be overcome, but what really disturbs them is how Yeshayahu could have predicted that two hundred years later, Koresh would be crowned king of Persia. To these critics, the prophet is nothing more than a political analyst. A political analyst may be able to predict the outcome of the current war, or perhaps the next election in the United States. An analyst with a real imagination could perhaps predict the outcome of the United States presidential race in eight years. Who could possibly know who will become President of the United States in two hundred years? Does anyone know for certain that there will even be a United States in two hundred years? 'Stylistic differences' are just an excuse. Yeshayahu proves that prophecy exists, which is something the human mind cannot comprehend. The critics were therefore left with no choice but to invent the other Yeshayahu. A person who denies the idea of prophecy cannot possibly believe in the Torah, for the Torah in its entirety is a prophecy given to Moshe Rabenu.

A person can observe every detail of the Oral Torah without believing that it was given to Moshe Rabenu at Har Sinai. Some believe that the *Torah Shebe'al Peh* simply developed over the generations. While there were many enactments of the *Anshei Knesses HaGedolah* and other Sages, the *mitzvos* from the Torah such as the thirty-nine categories of prohibitions on *Shabbos*, many details of the laws of *tefillin* and *shechita*, as well as the general interpretation of the Written Law are '*halacha leMoshe miSinai*.' I am not saying that Moshe Rabenu himself commanded us to fulfill the *mitzvos d'rabbanan* such as lighting Chanukah candles, but many Torah commandments which are not written explicitly were handed down to Moshe Rabenu at Sinai. Although there is some value in keeping *mitzvos* simply because 'my father did so,' this cannot serve as the basis of our observance. We must believe firmly that the interpretation of the Written Law was given to Moshe at Har Sinai.

Simply Mistaken

In *Sicha* Two of this *parsha* we discuss the incident recorded in the Torah as "Reuven went and lay with Bilha, his father's concubine." Chazal tell us כל האומר ראובן חטא אינו אלא טועה – "Whoever claims that Reuven sinned is simply mistaken."[16] If someone believes that Reuven sinned, not only is he mistaken in his understanding of this section of the Torah, but his entire outlook on the Torah is flawed. Could one think for a moment that the Kohen Gadol would carry the name of Reuven on his חושן המשפט – his 'breastplate of judgment,' if Reuven were guilty of the grave sin ascribed to him by the simple reading of the Torah's words? His name would surely have been hidden!

One who does not see this blatant contradiction cannot comprehend the vast difference between holiness and impurity. Chazal tell us that when Yosef considered sinning with Potiphar's wife, the image of his father appeared to him. Yaakov told him that the names of his brothers were destined to appear on the breastplate of the Kohen Gadol, and warned him that his name would be omitted if he sinned. This is clear proof that Reuven's name would not have appeared if he had truly sinned, as the *pasuk* implies. The *psukim* clearly cannot be understood literally. In the long run, Reuven was mistaken, yet he had reasons for doing what he did – he was concerned for his mother's honor. Great people of Reuven's stature do not succumb to such base instincts and anyone who believes otherwise is simply mistaken about the entire Torah. The same applies to

Dovid HaMelech. It is inconceivable that Dovid was able to commit a grave sin at night and then author the Divinely inspired book of *Tehillim* in the morning. As with Reuven, whoever thinks otherwise does not have any idea of the vast distance between holiness and impurity. He has a fundamental misperception of the entire Torah.

A person can observe all the dictates of the Torah, such as not mixing milk and meat, *Shabbos, maaser,* yet be simply mistaken and not have internalized even a fraction of the Torah.

Judging Diamonds

Although the Tanach's description of the infractions of *tzaddikim* such as Reuven and David should not be taken literally, we may still wonder why it uses such harsh language. The answer is that they are judged on their level. When speaking of scrap metal, we say how many tons it weighs – being off by a few kilograms in either direction is of little significance. In addition no one cares if it is dented or marked. We cannot compare this to a diamond, in which the slightest scratch can reduce its value tremendously. The *tzaddikim* are like diamonds. What we would consider minor infractions, tiny scratches, are major sins on their level. The Tanach therefore describes their shortcomings in terms which we would use to describe the violation of major prohibitions in ourselves.

HaRav Chaim Rabinowitz shlit"a, author of *Daas Sofrim*, compares this to a woman who reports that her child is able to speak. If the child is eight months or a year old, even uttering a few words such as אבא and אמא is a great accomplishment. If his speaking ability has not developed further by the time he is thirty years old, his mother would run to doctors and psychiatrists, and spend many hours *davening* at *Kever Rachel* and the *Kosel.* When we talk about a man of thirty who is able to speak, we mean perhaps that he has a gift for public speaking. In comparison to these spiritual giants, we can only say אבא and אמא.

Understanding Things In Context

When we are learning Torah and come across a new word or expression, it is important to know the context in order to figure out its meaning. The word חמרא, for example, which is found in the Gemara, can mean either 'wine' or 'a donkey.' How can we know which definition the Gemara is referring to? It has been said in jest that if a person's head is in the farm, he will interpret it to mean 'a donkey,' while if his head is in the barrel, he will interpret it to mean 'wine.' There are instances when it is unclear what the Gemara means. However, it is hard to believe that a person could misinterpret the Gemara's instruction to use חמרא for Kiddush to mean that Kiddush must be recited over a donkey rather than a cup of wine.

Interpretations of precisely the same words may vary depending on who said them, and who or what he was referring to. As we have just mentioned, descriptions of ordinary people do not mean the same thing when used to describe Reuven and Dovid HaMelech. Whoever does not realize this distinction may not necessarily be branded an *apikores* but he is simply mistaken.

From our discussion it is clear that actions as well as thoughts and beliefs are of primary importance. A minor alteration, such as writing the name 'Tzofnas Paneach' rather than 'Yosef,' can result in a difference as vast as the gap between heaven and earth. Proper belief will more than likely spur someone to proper action. Why should a non-believer have any reason to be stringent in his observance of *mitzvos*? Strict observance generally comes from belief in the great reward associated with each mitzvah and the worlds it can create. A person who truly believes in Hashem will go to significant lengths and make great sacrifices to observe every detail of a mitzvah. In this manner he will perfect his soul and merit entry into the Next World.

A person whose soul is not perfected has no tool with which to absorb anything from עולם הבא. One whose heart is sealed cannot receive the Divine Light of the Next World, just as no light from the outside can penetrate a sealed room without windows. The fact that the sun is shining brightly outside is of no significance when it cannot enter the room. To receive a share in the Next World, we must open our hearts. We must realize the significance of our every act and thought, and work constantly to improve ourselves and rise to higher levels. With Hashem's help, we will merit the arrival of

Moshiach and receive our share in the World to Come speedily in our day. Amen.

Notes

1   *Bereishis* 48:8

2   Rashi, citing *Tanchuma* 6.

3   Ibid. 9

4   *Kallah Rabbasi* 3

5   *Bereishis* 48:9

6   *Bereishis* 48:19

7   Ibid.

8   *Hoshea* 11:3

9   *Yeshayahu* 6:3

10   *Bereishis* 28:12

11   *Tehillim* 8:6

12   *Mishle* 15:24

13   See *Yoma* 39a

14   *Vayikra* 19:17

15   Ibid. 18

16   *Shabbos* 55b

Misunderstanding The Entire Torah!

Impetuosity Disqualifies

Yaakov Avinu blesses his sons before his death:

ראובן בכרי אתה כחי וראשית אני יתר שאת ויתר עז.
פחז כמים אל תותר כי עלית משכבי אביך

"Reuven, you are my firstborn, my strength and my initial vigor, foremost in rank and foremost in power."[1]

As the firstborn you were worthy of receiving a greater share than your brothers; the *kehuna* and the monarchy, but because of your "water-like impetuosity, you cannot be foremost."[2] Because Reuven acted in haste, that additional share was taken from him and granted to others, the *kehuna* to Levi and the monarchy to Yehuda. Where do we find his impetuosity? "Because you mounted your father's bed,"[3] referring to the incident recorded in *Parshas Vayishlach*:

וילך ראובן וישכב את בלהה פילגש אביו

"Reuven went and lay with Bilha, his father's concubine."[4]

Our Sages dispute precisely what took place. Some are of the opinion that, contrary to the literal meaning of the *pasuk*, Reuven was not guilty of illicit relations with Bilha. The *Ksav veHaKabala* shows that a careful reading of the *pasuk* in fact proves that there were no physical relations between them. He points out that when the Torah tells us that someone went – הלך, it implies he left a location. On the other hand, the word לבא – to come, emphasizes arrival at a specific destination. For example, when Moshe was commanded to meet Pharaoh outside his palace by the river he was told לך אל פרעה – "Go to Pharaoh,"[5] while when he was commanded to meet him inside his palace he was told בא אל פרעה – "Come to Pharaoh."[6] In the Torah's account of the above incident it says וילך ראובן – "Reuven went." This seems to indicate quite clearly that no wrongful act took place, for Reuven simply took Bilha out of Yaakov's domain. He he entered her own private domain, the Torah would have said ויבא ראובן – "Reuven came." What was Reuven guilty of? "He disturbed his father's bed and Scripture regards him as if he lay with her."[7,8]

Some of our Sages are of the opinion that Reuven did have relations with Bilha,[9] which is one of the most severe prohibitions a person can transgress. Although the *pasuk* states clearly that Bilha was not Yaakov's wife, but his concubine, the Rishonim dispute the exact status of a concubine. It is either a relationship without *kiddushin* or it is true *kiddushin* but without the benefit of a *kesuva*. The latter definition would classify Bilha as a full-fledged married woman,[10] making Reuven guilty not only of having relations with a married woman, but, in addition, of having relations with his father's wife! Even according to the view that a concubine is an unmarried woman, Reuven was not totally free of guilt. Firstly, Rav Yehuda is of the opinion that even a woman who had been raped is forbidden to the rapist's son. How much more so in the case of Bilha, who had a long-term relationship with Yaakov.[11] For Reuven to have relations with her, although not in violation of a *lav* (a negative commandment), and certainly not of an act punishable by *kareis*, is definitely forbidden. Even the Sages who reject Rav Yehuda's view, maintaining that a woman who had been raped or seduced is not forbidden to the son, would not permit having relations with any unmarried woman, since she may, for example, be in a state of *nidah*. Even if she were not, the Rambam views relations with any unmarried woman

---

7   This opinion in the Gemara explains that following Rachel's death, Yaakov moved Bilha's bed into his tent. Reuven, viewing this as an affront to his mother Leah's honor, removed Bilha's bed and replaced it with Leah's.

as a violation of the prohibition: "There shall not be a promiscuous woman among the daughters of Israel."[12]

Conversely we may ask, if Reuven's sin was indeed so severe, why did Yaakov use such delicate language as "water-like impetuosity" in his rebuke? Was Reuven's action no worse than that of a child who runs around wildly and falls, tearing a hole in his pants? We are speaking of one of the most serious violations in the Torah! We would have expected much sharper words of admonition than "water-like impetuosity"!

In The Merit Of This *Teshuva* ...

The explanation is that Yaakov rebuked him prior to his death, many years after the incident had taken place, which was sufficient time for Reuven to have undergone a *teshuva* process involving much suffering and fasting.[13] Chazal add that it was in the merit of this *teshuva* that he became the ancestor of Hoshea, the prophet who implored the Jewish people שובה ישראל עד ה' אלקיך – "Return, Israel, unto Hashem your God."[14] With this understanding, it becomes clear why Yaakov did not use sharper language in his rebuke; Reuven was a *baal teshuva* and it is forbidden to remind a *baal teshuva* of his misdeeds.[15]

We can now ask the opposite question: if Reuven had indeed repented for his action, why did Yaakov rebuke him at all, even gently? He had done *teshuva*! What more could be expected of him?

While Reuven may have repented, a *teshuva* sufficient to eradicate all the damage caused by the sin is very difficult. On the one hand we learn that repenting is not difficult: כי קרוב אליך הדבר מאד בפיך ובלבבך לעשותו "The matter is very near to you – in your mouth and your heart – to perform it."[16] However *teshuva* is "a ladder set earthward, its top reaching heavenward."[17] Climbing the bottom rungs of the ladder is an easy task, but ascending to higher rungs becomes progressively more difficult. Reuven may have repented, but Yaakov learned through *ruach hakodesh* that Reuven had not totally cleansed himself from this sin, and he therefore rebuked him.

Even spiritual giants of the world were unable to reach the top of the *teshuva* ladder. Adam HaRishon, for example, violated the one "easy mitzvah" that Hashem gave him – not to eat from the Tree of Knowledge.[18] Chazal teach us that "Adam HaRishon was an exceedingly pious man. When he saw that death came into the world because of him, for his sin of eating from the Tree of Knowledge, he fasted for one hundred and thirty years, and abstained from marital relations for one hundred and thirty years, and wore belts of fig branches on his skin for those one hundred and thirty years."[19] Adam's *teshuva* was certainly effective, for he was granted life in the Next World, yet it was still not enough to restore the world to its state prior to his sin. He was unable to rescind the decree of "By the sweat of your brow shall you eat bread,"[20] or that of "For you are dust, and to dust shall you return."[21] People still need to work for a living and they still die at the end of their days.

The Atonement Of Yeshayahu Hanavi

Similarly, Yeshayahu HaNavi committed what appears to have been an insignificant transgression. He said of *Am Yisrael*, "I dwell among a people with impure lips."[22] The very next *pasuk* describes his punishment: "One of the *seraphim* flew to me and in his hand was a coal; he had taken it with tongs from atop the altar."[23] The coal was so hot that even a *seraph*, an angel who himself is made entirely of fire, was unable to hold it with his hands, but needed tongs to grasp it. My esteemed teacher, HaRav Eliyahu Dessler, zt"l explained that this signifies that the coal was on a higher spiritual level than the angel. "He touched it to my mouth."[24] The angel took the high spiritual level of the coal and touched it to Yeshayahu's lips. "He said: 'Behold, this has touched your lips; your iniquity has gone away and your sin shall be atoned for.'"[25] It appears that Yeshayahu's transgression had effectively been removed and his sin had been atoned for, yet Yeshayahu knows that this is not the case and he must now begin the process of completely wiping out his sin.[26]

---

26 For an elaboration of this subject, see Titharu, – HaRav Nebenzahl's sichot on the Ten Days of Repentance p. 93

Immediately thereafter Hashem asked him, "Whom shall I send, and who shall go for us?"[27] Who will go to rebuke the Jewish nation?[28] Although other prophets such as Moshe Rabenu, Yirmiyahu, and Yechezkel all tried to avoid these missions, Yeshayahu volunteered his services: "And I said, 'Here I am! Send me!'"[29] We must realize that a prophet's job involved much more than being honored with *Shlishi* or *Shishi* each *Shabbos*. At times he would need to go out among the people to admonish them, exposing himself to potential suffering and persecution. Yeshayahu himself related, "I submitted my body to those who smite and my cheeks to those who pluck; I did not hide my face from humiliation and spittle."[30] I have taken upon myself the mission of prophecy, knowing full well that I am opening myself up to being smitten, to having my beard torn out, and to being spat at. For eighty years Yeshayahu was willing to suffer all the persecution and suffering involved in this mission in order to eradicate his sin. Presumably he was not persecuted the entire time, for part of his prophecy took place during the reigns of Uziyah, Yotam, and Chizkiyahu, who were righteous kings of Yehuda. The humiliation Yeshayahu was referring to probably occurred when the wicked kings Achaz and Menashe ruled over Yehuda. Furthermore, during those entire eighty years, the *Beis HaMikdash* was standing, meaning that Yeshayahu was prophet for eighty Yom Kippurs in which the שעיר המשתלח was sent to *Azazel*.[31] (It is probably inaccurate to assume that there was a שעיר המשתלח each year, for Achaz had put a stop to the service,[32] but the goat was certainly dispatched during the reigns of the righteous kings.) We do not doubt for a moment that Yeshayahu did *teshuva* as well. Even with all this, Yeshayahu was not granted complete atonement. At the conclusion of the eighty years, Menashe, king of Yehuda smote him in the mouth and killed him. All this was in retribution for the less than honorable way he spoke of *Am Yisrael*.[33] Yeshayahu's *teshuva*, persecution and suffering, and eighty Yom Kippurs in which eighty goats were offered, were not

---

31   The שעיר המשתלח, literally the goat dispatched (into the wilderness) atones for the less severe sins, even when not accompanied by *teshuva*. See Rambam, *Hilchos Teshuva* 1:2.

sufficient to provide a complete *tikkun* for his sin. Total erasure of a sin, even one as minor as Yeshayahu's, is very difficult.

A similar phenomenon occurred after the sin of the Golden Calf. Moshe Rabenu meted out justice to those guilty of worshipping the calf, and three thousand people were killed. In addition, Moshe ascended Har Sinai to pray to Hashem to forgive the Jewish nation. While Hashem granted forgiveness, the nation did not return to the level it had been on before the sin. The *teshuva* and *tikkun* of Moshe Rabenu and the other *tzaddikim* of the generation – Aharon, Yehoshua, and others, was not enough to cleanse the people entirely. It was sufficient to allow *Am Yisrael* to be saved from destruction and to be given the second set of *luchos*, to bring them into *Eretz Yisrael* and build the *Mishkan*, but it could not return us to our previous situation, in which we were free from the clutches of the angel of death and free from the oppression of other rulers.[34]

"How Can We Live With Our Sins?"

In this light we can understand the dispute that took place between *Am Yisrael* and the prophet Yechezkel. Yechezkel spoke to the people of his generation, saying, "Thus have you spoken, saying, 'Since our sins and our iniquities are upon us and we are wasting away because of them, how can we live?'"[35] The people did not believe that *teshuva* could fully correct the blemishes their sins had caused. They finally believed Yechezkel when he swore in the Name of Hashem, "Say to them: 'As I live – the word of Hashem Elokim – I do not desire the death of the wicked one, but rather the wicked one's return from his way, that he may live. Repent, repent from your evil ways! Why should you die, O House of Israel?'"[36] Why did they not believe at first that *teshuva* has the ability to correct sins? Because they understood the depths of corruption caused by sin; they could not see how *teshuva* could possibly change that. We are aware of Yechezkel's prophecy and the many sayings of Chazal relating to the power of *teshuva*. To us it all seems so easy: we fast on Yom Kippur, recite *viduy*, recite *selichos* (the Sephardim for a month, the Ashkenazim for approximately a week), and then Yom Kippur is over and we eat a scrumptious meal, as if nothing had ever happened! If we truly repented on Yom Kippur, why has the *Beis Ha-Mikdash* not been rebuilt? Why was it destroyed in the first place? Did the people of that generation not repent every year? While it is good to know that the Gates of Repentance are always open, we must realize that *teshuva* does not end on Yom Kippur. Even after Yom Kippur, we need to continue working on our *teshuva*. Complete and total *teshuva* is very difficult to attain and requires much hard work and effort on our part.

Apple Tricks

Rabbi Levi Yitzchak of Berditchev questioned how on Yom Kippur we can make the *bracha*:

מלך מוחל וסולח לעוונותינו ולעונות עמו בית ישראל

"Blessed are You Hashem, the King Who pardons and forgives our iniquities and the iniquities of His people, the Family of Israel."

How can we be so sure that this year Hashem will grant us forgiveness? If He does not, we will have recited a *bracha levatala*. Rav Levi Yitzchak explained with a parable. Once upon a time there was a child who very much craved an apple. Of course he could have asked his mother for one, but he was afraid that she might not agree to give it to him. After giving the matter some thought, the child came up with a brilliant idea. Standing next to her, he recited out loud: ברוך אתה ה' אלקינו מלך העולם בורא פרי העץ! Of course the mother did not want her beloved son to be guilty of reciting a *bracha levatala*, so she had no choice but to give him his precious apple. When we recite the *bracha*, "The King Who pardons and forgives our iniquities," we are, so to speak, forcing Hashem to forgive us. (I would like to point out that the story of the child and the apple is good for purposes of illustration, but from a purely *halachic* perspective we are not permitted to recite a *bracha* on a food before it is in our hand.)

We know that we are required to recite a *bracha* even on a minimal quantity of food. The same may be said of the *bracha* we recite on Yom Kippur – it applies even to the lowest level of *teshuva*. Although

Hashem forgives us for any level of repentance, we must realize that the fact that *Am Yisrael* has been repenting for so many generations, yet we have not yet merited a total redemption is clear proof that our *teshuva* is far from complete. *Am Yisrael* not only did not do enough *teshuva* – they continued sinning!

To return to Yaakov's rebuke of Reuven, there is an additional explanation for Yaakov's chastising him even though he repented. Every sinful act contains two components – the act itself and the negative trait that led to the act.[37] It is possible that Yaakov's words were gentle because he was not rebuking him for the act. For that Reuven had indeed repented. Yaakov rebuked Reuven for the character trait that was responsible for the act. When Yaakov accused Reuven of "water-like impetuosity," he was telling him that he may have atoned for his sin, but he had not sufficiently worked on his negative characteristic. It is for this reason that he "cannot be foremost." He was not worthy of the *kehuna* or of kingship. A king cannot act in haste. He needs to think matters through. A king who acts hastily may lead his people into a war which they have no chance of winning, or he may raise or reduce taxes without justification.

Sober Service

A Kohen too cannot be hasty. He must be fully mindful of his actions and must have the proper intention when bringing offerings, "in order to distinguish between the sacred and the profane, and between the contaminated and the pure."[38] The *pasuk* distinguishes between service that is holy and that which has been profaned.[39] It is for this reason the Torah forbade the Kohen to serve in the *Beis HaMikdash* while under the influence of wine.[40] Similarly a king may not drink too much wine, as we see in Batsheva's criticism of Shlomo: "It is not proper for kings who belong to God, it is not proper for kings to drink much wine."[41] A king and a Kohen must be sober and self-controlled in order to fulfill their roles. The functions of *kehuna* and *malchus* cannot be carried out impetuously and so they were taken away from Reuven and given to his brothers.

"Whoever Said Reuven Sinned ..."

Chazal tell us, "Whoever said Reuven sinned is simply mistaken."[42] What does this mean? If Reuven was punished, he must have done something wrong. We mentioned earlier that there is an opinion in Chazal which claims that Reuven did not actually have relations with Bilha, but was simply guilty of moving his father's bed out of Bilha's tent and in to Leah's. Chazal explain: "Reuven sought (to right) the affront to his mother. He said, 'If my mother's sister was a rival to my mother, shall the maidservant of my mother's sister be a rival to my mother?'"[43] Rachel may have been worthy of rivaling my mother Leah, for she too is counted among the matriarchs. But Bilha – Rachel's maidservant! What right does she have to take the place of Rachel? She is not one of our holy matriarchs! He therefore went and moved his father's bed.

Even according to the view that Reuven did indeed have relations with Bilha, events are not as they appear. We are not speaking of a person acting out of lust; rather it was a form of protest against the affront to his mother's honor. Of course, his whole perspective was mistaken. In addition to being his father, Yaakov was Reuven's Rav, the *gadol hador*, and a prophet. Reuven should have relied on Yaakov's judgment. If Yaakov believed that it was appropriate to live with Bilha rather than with Leah, he must have had his reasons.[44] At the very least, out of respect for his father, he should have asked Yaakov his reasons and not taken matters into his own hands, either by moving Yaakov's bed or by having relations with Bilha.

When Chazal said "Whoever said Reuven sinned is simply mistaken," they meant that even if he acted literally as the text implies, he was not impelled by the same drives that motivate others to act in such a manner. He intended to defend his mother's honor, although this was not the correct way to go about it.

Misunderstanding The Entire Torah

This leads us to a deeper understanding of "Whoever said Reuven has sinned is simply mistaken." Chazal are teaching us that someone who thinks this is mistaken not only in his understanding of this particular incident but in his approach to the entire Torah! He "is simply mistaken" in his understanding of the Torah, for the Torah teaches us the vast distance between holiness and impurity. An entire world separates them and they cannot coexist. A man who sins with his father's wife, by giving in to his base desires, is not worthy of having his name appear on the *choshen* and *ephod* stones worn by the Kohen Gadol as a remembrance before Hashem, as Reuven's did.[45] One who does not understand this has missed the point of the entire Torah.

The same may be said of Dovid HaMelech, of whom Chazal too say: "Whoever has said Dovid has sinned is simply mistaken."[46] Here as well, to be "simply mistaken" means to misunderstand the entire Torah. It does not stand to reason that Dovid can be guilty of all the terrible sins which the Tanach seemingly attributes to him – illicit relations, murder, and others – and at the same time be "the anointed one of the God of Yaakov, and the pleasing composer of the songs of Israel." Whoever thinks so "is simply mistaken" in his understanding of the entire Torah! The vast distance that separates sanctity and impurity does not permit these things to go hand-in-hand.

The Rambam writes "Prophecy only comes to ... one who is strong in his character, whose inclination will not overpower him with anything in this world, rather his mind can always overpower his inclination."[47] Dovid HaMelech was a prophet.[48] If prophecy can only come to someone who keeps his *yetzer hara* in check, then his failure in any area can only be due to a miscalculation on his part and not due to his *yetzer hara*'s getting the better of him.

What did Dovid have in mind (erroneously) in the incident with Batsheva? He saw with *ruach hakodesh* that "Batsheva the daughter of Eliam was suited since the Six Days of Creation to Dovid,"[49] and that *Moshiach* was destined to descend from her and from himself. What about the fact that she had a husband? Uriah was subject to the death penalty for having rebelled against royalty.[50] In my humble opinion, Uriah's rebellion is in his telling Dovid:

חיך וחי נפשך אם אעשה את הדבר הזה.

"By your life and the life of your soul I will not do such a thing."[51]

The word for "your life" is generally spelled חייך (with two *yuds*), but in this *pasuk* the word contains only one *yud*. A word with a missing letter is referred to as חסר – lacking. The implication here is that something was lacking in Uriah; he did not value the life of the king sufficiently. Therefore Dovid sent Uriah "directly in front of the fierce fighting"[52] ultimately leading to his death. Dovid was carrying out the punishment that Uriah deserved. We learn in the Gemara, "Whoever goes out to fight a war of the House of Dovid writes a bill of divorce for his wife."[53] If the soldier does not return, the woman is retroactively divorced from the time the *get* was given, therefore Batsheva was not actually a married woman.

A *Chillul Hashem*

What sin was David in fact punished for? For the great *chillul Hashem* which he caused. "However, because you have thoroughly blasphemed the enemies of Hashem in this matter."[54] The enemies of Israel can now accuse David of having killed Uriah in order to take his wife. They do not understand that Uriah deserved the death penalty for having rebelled against royalty. "You should have had him judged via the Sanhedrin."[55] A public trial would have demonstrated to everyone that he was guilty. Sending him to the front line in the war against Amon gave the enemy grounds to claim that "The anointed one of the God of Yaakov, and the pleasing composer of the songs of Israel" was a murderer, guilty of illicit relations! This was not the way to carry out justice. There is no greater *chillul Hashem* than this! To this very day our enemies speak this way of Dovid HaMelech.

In his psalm of repentance, Dovid declares, "Against You alone did I sin."[56] His guilt was only *bein adam laMakom*, in the terrible *chillul Hashem* that he caused.[57] There was no transgression *bein adam lachavero* – in having Uriah killed and in taking his wife. If we analyze Chazal's comment on the prophet Nathan's rebuke of Dovid, we will gain a clearer understanding of Dovid's sin. "While him you have killed by the sword of the children of Amon."[58] Our Sages explain that the prophet is emphasizing that David's wrongdoing was not in having killed Uriah. Uriah had it coming to him. Nathan

HaNavi was rebuking Dovid for having Uriah killed via the sword of Amon.[59] The Amonites' custom was to inscribe the symbols of their *avoda zara* on their swords. Whenever a Jew was killed by their sword, they claimed that their god had defeated the God of Israel, God forbid. Whether or not the symbol of the other nations' *avoda zara* is inscribed on their swords, when they defeat *Am Yisrael* they proclaim: ידנו רמה ולא ה' פעל כל זאת – "Our hand was raised in triumph and it was not Hashem Who accomplished this."[60] This was the great *chillul Hashem*.

From a Jewish perspective, when Jews are killed by non-Jews, as happened during the Holocaust and other tragic periods in Jewish history, they are considered as having died *al Kiddush Hashem*. From the perspective of the non-Jews, however, this is a tremendous *chillul Hashem*! They see Jewish people murdered and they believe that their god is superior. They say: לכו ונכחידם מגוי ולא יזכר שם ישראל עוד – "Let us cut them off from nationhood, so Israel's name will not be remembered any longer."[61]

There is no question that those who died at the hands of the Crusaders died sanctifying Hashem's Name, yet the non-Jews cannot see this. To this very day, the nations of the world ask, "Where was God in Auschwitz?" Anyone studying that tragic period cannot but be amazed at how much *Kiddush Hashem* there was. What took place during World War II was the greatest sanctification of Hashem's Name since the days of *Akeidas Yitzchak*. The same may be said of the Communist regime of the Soviet Union. In the eyes of the world, however, this was a desecration of Hashem's Name – so many Jews were killed in Auschwitz and other infamous places. The same applies to the many Jews killed in our Holy Land in war and acts of terror. We refer to them as having died *al Kiddush Hashem* but from the perspective of the Ishmaelites, a *chillul Hashem* has taken place. This was where Dovid erred; he did not take into account sufficiently how the other nations would react to the way Uriah was killed.

After all we have said, we must keep in mind that Dovid and Reuven may have erred, but they remained pure. Reuven's name is still worthy of being inscribed on the stones of the *ephod* as well as on the *choshen*, so that the Kohen Gadol carries it as a merit, together with that of the other tribes, in order to protect us. Dovid HaMelech too remained unblemished. and we await, speedily in our day, *Moshiach* who is destined to descend from him and Batsheva. Of course all that we have discussed is only within the limitations of what our minds can grasp. We can never uncover the depths of the thought processes of Reuven, Dovid HaMelech, or any of the other giants of Israel. We are not fit to judge their actions. May we be worthy that their merit will stand for us and the entire nation of Israel. May we be worthy of Dovid's descendant, *Moshiach*, speedily in our day. Amen.

Notes

1   *Bereishis* 49:3

2   Ibid. 4

3   Ibid.

4   *Bereishis* 35:22

5   *Shemos* 7:15

6   *Shemos* 7:26, 9:1, 10:1

8   *Shabbos* 55b

9   Ibid.

10   See Rashi and Ramban on *Bereishis* 25:6.

11   See *Yevamos* 97a.

12   *Devarim* 23:18. See Rambam *Hilchos Ishus* 1:4.

13   See Rashi *Bereishis* 37:29.

14   Hoshea 14:2. See *Bereishis Rabba* 84:19.

15   See *Baba Metzia* 58b.

16   *Devarim* 30:14. See Ramban there.

17   *Bereishis* 28:12

18   See *Shabbos* 55b.

19   *Eruvin* 18b

20   *Bereishis* 3:16

21   Ibid. 19

22   *Yeshayahu* 6:5

23   Ibid. 6

24   Ibid. 7

25   Ibid.

27   Ibid. 8

28   See Rashi there.

29   *Yeshayahu* 6:8

30   *Yeshayahu* 50:6

32   See *Sanhedrin* 103b.

33   See *Yevamos* 49b.

34   See *Shemos Rabba* 32:1.

35   *Yechezkel* 33:10

36   Ibid. 11

37 See Rambam *Hilchos Teshuva* 7:3.

38 *Vayikra* 10:10

39 See Rashi there.

40 See *Vayikra* 10:9.

41 *Mishle* 31:4

42 *Shabbos* 55b

43 Ibid.

44 See Rashi's commentary to *Shabbos* 55b, which states that Yaakov was directed by the Divine Presence.

45 See *Shemos* 28:12, 29.

46 *Shabbos* 56a

47 *Hilchos Yesodei HaTorah* 7:1

48 See *Moed Katan* 16b and Rashi there.

49 Sanhedrin 107a

50 See *Shabbos* 56a and see Rashi and *Tosafos* there, who differ regarding precisely in what way he rebelled.

51 *Shmuel* II 11:11

52 *Shmuel* II 11:15

53 *Shabbos* 56a

54 *Shmuel* II 12:14

55 *Shabbos* 56a

56   *Tehillim* 51:6

57   See *Zohar Shemos* 106:2.

58   *Shmuel* II 12:9

59   See *Zohar* Shmos 107:1.

60   *Devarim* 32:27

61   *Tehillim* 83:5